# Using Diagrams in Psychotherapy

*Using Diagrams in Psychotherapy* presents the Visually Enhanced Therapy framework, a unique approach to communicating information in psychotherapy. The framework brings visual information processing principles and techniques into the practice of psychotherapy to help therapists communicate more effectively with clients. Replete with illustrations and therapist thought boxes designed to help readers translate theory to practice, the book presents visual strategies that enable clients to become more actively engaged in therapy sessions and to better retain information. This is a thorough, user-friendly resource with numerous diagrams and worksheets for implementing visually oriented interventions across a broad range of clients, clinical settings, and clinical problems.

**Charles M. Boisvert, PhD,** is a professor of clinical mental health counseling in the Department of Counseling, Educational Leadership, and School Psychology at Rhode Island College and a practicing clinical psychologist at the Rhode Island Center for Cognitive Behavioral Therapy (RICBT) in North Kingstown, Rhode Island.

**Mohiuddin Ahmed, PhD,** has over 40 years of psychotherapy and consultation experience with varied populations of all ages in inpatient and outpatient practice settings. Following his retirement from Taunton State Hospital in Massachusetts and Community Care Alliance in Rhode Island, he continues to be active in mental health publications and maintains a part-time psychology consultation practice.

# Using Diagrams in Psychotherapy
## A Guide to Visually Enhanced Therapy

**Charles M. Boisvert**
**Mohiuddin Ahmed**

NEW YORK AND LONDON

First published 2019
by Routledge
711 Third Avenue, New York, NY 10017

and by Routledge
2 Park Square, Milton Park, Abingdon, Oxon, OX14 4RN

*Routledge is an imprint of the Taylor & Francis Group, an informa business*

*Library of Congress Cataloging-in-Publication Data*
Names: Boisvert, Charles M., author. | Ahmed, Mohiuddin, author.
Title: Using diagrams in psychotherapy : a guide to visually enhanced therapy /
    Charles M. Boisvert, Mohiuddin Ahmed.
Description: New York, NY : Routledge, 2019. | Includes bibliographical references
    and index.
Identifiers: LCCN 2018022569 (print) | LCCN 2018023197 (ebook) |
    ISBN 9781351203357 (eBook) | ISBN 9781138565623 (hbk) |
    ISBN 9781138565647 (pbk) | ISBN 9781351203357 (ebk)
Subjects: LCSH: Psychotherapy. | Psychotherapist and patient.
Classification: LCC RC475 (ebook) | LCC RC475 .B67 2019 (print) | DDC 616.89/14–dc23LC
    record available at https://lccn.loc.gov/2018022569

ISBN: 978-1-138-56562-3 (hbk)
ISBN: 978-1-138-56564-7 (pbk)
ISBN: 978-1-351-20335-7 (ebk)

Typeset in Frutiger
by Apex CoVantage, LLC

For Charles Boisvert: He dedicates this book to his loving wife, Rachel, a dedicated mother, wife, and social worker. She provided helpful feedback on prior drafts of the book and tolerated many long nights of writing. She has been a source of great support and strength over the years. He also dedicates this book to his two beautiful children, Gregory and Kimberly. They are an inspiration and two beacons of light in his life.

For Mohiuddin Ahmed: He dedicates this book to Dr. Josefina Resurreccion Ahmed, an educationist by training and profession who not only provided a loving companionship of spousal relationship of 49 years but provided Ahmed insight and understanding as how to incorporate teaching strategies and behavioral objectives into his clinical practice. Much of it influenced Dr. Ahmed's work in developing the mind stimulation therapy model in collaboration with Dr. Boisvert.

# Contents

# Figures

# About the Authors

## Charles M. Boisvert, PhD

Charles M. Boisvert, PhD received a B.S. in psychology from Le Moyne College, an M.A. in counseling from Rhode Island College, and a PhD in clinical psychology from the University of Rhode Island. He completed an internship in clinical psychology at the Edith Nourse Rogers Memorial VA Medical Center in Bedford, Massachusetts, and a two-year post-doctoral fellowship in clinical psychology in the Department of Psychiatry and Behavioral Medicine at the Lahey Clinic Medical Center in Burlington, Massachusetts. Dr. Boisvert has worked in a variety of clinical settings, including working for 12 years in community mental health centers, providing services to a diverse range of clients. Dr. Boisvert is a professor of clinical mental health counseling in the Department of Counseling, Educational Leadership, and School Psychology at Rhode Island College and former director of the counseling programs. Additionally, Dr. Boisvert is a practicing clinical psychologist at the Rhode Island Center for Cognitive Behavioral Therapy in North Kingstown, Rhode Island. His research and clinical interests include science-practice relations in psychotherapy, using multimodal therapy interventions, the biopsychology of stress, psychiatric care in primary care, and predictors of psychotherapy outcome. He has several publications in peer-reviewed journals and serves as an ad hoc reviewer for *Professional Psychology: Research and Practice* and *Family Practice*. He has also served as an ad hoc reviewer for *Schizophrenia Bulletin*. In 2013 he coauthored with Mohiuddin Ahmed the book *Mind Stimulation Therapy: Cognitive Interventions for Persons With Schizophrenia*.

## Mohiuddin Ahmed, PhD

Mohiuddin Ahmed completed his undergraduate and graduate studies in philosophy in Bangladesh at Dhaka University (B.A. (Honors), and M.A.) and was awarded a Fulbright Scholarship to study in the United States. He completed his M.Sc. in clinical psychology at Long Island University in Brooklyn, his PhD in clinical psychology at the University of Pittsburgh, and his clinical psychology doctoral internship at the Winnebago Mental Health Institute in Wisconsin. He has had over 40 years of clinical experience working with varied clinical populations of all ages in the Philippines, Bangladesh, and the United States. He has worked in psychiatric inpatient and outpatient facilities, institutions for the developmentally disabled, and nursing homes and has provided consultation to mental health agencies, residential programs for adults with behavior disabilities, and special education programs. He has supervised many pre- and post-doctoral-level psychology graduate students. Dr. Ahmed has pioneered innovative models of clinical services for children, adolescents, and adults and has many publications in peer-reviewed journals describing some of his innovative clinical practice work. In 2013 he coauthored with Charles Boisvert the book *Mind Stimulation Therapy: Cognitive Interventions for Persons With Schizophrenia*. For his full biography and publication list, please see his website at www.psychology mentalhealth.com.

# Introduction

*I hear and I forget . . . I see and I remember . . . I do and I understand.*

—Confucius

We live in a visual world. We are by nature visual creatures and rely heavily on visual processing to navigate the world, adapt, and survive. Our visual system is among the most sophisticated systems in our body. Our brain devotes more of its resources to visual processing than to all the other senses combined (Garrett, 2014; Wade & Swanston, 2013). The eye itself has an intricate technology designed to process images, pictures, and visual stimuli to enable us to function in and adapt to the world around us (Wade & Swanston, 2013). Our visual system often trumps the other systems, such as our auditory and "verbal" systems.

> *Vision is our most dominant sense. We derive most of our information about the world . . . from the light that enters our eyes and the processing in the brain that follows . . . vision has the lion's share of . . . the work associated with our perceptual experiences.*
>
> (Wade & Swanston, 2013, pp. ix–1)

Consider the following (Garrett, 2014; Jensen, 2008; Wade & Swanston, 2013; Ware, 2008):

- Approximately 30–50% of the brain's cortex is devoted to vision.
- Vision accounts for two thirds of the brain's electrical activity.
- Eighty-five percent of our learning is through our visual system.
- We retain information better when we both hear and see the information.
- There are more brain neurons devoted to vision than to the other four senses combined.
- The visual cortex is the largest system in the human brain.

Most of us have heard the adage "a picture is worth a thousand words." This saying, in some ways, speaks to the sophistication of our visual system in its ability to process information more comprehensively and efficiently than our "auditory-verbal system." Research has indeed shown that diagrams, images, and pictures can communicate a considerable amount of information rapidly and efficiently. Images can serve a powerful explanatory function by facilitating our ability to process and understand information more quickly and comprehensively than, for example, relying on words alone (Dansereau & Simpson, 2009; Larkin & Simon, 1987; Tufte, 2006). For example, by showing a person a picture of a map, they can understand more quickly and easily where something is located compared to using words alone to explain the location. Our brains in some ways are programmed to attend to visual information and stimuli, particularly images, designs, and diagrams (Tufte, 2006). In his book *Visual Thinking for Design* (2008), Colin Ware stated:

> *Although we can, to some extent form mental images in our heads, we do much better when those images are out in the world, on paper or computer screen . . . often to see a pattern is to understand the solution to a problem.*

(p. ix)

We all benefit from visual aids to assist us in processing information. In our everyday functioning, we routinely use various visual strategies and written materials to organize our day, plan activities, and remember tasks. Using PowerPoint and other visual aids is routine and anticipated when one attends, for example, a presentation, takes a class, or leads a business meeting. In these learning environments, visual aids are commonly used to enhance communication, engage the audience, and facilitate a meaningful exchange of information. With modern-day advances in information sharing through, for example, computer technology, texting devices, and the Internet, the processing of visual information has become commonplace and even necessary to maximize one's ability to communicate and function in the social world.

We are more likely to perceive and direct our attention to a visual cue or image compared to an auditory or verbal cue (Larkin & Simon, 1987; Wade & Swanston, 2013). For example, after you turned the page, your attention, at some point, may have been diverted from reading to noticing the following two circles depicted on the page. You may have gazed at the circles, read the information in the circles, and then returned to reading the paragraph.

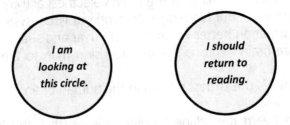

In this information and media age, we are readily attracted to visually cued products, such as iPads, laptops, iPods, smartphones, tablets, and computers. Today's technology appeals directly to our inherent inclination to navigate the world visually.

This book presents a unique approach to communicating information in psychotherapy called *Visually Enhanced Therapy (VET)*. VET is founded on a conceptual framework that brings "visual communication" into the psychotherapy arena by applying auditory and visual information processing principles, attention, memory, and learning processes and communication principles. In short, it is about using visually mediated communication strategies to augment the communication platform and learning environment in psychotherapy, ultimately enhancing the client's ability to remember, understand, and use the information exchanged during the psychotherapy dialogue.

## PSYCHOTHERAPY: A COMMUNICATION PLATFORM WITH IMPLICIT GOALS AND ASSUMPTIONS

Psychotherapy has historically relied on verbal communication and "auditory processing" as the primary and often only communication modality. The roots of psychotherapy, which grew out of Freudian psychoanalysis, had no particular requirements of the patient except to discuss "anything" that came to mind. The therapist did not even look at the patient and intentionally was not visually cued. Psychotherapy came to be known as "the talking cure." Talking and listening within a therapy relationship to achieve some sort of change in the patient continues to be foundational to psychotherapy. Simply being able to share one's feelings and experiences and to feel supported and understood by another can be powerfully therapeutic and has been a central facet of psychotherapy beginning with Carl Rogers (Rogers, 1951) and supported by decades of psychotherapy "relationship research" (Duncan, Miller, Wampold, & Hubble, 2010; Norcross, 2011; Wampold, 2001).

The relationship or therapeutic alliance has been considered the primary vehicle of change, and in some ways the verbal dialogue itself is considered to be the fuel that propels and sustains this therapeutic alliance, the quality of which is a strong predictor of therapy outcome (Anderson, Ogles, Patterson, Lambert, & Vermeersch, 2009; Anderson, Lunnen, & Ogles, 2010; Norcross, 2011; Wampold, 2001). In therapy, the verbal dialogue is considered the quintessential vehicle to effect change and achieve goals. We use the verbal medium to convey information, ask questions, problem solve, clarify information, understand concepts, gain insight, and express emotions. An implicit assumption is that the verbal medium is sufficient to achieve our goals and that through this medium alone the client will understand, integrate, and implement the themes and goals of the verbal dialogue. The client, through this process, is expected to "put into action" what was verbalized during the session and achieve their goals by "applying the verbal dialogue" outside of the session.

We know that therapy, which at its core relies primarily on auditory processing, is effective for the vast majority of clients (Duncan et al., 2010; Lambert & Ogles, 2004; Wampold, 2001). We recognize the therapeutic value of the verbal dialogue in and of itself and that it may be the primary or only communication vehicle used by most therapists. We do not wish to underestimate the therapeutic value of verbal communication. However, we believe that therapeutic communication and information processing can be enhanced when therapists use visually mediated communication strategies, such as diagrams, worksheets, and visual aids, to supplement traditional verbal therapy.

Consider the following:

*An instructor starts a course by saying, "This semester I do not want you to write anything down and neither will I. Just listen to me for the next 15 weeks and remember and incorporate all I have said so that you can use it and apply it. I will give you a cumulative exam at the end of the course to see how much you have remembered. Just listen well and you will learn."*

*A coach says to the team, "To learn this game, develop skills, and play well on the field, I want you to just listen to what I have to say. I will discuss the skills you will need, how you should develop them, and teach you strategies that will make you a better player. However, I am not going to show you anything or demonstrate anything during our practice sessions. Just listen well and you will learn."*

In some ways relying solely on the verbal dialogue in therapy would be akin to a teacher not using visuals or allowing note-taking during class but still expecting the students to learn the material, or akin to a basketball coach just discussing how to play the game of basketball and the skills required to become a better player but not using any visual models, skill demonstrations, or "X's and O's on a clipboard" but still expecting the players to learn how to play the game. If therapy is in some ways a psychoeducational process where information is exchanged, concepts are discussed, skills are taught, goals are identified, and steps are formulated to reach these goals, then relying strictly on verbal processing may not always be the most optimal method.

In one of my therapy classes, I (Charles Boisvert) start the class with an exercise where each student is asked to talk for 1 to 2 minutes, sharing something about themselves or their clinical background while the other class members listen. We go around the classroom until every student has spoken. The exercise usually takes about 5 to 8 minutes, depending on the number of students in the class. At the end of the exercise, I ask the students to take out a piece of paper and to write down every full sentence they can recall from the exercise. Typically, most students cannot recall one full sentence from the exercise. Most of the time there is only one or two students who think they may have the gist of one full sentence, but often they are unsure. I use the exercise to illustrate the challenges we have in remembering details of conversations and how, despite this, we tend to put a lot of "verbal energy" into sharing details in conversations. I emphasize to my students the importance of slowing the therapy process down and finding ways to maximize the way we "use the therapy dialogue." We then discuss how clients may have trouble processing all the verbal information in the session and remembering afterward what they had discussed. The exercise helps students become more aware of the challenges that both therapists and clients can

4

have in processing verbal information during therapy sessions. Consider the following statements made by clients during actual therapy sessions:

- *"I wish I could write all this down."*
- *"Can we tape-record the session? . . . It's hard to remember everything."*
- *"Can I take a picture of those statements we just wrote down so that I can remember them?"*
- *"Could you make a copy of that diagram for me?"*
- *"Let me write that down."*
- *"I remember the circles from last session and have been trying to shrink that outer layer of stress we talked about."*
- *"I knew you would get it out of me . . . I just needed to see it on paper."*
- *"Oh good, we get the white board today."*
- *"Wait a minute. Before we end, can I use my iPhone to take a picture of that diagram?"*
- *"Thanks for writing that on the white board . . . it helped me understand it better."*
- *"Can I borrow a notecard from your desk and write down those statements we just mentioned."*
- *"That was a good session . . . writing it down helped me see the pros and cons more clearly."*
- *"I've been showing those time circles to everyone."*

In some ways these anecdotes illustrate our propensity to seek visual information and to recognize the importance of it in communication. Implicit in these statements is that clients may perceive the verbal dialogue itself as falling short in enabling them to adequately process the information and to "internalize" and remember important facets of the therapy dialogue. These anecdotes may illustrate as well that clients somehow view therapy as an educational environment whereby they will receive pertinent information to help them achieve their goals.

## PSYCHOTHERAPY AS PSYCHOEDUCATION

During their schooling, psychotherapists learn a core body of knowledge about the theory and practice of psychotherapy. For example, therapists learn about various therapy interventions and "empirically supported treatments," the process and outcome of psychotherapy, and factors that influence the therapeutic alliance. This knowledge provides the foundation to enable therapists to effectively practice their trade. To the extent that psychotherapy entails sharing this information with clients, it is *psychoeducational*. To the extent that psychotherapy entails explaining to clients the nature of their problem and the recommended treatment, it is *psychoeducational*. To the extent that psychotherapy entails helping clients learn coping strategies, it is *psychoeducational*. Indeed, we believe that in many ways psychotherapy is fundamentally a psychoeducational process, a process of explaining the rationale for treatment, formulating goals, helping clients gain insight and understanding into their thoughts, emotions, and behaviors, identifying problem areas, and teaching coping strategies. What emerges is a sort of "learning environment."

> This book provides practical suggestions and recommendations to illustrate how therapists working with any clinical population can use visually mediated strategies to enhance communication and information processing in the therapy session.

We believe that therapists can maximize therapy communication and information processing within this learning environment by using strategies and activities that are known to enhance learning, understanding, memory, and information processing. Augmenting verbal communication with verbal-visual communication (e.g., diagrams, worksheets, written lists of coping strategies, word processing activities) can ultimately facilitate the exchange of information, enhance the chances of clients remembering the dialogue, and enhance clients' ability to use the information outside of the therapy session.

The value of using multimodal communication methods became increasingly evident to us as we noticed how these communication methods seemed to more actively engage clients by augmenting auditory processing and improving clients' ability to focus on relevant and practical therapy goals. A natural extension of this was to more directly and deliberately use visual methods to engage clients in the therapy session. Their attention to visually mediated methods, such as diagrams, became apparent as the diagrams seemed to quickly capture clients' attention and enable them to more clearly express their thoughts and feelings. Clients could more easily process the verbal dialogue and engage more directly in a goal-focused discussion. This further inspired the book's main theme of using *visually mediated strategies* to augment traditional verbal therapy.

Although there are numerous workbooks, "empirically supported treatments," and protocol-driven therapies that may, for example, rely periodically on using visuals, this book differs from customary "treatment manuals" or problem-focused workbooks. Our book is designed to help clinicians address a broad range of clinical problems and themes across diverse client populations, clinical settings, and age groups. This book presents ways to communicate more effectively with your clients and to visualize the information and themes of the therapy dialogue that emerge during the session. We do not argue whether one therapy approach is superior to another but rather how one can use visuals to maximize communication in any therapy format, with any clinical population, and using any theoretical model.

VET is designed to enable clients to better understand and communicate their feelings and thoughts, better understand therapy concepts, and more effectively remember and use coping strategies. This is achieved by augmenting the verbal dialogue with diagrams, images, and goal-setting charts and by using in-session writing exercises and homework sheets to reinforce therapy goals and coping strategies. We discuss multiple ways that you can use these visuals, handouts, and diagrams to assist both you and your clients in remembering, understanding, and using the information discussed in the session. For example, we discuss how you can use these visually mediated strategies to convey a concept, explain various mood states and "mental processes," understand certain behavioral dynamics, or present universal therapy themes and coping strategies. Additionally, we discuss how you can use visuals spontaneously in session to diagram the dialogue and to help your client stay more focused during the session.

## STRENGTHENING INFORMATION RETENTION AND THE COMMUNICATION PLATFORM IN PSYCHOTHERAPY

In our prior research and clinical work, we have illustrated how using visually mediated strategies can enhance the therapy dialogue, more actively engage clients, and provide a common framework through which the client and therapist can focus the therapy discussion (Ahmed, 1998, 2002, 2016; Ahmed, Bayog, & Boisvert, 1997; Ahmed & Boisvert, 2003a). Visuals provide a structure that is not typically present in traditional verbal therapy. For example, using a white board or computer monitor to display the information in the session can quickly center the conversation and enable the verbal dialogue to stay more "theme-focused." The white board or computer monitor provides a sort of holding place for the information. This process of visualizing the verbal dialogue can reduce the chances of the therapist and client going astray in the sometimes random or idiosyncratic verbalizations of the client. The visuals also provide the therapist with a framework through which to structure the conversation and to minimize the impulse to sometimes "float around in the verbal world of the client."

A primary goal of the book is to assist therapists in strengthening information retention and the communication platform in psychotherapy. It is our belief that VET communication strategies will help maximize both the therapist's and the client's processing of the information by providing a more structured framework through which the therapist and client can communicate more clearly. We believe that this will help increase the chances of the client understanding and remembering the information discussed in therapy and ultimately benefitting more from the therapy dialogue. In Chapter 2 we discuss research in the fields of cognitive science, education, communication, and language and memory. We discuss how research findings in these areas can inform our understanding of the brain's memory systems and information processing abilities and how these findings can potentially inform the practice of psychotherapy. In Chapter 3 we discuss ways to become a visually oriented therapist and provide guidelines for how to equip your therapy station with visual materials.

In Chapters 4–7 we discuss specific ways that you can use visually mediated communication strategies in your therapy sessions. It is likely that you will be familiar with several of the therapy topics and coping strategies described in this book. Many of the topics we present have been recognized as common therapy problems, such as worry, rumination, pain, panic, and mood regulation (Barlow, 2014; Beck, 2011; Bourne, 2015; Leahy, 2018; Leahy, Holland, & McGinn, 2011; Mckay, Davis, & Fanning, 2011; Nathan & Gorman, 2015; Roth & Fonagy, 2004). We also present other universal experiential themes, such as mindfulness, uncertainty, and stress, which many of your clients will likely relate to and understand. To help explain these problems and many other therapy topics, we provide over 100 diagrams and easy-to-remember terms, such as *the map of the mind*, *anger arrows*, *depression ditches*, and *time circles*.

We use the term *visual* to refer to any visually cued method that a therapist can use to facilitate communication in the therapy session. These methods could include drawing a diagram, using a handout or worksheet, using the computer to visually reflect elements of the therapy conversation, using an electronic device to present information, or using a movement exercise to focus attention.

In Chapter 4 we discuss ways to use visuals to gather information in the session, such as identifying client values, brainstorming goals, and gathering relevant historical information using timelines, pie graphs, and goal-setting charts. In Chapter 5 we illustrate various ways to use visuals to address and explain universal therapy topics, such as mindfulness, stress, ambivalence, communication, and uncertainty. In Chapter 6 we discuss ways to use visuals to address common clinical problems, such as worry, rumination, pain, mood regulation, urges, and low motivation. In both of these chapters, we provide teaching points to explain the topic and guides for drawing or displaying a particular diagram that illustrates the topic. For each topic we have also developed an in-session worksheet to use with your clients to assist them in applying the topic to their lives and a coping strategy handout that your clients can use after the session to practice new coping skills.

You may find it easiest to use the handouts and worksheets in Chapter 4 with new clients to assist you in gathering important background and historical information and identifying relevant therapy goals. For your already established clients, you may prefer to begin with Chapter 5 or Chapter 6, which illustrate how to use visuals to further discuss and explain common therapy topics and problem areas. Even if you have already covered certain topics or problem areas with your clients, you can use the visuals in Chapters 5 and 6 to further reinforce information you have covered. Using the visuals is also a way to check your client's understanding of concepts you have previously covered in therapy. You may also find that some of the diagrams and visuals can further your client's understanding of the particular topic or clinical problem area. For example, if you have covered the topic of worry, you could use some of the worry diagrams to further reinforce or discuss this topic and to perhaps develop some new coping strategies to assist your client in managing the problem more effectively.

In Chapter 7 we discuss how to use visuals spontaneously in session and how to use common diagrams, such as a tree, a barometer, and a Venn diagram to illustrate common therapy themes. We also provide several case examples of various ways we have used diagrams, drawings, and writing strategies in therapy sessions. The case examples and suggestions we provide are drawn from actual clinical experience using visuals in therapy sessions. We conclude the chapter by offering various tips on how to use visuals and visually mediated activities to more actively engage your clients in the therapy session. In Chapter 8 we discuss using various multimodal strategies with special clinical populations, such as behaviorally challenged children and adolescents, clients with schizophrenia, geriatric patients, dually diagnosed clients, and developmentally disabled clients. We draw from some of our prior work with these populations, who historically have not benefitted optimally from traditional verbal therapy approaches. In this chapter we also discuss using visual observation and body movement exercises with these client populations to promote more adaptive skills and to enhance their ability to "visually navigate" the social and physical world. Chapter 9 closes the book with a review of the components of the VET model, provides a diagram that illustrates the various components of the VET model, and offers some general recommendations for using visually mediated strategies.

The following is a brief description of the nature of the handouts and worksheets in the appendices. You can use any of the handouts or worksheets as needed to address a relevant clinical issue with your clients and to assist them in developing more effective coping strategies.

*Appendix A: Information-Gathering Tools.* Information-gathering (IG) worksheets are worksheets used to gather information on your client's background, values, goals, and daily activities. The IG worksheets include timelines, pie charts, and goal-setting worksheets and can be completed during the session or, if needed, finished outside of the session.

*Appendix B: Universal Therapy Topics: Diagrams, Worksheets, and Handouts.* This appendix includes in-session (IS) worksheets and coping strategy (CS) handouts to use with your clients when reviewing the various topics of mindfulness, ambivalence, uncertainty, stress, and communication. The *in-session worksheets* are used to apply the topic to your client's current life situation. The *coping strategy handouts* are used for homework to assist your client in practicing the coping strategy associated with the topic.

*Appendix C: Common Clinical Problems: Diagrams, Worksheets, and Handouts.* This appendix includes IS worksheets and CS handouts to use with your clients when reviewing the various clinical topics of worry, pain, rumination, mood regulation, motivation, self-esteem, panic, and urges. The *in-session worksheets* are diagrams to use to apply the topic to your client's current life situation. The *coping strategy handouts* are used for homework to assist your client in practicing the coping strategy to manage the clinical problem.

*Appendix D: Miscellaneous Diagrams.* These diagrams and handouts address various topics, such as shyness, regret, communication, mood monitoring, disorganization, cognitive defusion, traffic stress, and family background. Various diagrams are used, such as the Venn diagram, the genogram, the tree, the barometer, and others.

*Appendix E: Mind Stimulation Exercises and Handouts.* This appendix includes various handouts, such as body movement exercises, paper-and-pencil cognitive exercises, coping statement handouts, and self-assessment tools. These various materials can be used with the special clinical populations addressed in Chapter 8 as well as with many other clients.

*Appendix F: Brief Assessment Tools.* These tools can be used to assess your clients' progress in reaching their therapy goals.

*Appendix G: Objectifying Therapy: Using Common Objects to Convey Therapy Concepts.* We provide a table describing how common objects can be used in therapy sessions to "visually" convey various therapy themes and concepts.

*Appendix H: Coping Cards.* These sheets contains 10 cards roughly the size of a credit card that clients can easily carry in their pockets, purses, or wallets. The cards are designed for the therapist to give to clients during sessions so that clients can write down a coping strategy and carry it with them as a reminder.

*Appendix I: Mini (Wallet) Diagrams.* These are wallet-size pictures of eight different diagrams discussed in the book. Your clients can use these as quick reminders of the coping strategies associated with the diagram. These mini diagrams include the following: time circles, the barometer, the tree, pain circuits, rumination, urges, communication, and worry.

## UNIQUE FEATURES OF THE BOOK

This book differs fundamentally from other workbooks or manuals. Although other workbooks and manuals may provide some worksheets and handouts for clients, this book is specifically designed to use writing exercises and drawings to actively engage both you and your client during the therapy session. The book will teach you various ways to creatively use writing and drawings during the actual therapy session. This differs from other traditional therapy methods that focus primarily on "discussing issues" and that assume the client will "engage" with the material after the session by remembering it and applying it. In the strategies we discuss, the active engagement starts right in the session, and the methods provide you with specific and concrete ways to stimulate your client's thinking, information processing, and active involvement during the actual session. We encourage you to use these visually mediated methods creatively and spontaneously but also in planful ways as you reflect on your clients' needs and prepare for your therapy sessions. We also encourage you to pick and choose any of the diagrams, handouts, or exercises you think will best meet your clients' needs.

The book is not laden with clinical jargon or esoteric concepts and is designed to be user-friendly, "language accessible," and visually appealing. The strategies and diagrams are easy to implement and are applicable to a wide range of clinical populations, ages, and clinical problems. You should find that most of the areas covered will be relevant to your clinical practice and will be applicable to the work you are doing with your clients. Fundamentally, we encourage you to continue providing therapy using the theoretical model you have been trained in or subscribe to but to incorporate VET methods as adjunctive strategies to enhance your clinical practice. Our aim is to provide you with visually mediated communication strategies to enhance the psychoeducational facets of therapy and to assist you in focusing more effectively on therapy goals and themes that emerge in the session. We believe that VET will provide you with new methods to present, understand, and communicate information so that ultimately your client will remember and use the information discussed in the sessions more easily and effectively.

In Chapter 2 we discuss how research findings in the fields of cognitive science, education, communication, and language and memory support how visuals can be effective teaching tools by enhancing communication and facilitating learning. We suggest ways that these findings may apply to psychotherapy. We also discuss how research findings describing the limitations of working memory and auditory processing may have implications for the field of psychotherapy—a field that historically has relied on auditory processing as its core communication modality.

VET is designed to assist both you and your client in using a collaborative framework to communicate more clearly, remember information exchanged in the therapy, and actively use this information to formulate goals and coping strategies.

# 2

# Diagrams as Communication and Teaching Tools

## The Application of Research Findings to Psychotherapy

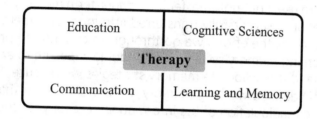

*There is in general no guarantee of the correctness of our memory; and yet we yield to the compulsion to attach belief.*

—Sigmund Freud, *The Interpretation of Dreams*

In this chapter we discuss how research findings from the fields of cognitive science, education, communication, and learning and memory can inform psychotherapy. The research findings we discuss provide the foundation for the framework of VET and the rationale for using visual strategies to augment information processing in psychotherapy. For each research section, we extract central themes and research findings that may be applicable to psychotherapy. As you read these research findings, we invite you to reflect on what they may imply when considered in the context of the "psychotherapy learning environment"—an environment that relies heavily on verbal and auditory processing. After each section, we conclude with a "Therapy Thought Box," suggesting how the research findings may apply to psychotherapy.

First, we discuss cognitive science research addressing the brain's auditory and visual information processing systems, cognitive load theory, and how language, attention, vision, and memory systems interact. We discuss, for example, how understanding the brain's memory and information processing systems may provide a conceptual framework from which we can design more effective psychotherapy communication strategies. We provide examples of how the therapist, for example, may be able to use visually mediated strategies to activate the client's memory systems and to recruit more effective information processing mechanisms to facilitate the client's retention of the information shared during the therapy dialogue.

## COGNITIVE SCIENCES

### Memory Systems: Working Memory and Long-Term Memory

Cognitive science researchers have suggested that our brains have two distinct yet interactive memory systems—one that enables us to hold information in mind to perform some operation on it (*working memory*) and another that stores our accumulated knowledge (*long-term memory*). These systems work in a coordinated fashion—for example, in enabling us to process information at the moment, perform a necessary task, and then potentially transfer the information into longer-term memory storage so it can be used later. Not all information that is operated on in working memory will be stored. For example, we may "memorize" a phone number just long enough to use it but not transfer it to longer-term memory for later retrieval. Whether information is successfully transferred into long-term memory depends on various factors, such as the efforts we go through to continue to process the information in our working memory systems, our ongoing exposure to and processing of the information, and the deliberate memory strategies we practice.

Baddeley (1992) defined working memory as "a brain system that provides temporary storage and manipulation of the information necessary for such complex cognitive tasks as language comprehension, learning, and reasoning" (p. 556). Baddeley (1992) also suggested that working memory has been found to require the simultaneous storage and processing of information and is divided into three subcomponents, including an "attentional system," a "visual system" that processes visual images, and a "verbal system" that stores and rehearses speech-based information. Researchers have suggested that our working memories essentially are comprised of both auditory and visual information processing systems (Baddeley, 1992, 1998). The auditory system processes language and information that is heard while the visual system processes information that is seen.

Research suggests that our working memory system is quite limited in the amount of information it can hold. In his seminal article, Miller (1956) described the limits to our working memory and its capacity to process information. He concluded that

> the unaided observer is severely limited in terms of the amount of information he can receive, process, and remember. However, it is shown that by the use of various techniques, e.g., use of several stimulus dimensions, recoding, and various mnemonic devices, this informational bottleneck can be broken.
>
> (p. 81)

Cowan (2010) stated that "working memory storage capacity is important because cognitive tasks can be completed only with sufficient ability to hold information as it is processed" (p. 51). Ma, Husain, and Bays (2014) suggested that "the quality rather than the quantity of working memory representations determines performance" (p. 347).

These findings as a whole suggest that our working memory is limited but can be enhanced and more easily transfer information into long-term memory when memory-enhancing strategies are used. For example, working memory seems to be maximized when information is presented in both auditory and visual modalities, such as using words *and* pictures to convey information (Mayer, 2005; Mousavi, Low, & Sweller, 1995; Sweller, 2003, 2005; Sweller, Van Merrienboer, & Paas, 1998). The way in which the information is organized can also affect the ability of our working memory to process the information (Ayres & Paas, 2012). Standing (1973) suggested that the capacity for "picture memory" is remarkably high and that visual memories are "robust" and can be retained in long-term memory.

## Cognitive Load Theory (CLT)

Cognitive load theory (CLT) has been a focus of study in both the cognitive sciences and the education fields. CTL is grounded in findings from memory research that have examined the interaction between working memory and long-term memory and how understanding this interaction can be used to identify strategies to facilitate learning (Ayres & Paas, 2012; Sweller, Ayres, & Kalyuga, 2011). The load placed on one's working memory is the *cognitive load*. Too much cognitive load can be created, for example, when information processing systems cannot efficiently process the information due to the complexity of the information or the poor organization of the information (Ayres & Paas, 2012; Sweller, 1988, 1993). Such processes as "split attention" or needing to simultaneously process multiple and poorly integrated or displayed sources of information have been shown to increase cognitive load and ultimately impede learning and information retention (Roodenrys, Agostinho, Roodenrys, & Chandler, 2012). Also, cognitive load can be increased when cognitive resources are diverted to processing information that is only marginally related to the learning task or when working memory resources are depleted due to being recruited for extraneous tasks (Artino, 2008). CLT researchers in the education field have focused on exploring instructional methods that reduce cognitive load by freeing up working memory, which enables learners to direct attention and cognitive resources to relevant learning tasks and goals (Artino, 2008).

### Therapy Thought Box

*The process of psychotherapy requires therapists and clients to engage their working and long-term memory systems to process the verbal information and the therapy dialogue. It requires clients to learn new information and to find ways to implement and apply this information. These memory and "learning" systems are needed to retrieve relevant information and historical material, determine what aspects of the current information to attend to, and determine how to apply the information to formulate therapy goals and strategies to reach these goals.*

*The fundamental principles of cognitive load theory and findings from memory research may have relevance to understanding communication processes in psychotherapy. Is relying on verbal processing alone less effective than we think because it ignores the limitations of human working memory and imposes a heavy cognitive load on both the therapist and the client? Think of running your session with the following questions in mind: "What do I want my client to remember from this session, and what am I doing to facilitate that? Will verbal repetition be enough?"*

*Specifically, using visuals to supplement the verbal dialogue may enhance short- and long-term memory systems and lessen the cognitive load of both the therapist and the client. For example, the therapist can become more focused on what the client is saying by using a visual to write down a theme verbalized by the client. The therapist can share how they are processing the client's information.*

*With the visual aid, the client now directs attention outward to process the visual display of their verbalizations. The client recruits their visual attentional system and simultaneously uses both auditory and visual processing. Ultimately, the visuals (e.g., using a white board or notepad to display information or using handouts to reinforce the information) can help maximize the client's retention of the therapy themes (see Figure 2.1 comparing traditional verbal therapy with visually enhanced therapy).*

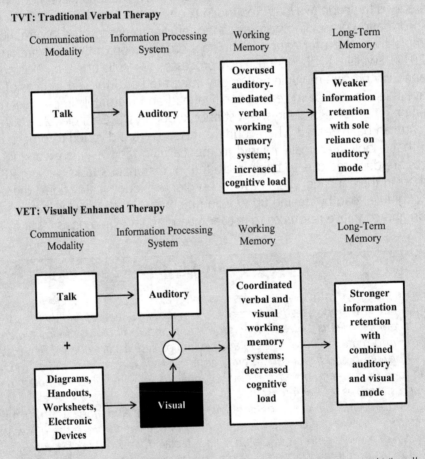

*Figure 2.1* Comparing Memory Systems in Traditional Verbal Therapy and Visually Enhanced Therapy

## Information Processing: Auditory and Visual Attentional Systems

Cognitive science research has examined the interaction between our auditory and visual information processing systems and how language, vision, attention, and memory interact. For example, Huettig, Mishra, and Olivers (2012) used tracking eye movements to study attention to common objects in one's visual field, how visual attention is guided or influenced by linguistic representations, and how our mental world interacts with input from the visual environment. They concluded that "a hallmark of human cognition is its ability to integrate rapidly perceptual (e.g., visual and auditory) input with stored linguistic and non-linguistic mental representations" (p. 1) and that "language-mediated visual orienting arises because linguistic and non-linguistic information and attention are instantiated in the same coding and substrate" (p. 9). They suggested that linguistic and non-linguistic (visual) representations are connected such that when we hear spoken words, long-term memory activates semantic structures, which in turn activate associated visual representations in memory. Similarly, Cavicchio, Melcher, and Poesion (2014) suggested that visual input has a rapid effect on language interpretation, and visual information can help "disambiguate the interpretation of information and that verbalizing words associated with a visual can help make the visual more salient and meaningful" (p. 9).

In a seminal article, Cooper (1974) found that "continuous speech is interpreted from moment to moment in the context of the contemporary visual field" (p. 84) and stated that

> when people are simultaneously presented with spoken language and a visual field containing elements or objects semantically related to the informative items of speech, they tend to spontaneously direct their line of sight to those elements which are most closely related to the meaning of the language currently heard.

(p. 84)

By studying eye-tracking moments, Tanenhaus, Spivey-Knowlton, Eberland, & Sedivy (1995) provided support for the integration of our visual and linguistic processing systems in deriving meaning from conversations. They found that "visual context affected the resolution of temporary ambiguities within individual words" (p. 1632). They also concluded that "referentially relevant nonlinguistic information immediately affects the manner in which the linguistic input is initially structured" (p. 1634) and that this paradigm can extend to "understanding conversational interactions during cooperative problem solving" (p. 1634).

### Therapy Thought Box

*The research that has examined the interaction between our auditory and visual attention systems may have implications for the visual-auditory interaction in routine therapy conversations, such as how visual stimuli like diagrams or illustrations may direct* attention and influence linguistic processing. Using visuals may serve to focus the client and direct their attention to the more pertinent details of the discussion. Visuals may activate more "relevant" linguistic opportunities that enable the client to further expand upon or explore the therapy topic or theme. This may then minimize the client's superfluous verbalizations and overlearned thinking habits that can be readily activated when relying solely on auditory and verbal processing in the session (see Figure 2.2).

Additionally, therapy supervision could focus more on determining how well the client is understanding and receiving the intended messages in therapy and what the therapist is doing to maximize the client's understanding and engagement in therapy as opposed to using the more traditional supervision focus on how well the therapist in training explains themes and issues (i.e., traditional supervision tends to focus more on the therapist's verbal facility in explaining the case versus the client's capacity for understanding).

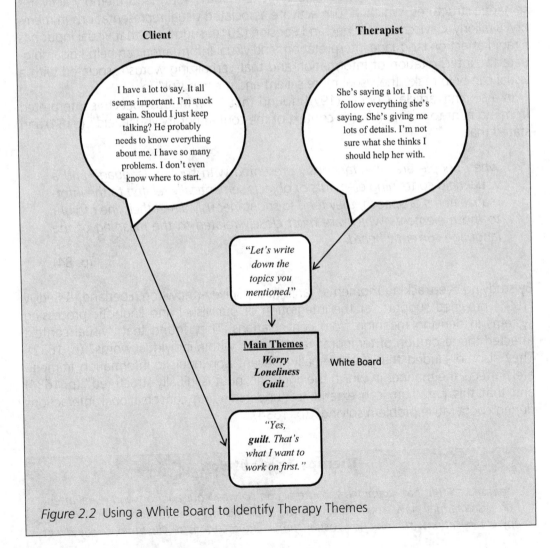

Figure 2.2  Using a White Board to Identify Therapy Themes

## EDUCATION RESEARCH

### Knowledge and Concept Maps

Research in the education field has shown the benefits of visual learning in increasing retention of information and engaging the learner more actively in the learning process. Researchers, for example, have found that various graphic organizers, such as knowledge maps (Chmielewski & Dansereau, 1998) and concept maps (Novak, 1990), have been used successfully in educational settings to promote knowledge retention and reading comprehension and to facilitate memory and recall of information. Knowledge and concepts maps essentially are diagrams presented in a "node-link" layout that represent ideas. They are used, for example, as communication aids in lectures and study materials, and they essentially help facilitate learning (Nesbit & Adescope, 2006). Research has also shown that students can improve their performance by having access to visual modalities, such as PowerPoint, to supplement verbal material (Susskind, 2005). Similarly, in other fields, such as the medical field, Hill (2006) found that using visual concept maps was useful in communicating medication information to patients.

In a meta-analytic review of the literature, Nesbit and Adescope (2006) found that using knowledge and concept maps increased students' knowledge retention. Stiller, Freitag, Zinnbauer, & Freitag (2009) found that visual texts reduced cognitive load on learners and increased retention performance. In the field of education, "visual literacy" has also been applied to the learning process. Burmack (2002) described visual literacy as a "person's ability to interpret and create visual information—to understand images of all kinds and use them to communicate more effectively" (p. v). Stokes (2001) reviewed literature on visual literacy and reported that using visuals in teaching enhances learning. Titsworth (2001) and Witt, Wheeless, and Allen (2004) concluded that student learning and memory retention for lectures is maximized when the presentation or lecture contains organizational cues and when students take notes. They made a case for writing as an enhancement strategy for maximizing student learning.

### Diagrams and External Representations

Researchers found that the pictures and diagrams can facilitate learning and information processing. For example, Fletcher and Tobias (2005) described the multimedia principle as "people learn better from words and pictures than from words alone." (p. 117) In a seminal article, Larkin and Simon (1987) discussed the communication value of visuals, such as diagrams, and stated that "one may be able to use the information in a verbal description to draw or image a diagram or use a diagram to infer verbal statements" (p. 66) and concluded that "diagrams can be superior to a verbal description in solving a problem" (p. 98). Stenning and Oberlander (1995) discussed how diagrams can "limit and focus abstraction" and facilitate information processing or "processibility" of a concept. In the computer field, research has supported the benefits of using diagrams to think and communicate more effectively and the role that diagrams can play in the learning process (Brna, 2001). In the legal arena, Faust and Ahern (2011) and Gass (2011) discussed how to use visuals and diagrams in the courtroom to enhance communication. Gass (2011) highlighted the adjunctive value of using visuals and the significant gain in jurors' information retention when they were exposed to information delivered in both verbal and visual modalities compared to just the verbal modality.

Zhang reviewed research on external representations (knowledge and structures in the environment, such as objects, diagrams, and written symbols) and how they provide a separate knowledge structure compared to internal representations (the knowledge structures in people's heads). Zhang (2000, 1997) discussed how external representations are intrinsic to many cognitive tasks and serve to guide and determine cognitive behavior. He suggested that external representations can serve as memory aids, extend working memory, form more permanent memories, and enable one to access information and skills that may be unavailable from internal representations. Zhang (1991) further added that this "external structure can a) serve as an external memory aid; b) provide information that can be directly perceived and used; c) anchor and structure cognitive behavior; and d) change the nature of the task" (p. 958).

## Diagrammatic Reasoning

Venn first introduced "diagrammatic reasoning" in his article "On Diagrammatic and Mechanical Representations of Propositions and Reasoning" (Venn, 1880). Hoffman (2011) discussed diagrammatic reasoning as a method to facilitate individual or social thinking processes in situations that are too complex to be coped with exclusively by internal cognitive means. He suggested that diagrammatic reasoning can reduce the cognitive load and is about "problem solving, decision making, knowledge development, and belief change by means of diagrams" (Hoffman, 2011, p. 193). He suggested that by communicating through a diagram, we can stimulate reasoning and other thought processes.

Hoffman (2011, p. 193) discussed diagrammatic reasoning as a process that can "facilitate thinking processes" by enabling one to do the following:

1. Reflect on something without being constrained by the limits of one's short-term, or working, memory.
2. Analyze a problem more thoroughly and systematically.
3. Clarify and coordinate confused ideas about a problem.
4. Clarify implicit assumptions and background knowledge that might be insufficient or inadequate.
5. Structure a problem space.
6. Change perspectives.
7. Identify "unintended and unexpected" implications.
8. Play with interpretations.
9. Discover contradictions.
10. Distinguish the essential from the peripheral.

One could replace the words "diagrammatic reasoning" with "therapy goals and processes." If diagrams can achieve these aims, then one could argue for their use in therapy, particularly short-term, problem-focused therapy approaches.

---

### Therapy Thought Box

*These findings have potential implications for how to maximize the learning environment in therapy. Organizing your clients' verbalizations and themes through illustrations, flowcharts, and topic-based diagrams may help them better understand relationships and connections between their thoughts, feelings, and behaviors. The diagrams can serve as an external memory aid and anchor the discussion. Encouraging writing in the therapy session can also reinforce information. For example, you could invite your clients to write out their goals, brainstorm solutions to problems, or write out various coping strategies discussed. They could bring a notebook to session or use, for example, index cards to record pertinent information. Clients could also be encouraged to use a personal journaling diary to express their thoughts and feelings without necessarily needing to share these thoughts with their therapist. They could use journaling for their own thought expression and organization and to promote the logical expression of their ideas.*

---

## COMMUNICATION RESEARCH

### Recall From Conversations

In the communication literature, we find a body of both empirical and theoretical research supporting the discovery that our memories tend to be poor for accurately recalling details of conversations. Recall for various types of conversations averages about 10%, and we tend to retain only global impressions of our conversations (Ross & Sicoly, 1979; Stafford & Daly, 1984). Miller, deWinstanley, and Carey (1996) found that people have a better memory for their own conversation versus their partner's conversation and that the longer the conversation, the less accurate the recall. They also found that we tend to recall only about 20% of the details from a conversation and that we inaccurately recall at the same rate that we accurately recall. Additionally, the personal importance one places on an event or conversation seems to improve the recall of the event (Conway & Bekerian, 1987).

### The Goals of a Conversation

Todman (2002) suggested that, in general, we bring limited attention resources to a conversation and have difficulty generating "ideal" utterances rapidly during a conversation due to the limited capacity of our working memory. This limited capacity of our working memory also prevents us from producing many potential utterances because we cannot hold them long enough in memory. He suggested that

> when the main goal is to convey information accurately . . . precision takes precedence . . . however, when social goals, such as enjoying the interpersonal interaction or creating a favorable impression predominate, what is said is often quick and approximate rather than precise.
>
> (Todman, 2002, p. 69)

He suggested that if our goal is to achieve a social connection, then we will more likely focus on maintaining "conversational momentum," relying on "reusable utterances" as opposed to providing lots of details.

## Therapy Thought Box

*As you reflect on these findings in the communication literature, consider the following questions: How much is my client really remembering? Will we both forget the majority of today's conversation? How can I help my client remember the information? What are the goals of the conversation? Could my client's 'reusable utterances' simply reflect their thinking habits that get activated during "un-cued" conversation? Without visual cuing to aid the conversation, your client's attention may continue to be directed inward. A "prolonged" supportive listening stance may serve to foster the relationship but unwittingly reinforce these overlearned thinking and conversational habits (see Figure 2.3).*

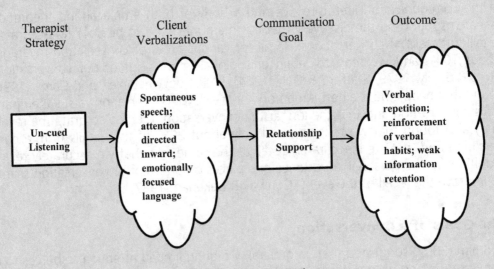

**Traditional Verbal Therapy**

| Therapist Strategy | Client Verbalizations | Communication Goal | Outcome |
|---|---|---|---|
| Un-cued Listening | Spontaneous speech; attention directed inward; emotionally focused language | Relationship Support | Verbal repetition; reinforcement of verbal habits; weak information retention |

*Figure 2.3* Un-Cued Therapy Communication Strategies

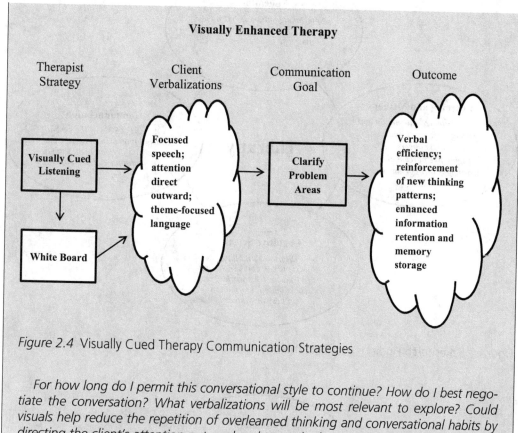

**Visually Enhanced Therapy**

Therapist Strategy — Client Verbalizations — Communication Goal — Outcome

Visually Cued Listening

White Board

Focused speech; attention direct outward; theme-focused language

Clarify Problem Areas

Verbal efficiency; reinforcement of new thinking patterns; enhanced information retention and memory storage

*Figure 2.4* Visually Cued Therapy Communication Strategies

*For how long do I permit this conversational style to continue? How do I best negotiate the conversation? What verbalizations will be most relevant to explore? Could visuals help reduce the repetition of overlearned thinking and conversational habits by directing the client's attention outward and toward relevant therapy goals and themes that emerge during the dialogue? (See Figure 2.4.)*

## A VISUAL SUMMARY OF THE RESEARCH

Figure 2.5 presents a visual summary of research findings that may have implications for psychotherapy. Notice that the entire *therapy circle* is not filled. The nonoverlapping and larger section represents the core facets of therapy, such as relationship building, active listening, nonverbal gestures, instilling hope, and general alliance building—all facets that represent the more traditional characteristics of verbal psychotherapy. The overlapping sections represent the psychoeducational facets of therapy, such as sharing information, explaining concepts and themes, designing coping strategies, and exploring various interventions that can assist clients in reaching their therapy goals.

The suggestions in the overlapping parts (see Figure 2.6) represent how these research findings potentially apply to the psychoeducational nature of therapy whereby the therapist is, for example, gathering information to identify treatment goals, the client is learning new information, and the therapist is teaching a skill or explaining a

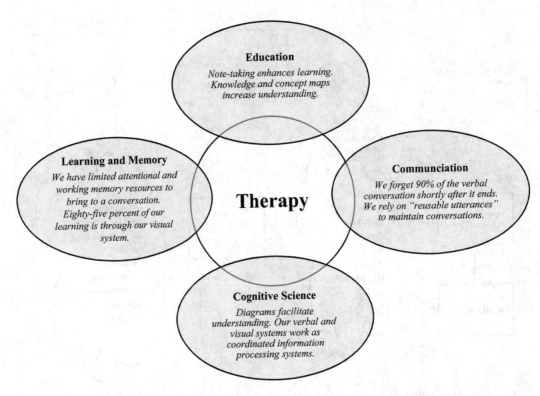

Figure 2.5 Research Findings in Allied Therapy Fields

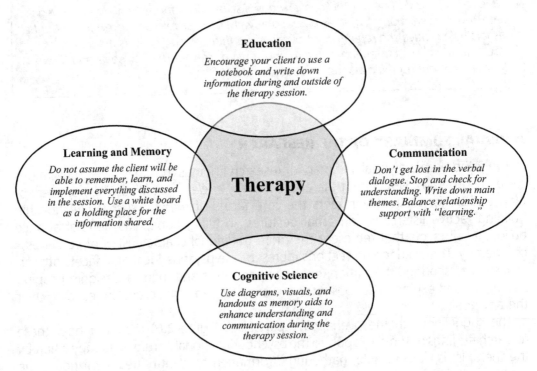

Figure 2.6 Potential Implications of Research Findings in Allied Therapy Fields

concept. To be effective in these areas of therapy, it is important to understand ways to best facilitate and maximize your client's processing of information.

Our aim in the remainder of the book is to show how therapists can enhance communication in therapy by using various visually mediated and multimodal communication strategies. In the next chapter, we discuss how to set the foundation to become a visually oriented therapist. We discuss the value of using visually aided strategies to help your clients focus their attention, enhance their communication, retain more information from the session, and more actively use coping strategies by more directly and deliberately using the information discussed in the session. We also discuss various types of visual methods and multimodal strategies and the purposes these may serve as well as ways to equip your therapy station with visually oriented materials.

# 3

# Becoming a Visually Oriented Therapist
## Setting the Foundation

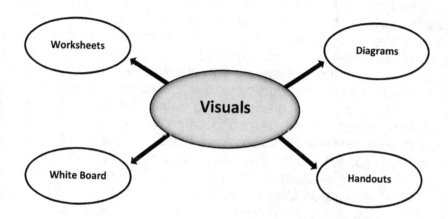

In this chapter we discuss the rationale for using visually mediated strategies, such as a white board, diagrams, and handouts, during your therapy sessions. We discuss the central role that attention plays in directing communication and thought processes and how, for example, using various visual aids can keep both you and your client more focused on therapy themes. Incorporating visually mediated strategies can also keep clients "linguistically centered" on core issues that emerge during the session. We begin by discussing some of Dansereau's work using what is called node-link mapping—a method used to present and convey information more clearly in therapy sessions. We then discuss how to broadly conceptualize visually mediated strategies and the multiple purposes that these strategies can serve in a therapy session. We discuss how using visually aided props, such as a white board, can help direct attention and provide a common visual field through which the therapist and client can collaboratively discuss and explore relevant therapy themes and goals. We also discuss writing as a "visual-motor" engagement strategy, which activates more sophisticated information processing systems in clients and provides them with a "vehicle" through which they can express and discuss material that may not be as easily or readily shared in a more traditional "conversational" therapy format. We conclude the chapter by discussing ways to equip your therapy station with visual materials and props to more actively engage your clients in the therapy encounter. We understand that you may already be using some visuals in your therapy sessions, such as worksheets, and encourage you to continue to use these. Our primary aim is to provide you with a rationale for using additional visually mediated strategies and techniques and to teach you ways to creatively incorporate these techniques into your clinical work.

## DANSEREAU: NODE-LINK MAPPING

Dansereau (2005) and Dansereau and Simpson (2009) have written about using node-link (box-line) graphic representations to convey information more clearly. They discussed three types of node-link displays that may be applicable to counseling: information maps (used by the "expert" to convey information about specialized topics); guide maps (fill-in-the-blank graphic tools that can be used to facilitate self-exploration, planning, and problem-solving), and freestyle maps (produced from scratch as a note-taking technique or vehicle to express and organize personal knowledge). Their research supports how using diagrams and maps may potentially enhance various aspects of counseling, including client engagement, understanding, follow-through, and insight into problems. Dansereau, Joe, and Simpson (1993) researched how node-link mapping and using visuals during drug abuse counseling can actively involve the client in problem-solving. They suggested that mapping can be useful when counselors and clients differ in verbal abilities, as the map provides a "visual bridge for the exchange of information" (Dansereau et al., 1993, p. 394). They discussed how using visuals is central to maximizing learning in these "educational-like" relationships and environments. Similarly, Czuchry, Newbern-McFarland, and Dansereau, (2009) discussed the advantages of using various visual "mapping" techniques versus standard treatment to improve outcomes in substance abuse treatment.

A version of a node-link map may look something like the example shown in Figure 3.1.

Dansereau, Dees, and Simpson (1994) discussed how cognitive modularity (mental processing systems for handling different types of information) influences how information is represented and exchanged in client-counselor interactions. They concluded that "for certain counseling activities, spatial-graphic representations are likely to be useful adjuncts to natural language" (p. 513). They support the idea that these spatial-graphic displays can supplement language during what they call declarative counseling episodes. Due to the complexity of information processing and processing language, they make the case that diagrams and visuals can serve as "place keepers" to maintain focus on counseling themes by streamlining attention. One could hypothesize that this can help minimize the chances of clients becoming tangential and as a result less apt to lose their place in the conversation. It may help clients rely less on overlearned thinking habits and minimize their tendency to access stored language habits.

The node-link map is one type of visual method that can facilitate communication in therapy. Next we discuss various other types of visuals one could use in therapy sessions as well as various uses for visuals in therapy sessions.

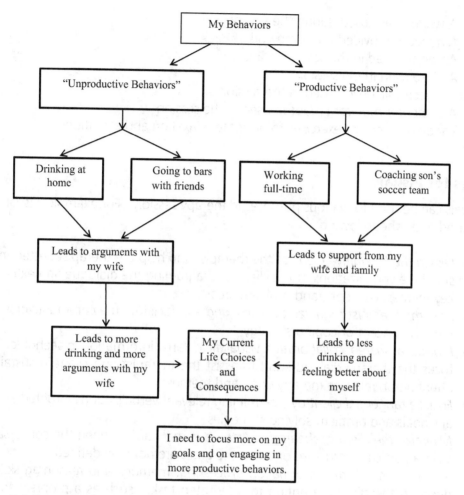

*Figure 3.1* Example of a Node-Link Map

## VISUALS BROADLY CONCEPTUALIZED

### Types of Visuals

We use the term *visual* to refer to any visually cued activity that a therapist could use to enhance communication during therapy sessions. A visual could be any of the following:

- A *diagram* drawn during the session
- A *worksheet* completed during the session

- A *white board* used during the session
- A *handout* provided for homework
- An *object* used in the session
- A *video* used in the session
- An *electronic device* used in the session
- A *computer monitor or laptop* used in the session
- Various *movement exercises* to promote relaxation and attention

## Uses for Visuals

Visuals can be used for various purposes in therapy sessions. For example, visuals can be used to do the following:

- *Lessen the "cognitive load"* of the therapist and help the therapist better understand the verbalizations of the client by diagraming the dialogue and extracting key themes, concepts, and problem areas
- *Help the therapist organize their thinking* and facilitate the communication of a therapy concept or coping strategy
- *Provide a shared collaborative visual field* (an "information placeholder") to focus the therapy dialogue and to assist the therapist and client in sustaining attention on relevant therapy goals and themes
- *Focus a tangential client* by streamlining relevant verbalizations targeted at therapy goals and problem-solving strategies
- *Minimize the client's rehearsal of "stored verbal habits"* when the conversation lacks a particular structure or when the goals are not well defined
- *Stimulate the client's information processing,* memory, and reasoning skills by directing the client's attention to a "written task," such as a problem-solving worksheet
- *Help a disengaged or low verbal client engage more actively* in the session by using the act of writing (e.g., writing out a list of goals, developing coping statements, listing stress management strategies)
- *Provide a medium, such as a computer (a visual device),* to generate handouts or printouts from the session that the client can use outside of the session to reinforce therapy goals
- *Record and remember tasks and take pictures, via the client's cell phone,* of diagrams and information written down during the session
- *Stimulate brain functioning via the computer* by finding tasks, games, and worksheets that clients can access in and outside of the session to stimulate their information processing (e.g., clients can find their favorite websites or favorite music lists and use this information to discuss interests and goals and to generate coping strategies)
- *Teach relaxation and redirection skills* through modeling various movement exercises

## FOCUSING ATTENTION

There are various ways to focus attention during therapy sessions. Did you ever notice, for example, that you may sometimes use nonverbal gestures in the therapy session to illustrate a point or to convey a particular concept? In some ways by using hand gestures you are trying to visually convey a concept or image to your client—a concept that may not be adequately explained through words alone. For example, by motioning high with one hand and low with the other hand, you may signify an imbalance in the client's thinking (e.g., raising one hand high may convey that the client uses lots of negative self-talk and lowering the other hand may convey that the client uses little positive self-talk). Similarly, you may use hand gestures to illustrate where your client is now and where they want to end up as a result of therapy. For example, by spreading your hands apart, you can illustrate the distance the client needs to travel to change. The outstretched right arm can represent where they are now, and the outstretched left arm can represent where they want to be. The outstretched arms can visually represent the path to change, and you can move the arms closer together to represent small incremental change and to illustrate the concept of patience and realistic expectations. You may also use outstretched hands to represent ambivalence or polarities, such as part of the client that feels confident and part of the client that feels unsure. Using nonverbal gestures can help direct the client's attention to the conversation and more actively engage the client in the conversation.

We will discuss ways to use a variety of visual techniques and multimodal strategies to engage your client in the therapy session. For example, we will discuss using a white board to list therapy themes and issues and to focus the client's attention at the very start of the session. By becoming more focused at the beginning of the session, both you and your client can more easily focus on therapy themes and goals. By providing a consistent structure and using visually aided methods, you can assist your clients in focusing the conversation and directing their attention to the most relevant therapy topics. Asking questions that are more theme focused can also help elicit more relevant information and keep the client "on track" in exploring therapy issues and working toward therapy goals. Moreover, adding a consistent structure through visually aided techniques can help "bridge the sessions" by reminding the client of what was discussed during the last session. There is value in using various communication methods and modalities during a therapy session. It is important to be flexible in using these various methods to help maximize communication and information processing during the session and to meet your client's specific needs. You will notice, however, that some methods and questioning techniques will better achieve certain communication goals and will be more likely to focus both you and your client on the primary therapy themes. Consider, for example, the difference between asking these two different questions to start the therapy session:

1. *"How are you doing?"*
2. *"Last time we discussed ways to manage your irritability . . . how did you do practicing the coping strategies?"* or *"What did you remember from our last session that you found helpful to practice?"*

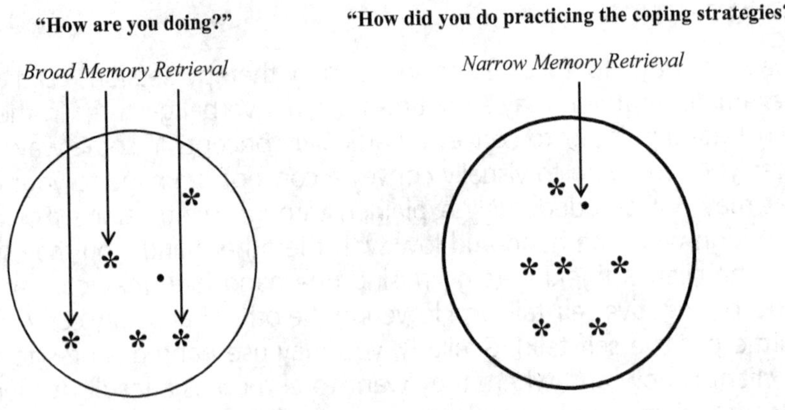

*Figure 3.2* Memory Retrieval Based on the Type of Question Posed by the Therapist

- The client is more likely to discuss the nature of the coping strategy discussed last session, how it was implemented, and the degree to which it helped the client manage the problem.
* The client could potentially discuss any of a variety of themes that come to mind from the past week, such as a change in work schedule, an argument with their partner, receiving an unexpected bill, a good week of sleep, their son receiving a school award, or hearing from a good friend. Some of these will be more or less relevant to the client's therapy goals.

The diagram illustrated in Figure 3.2 presents the various responses that could be elicited based on the different questions. The broad question "How are you doing?," although open-ended and potentially therapeutic, can elicit a wide range of responses, some of which may be potentially tangential and "distracting." For some clients, open-ended questions such as this may "feed into" their difficulties in redirecting themselves from habitual "ruminations" or their difficulties in resolving their "ambivalence." These clients often need more active cues and structured conversation to help them better focus in therapy. Therefore, the question "How did you do practicing the coping strategies?" centers the client on the goals from the last session and is more likely to elicit pertinent and relevant verbalizations associated with the client's therapy goals.

Displaying, for example, a white board with the therapy themes listed at the start of the session can help focus both you and your client. It may also help minimize "reusable utterances" and reiterations of problem areas by keeping the client more centered on solutions and coping. We do not wish to undermine or minimize the potential value of spontaneous verbalizations and exploration, yet we believe that by setting the tone and focus initially in the session, one can more easily focus the client's thought processes and initiate more goal-directed conversation. There is generally

32

ample opportunity throughout a therapy session for spontaneous empathy and support as your client continue to discuss their therapy issues.

## MANAGING EYE CONTACT

Did you ever notice the ebb and flow of eye contact during a therapy session? For example, the initial dialogue may look something like the representation shown in Figure 3.3 where eye contact is sustained between both parties as an issue or theme is discussed.

When the dialogue stops, there is often a natural break in eye contact. There appears to be an internally directed process that is activated whereby a search ensues for both the therapist and the client to recruit words, language, and responses that will keep the conversation going (see Figure 3.4).

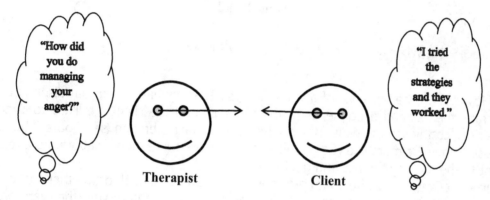

Figure 3.3 Eye Contact During a Therapy Dialogue

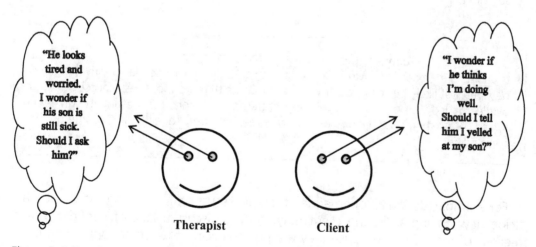

Figure 3.4 Eye Contact Is Broken After the Dialogue Stops

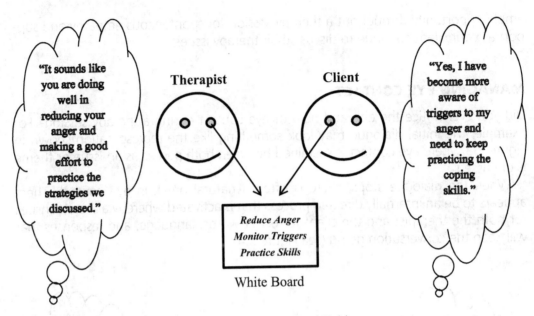

*Figure 3.5* The White Board Provides a Common Visual Field

However, in the presence of a visual field, such as a white board that displays the therapy themes and dialogue, both the therapist and the client are likely to direct their eye contact to the white board when eye contact is broken (see Figure 3.5). As a result, they are more likely to recruit and produce verbalizations that are more relevant to the therapy themes and goals.

In some ways the white board provides a common visual field for the therapist and client to direct attention to when they break eye contact. Otherwise, the client and therapist will tend to look away, gaze, spontaneously reflect, and then "decide" what to say next.

> During this "recruitment process" that occurs in spontaneous dialogue, various thoughts and images are vying for attention. Some of the client's maladaptive thinking patterns will likely be reinforced by those thoughts that are most easily accessible and overlearned. These overlearned thinking patterns and habits can be unwittingly reinforced by the therapist's head nods, covert agreement, and "directives" to continue the conversation.

For example, during an open-ended therapy discussion focused on the client practicing new coping skills, the client may start to discuss a lack of confidence and feelings of inadequacy because they are not practicing the anger coping strategies enough or because they had been unable to reach their overall goals because they yelled at their son this week. Allowing the client to continue discussing these negative themes can unwittingly reinforce these patterns and contribute to the "run-on sentence" of the client's mind. Using a visual, such as a white board or other visually mediated interventions, in the session can help focus the client's attention and minimize potentially "distracting ruminations" and "redundant verbalizations." Through the white board, the therapy topic is visualized, and attention is directed toward the topic. This helps "restrain" the client from soliciting overlearned and potentially unproductive thinking habits that can reinforce negative emotions.

## VISUALS: DISAMBIGUATING AND EXTERNALIZING THE DIALOGUE

Visually mediated devices or methods provide an alternative "information and attentional site" external to the client's competing "internal attentional systems." Visual cues by nature tend to be less ambiguous and easier to process compared to auditory cues due to the nuances and ambiguities often imbedded in language and auditory processing. Visual methods can provide a more "consensually formatted information platform" from which the therapy dialogue can develop. As such, the therapist and client may not have to grapple as much for topics or "mentally choose," through spontaneous dialogue, what is most relevant to discuss. The conversation can progress in a more linear and structured format. By externalizing the information, the client may be better able to recruit problem-solving strategies and "goal-directed verbalizations." When distracting competing thoughts or emotionally laden reactions are spontaneously activated in the client, the therapist and client can more easily redirect the conversation through the use of the visual prompts.

## VISUALS: ENHANCING WORKING MEMORY AND INFORMATION RETENTION

Visual cues can activate memory and information processing systems that would likely be "dormant" or less accessible during traditional verbal therapy. Figure 3.6 illustrates the memory demands placed on the client in processing information during a traditional verbal therapy session. The client is challenged to remember information in the absence of any visual cues or reminders. Alternatively, Figure 3.7 illustrates the potential benefit of using visuals cues in the therapy session to facilitate information retention.

## WRITING AS A VISUAL-MOTOR ENGAGEMENT STRATEGY

Using writing in the session will almost guarantee that your client will become more focused and attentive. During the writing process, as compared to a verbal process, when breaking eye contact, the client will almost automatically return to the written

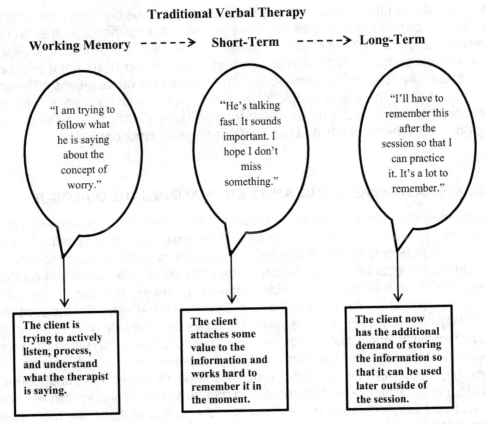

**Traditional Verbal Therapy**

**Working Memory** - - - - -> **Short-Term** - - - - -> **Long-Term**

"I am trying to follow what he is saying about the concept of worry."

"He's talking fast. It sounds important. I hope I don't miss something."

"I'll have to remember this after the session so that I can practice it. It's a lot to remember."

**The client is trying to actively listen, process, and understand what the therapist is saying.**

**The client attaches some value to the information and works hard to remember it in the moment.**

**The client now has the additional demand of storing the information so that it can be used later outside of the session.**

*Figure 3.6* Memory Demands Placed on the Client During a Traditional Verbal Therapy Session

words and visual cues and use these cues to stay focused on the specific tasks and goal of the exercise. The writing and visual tasks in some ways establish parameters and clear goals. A verbal task or encounter, on the other hand, usually has less specific parameters and vaguely defined goals. In traditional verbal exchanges, the goal can change quickly, unexpectedly, and for unclear reasons, some of which are idiosyncratic to either the client or the therapist. For example, when engaged in a dialogue, the therapist or client could extemporaneously switch the topic and introduce a new topic or theme without consulting the other and have little intention of revisiting, resolving, or discussing the theme or topic that preceded the conversation shift.

If we structure the dialogue by writing down, for example, goals, coping statements, and ways to manage stress, the client will tend to become more focused and attend more directly to these themes through the writing process. This is a natural tendency associated with the universal experience of writing, which promotes and facilitates a certain focused "attentional stance." Consider, for example, a teacher who asks their students to begin a writing exercise. The simple act of picking up a pen or pencil activates attentional systems. The students will tend to become quickly focused. Students who otherwise may have been distracted and unable to follow the

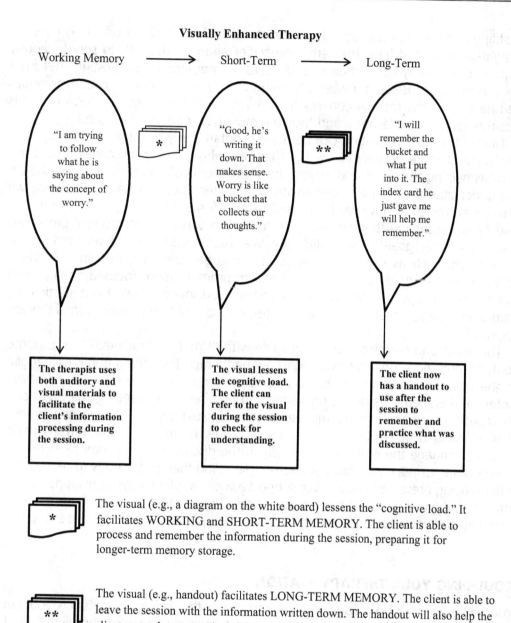

**Visually Enhanced Therapy**

Working Memory  →  Short-Term  →  Long-Term

"I am trying to follow what he is saying about the concept of worry."

*

"Good, he's writing it down. That makes sense. Worry is like a bucket that collects our thoughts."

**

"I will remember the bucket and what I put into it. The index card he just gave me will help me remember."

The therapist uses both auditory and visual materials to facilitate the client's information processing during the session.

The visual lessens the cognitive load. The client can refer to the visual during the session to check for understanding.

The client now has a handout to use after the session to remember and practice what was discussed.

\* The visual (e.g., a diagram on the white board) lessens the "cognitive load." It facilitates WORKING and SHORT-TERM MEMORY. The client is able to process and remember the information during the session, preparing it for longer-term memory storage.

\*\* The visual (e.g., handout) facilitates LONG-TERM MEMORY. The client is able to leave the session with the information written down. The handout will also help the client remember to practice what was discussed.

*Figure 3.7* Using Visual Cues to Facilitate Information Retention in the Therapy Session

verbal dialogue in class now are more likely to become focused and engaged. Similarly, using writing and visually aided prompts in therapy sessions can help minimize the chances of the client as well as the therapist being susceptible to their own idiosyncratic thoughts, impressions, and interests. We are not making the argument that spontaneous verbal exploration is of no therapeutic value and does not foster rapport building and alliance building. It has considerable value for clients who may be more insight-oriented and have the verbal capacities and ego strength to spontaneously explore emotionally laden themes and issues. Rather, we are suggesting that from an information processing framework, using visually aided communication strategies can help focus the therapy conversation, minimize "spontaneous discussion that is less therapeutically relevant," and facilitate more goal-directed dialogue.

During the session, writing can be done spontaneously by either the therapist or the client or more deliberately by the therapist who is trying to convey a concept, such as helping the client understand the components of anxiety or helping the client understand the nature of certain stress management strategies. In this book we provide examples of how we have used various forms of writing and diagrams to visually represent the therapy dialogue, to explain various psychological processes, and to facilitate "goal-focused" dialogue. We also discuss how we have used unique worksheets, such as synonyms, general knowledge questions, or math exercises, to stimulate clients' thought processes and to promote more focused engagement during the therapy session. These "cognitive worksheets" have been particularly helpful in engaging clients who have not responded well to traditional verbal therapy approaches.

Therapists and clients can often struggle with "What do I say next?" in response to the information and ideas exchanged during therapy. Everything that is exchanged in the therapy encounter can be of potential interest, and any response can have potential therapeutic value. Using visuals can be effective in keeping the client and therapist focused and can minimize spontaneous explorations of "curiosity themes" that, if pursued, may have less therapeutic value. Moreover, collaboratively using visuals to engage the client more actively in the discussion may promote increased "ownership" of the issues discussed as the client and therapist actively review or edit what is being presented visually. We support a wide range of ways to respond to and interact with your clients. What we are introducing are additional methods to assist both you and your clients in getting the most therapeutic value out of the session.

## EQUIPPING YOUR THERAPY STATION

You will need your own visual cues to remember the variety of materials you can use in therapy sessions with your clients and to actively engage your clients' right in the moment during a therapy session. You will likely benefit from equipping your office with various visual and writing materials, such as Post-it notes, index cards, and a white board. *If you don't see it on your desk station, then you probably won't remember to use it during the session.* Here is a recommended list of materials to have available during your therapy sessions:

- 14×11 white board with colored markers and an eraser
- Legal notepad
- Jar with pencils and pens

- Index cards: 3x5 and 4x6
- Post-it notepad
- Package of orange sticky dots*
- Manila folders for clients to keep handouts
- Goal sheets
- Weekly schedule grids
- Blank sheets of paper
- Copies of VET handouts and worksheets
- Computer station: two chairs set up side by side (used for computer-facilitated therapy; see Chapter 8)
- Basket of objects (optional; see Appendix G)
- Easel with a large pad (if office space can accommodate)

---

*Using sticky dots as visual cues to help clients remember coping strategies was first introduced to me (Charles Boisvert) by my clinical supervisor, John Garrison, Ph.D., during my clinical psychology post-doctoral fellowship at the Lahey Clinic Medical Center in Burlington, Massachusetts.

## YOUR "VISUAL VOICE": BECOMING COMFORTABLE WITH THE WHITE BOARD

To start using the white board, diagrams, and other visually mediated strategies, we recommend the following strategies and methods so that you become comfortable with the process:

1. Display the white board with the main themes discussed from the last session.
2. Place it on a holder so that clients see it when they enter your office.

---

**Sample phrases for spontaneously introducing the white board:**

*"I'm envisioning a few things when you say that," "I'm thinking of a circle here to represent what you're saying," "Let's use the X's to represent those negative statements and the O's to represent positive statements," "Let me write this down for a minute and see if it makes sense," "It might look something like this," "Here's a way you may be able to visualize it," "As you were explaining that, I was envisioning two circles like this," and "Let's record that on your mood meter here."*

3. Say something like the following when referring to the white board:
   - "I posted a few of the main themes we discussed so that we can decide what you may want to work on this session."
   - "I thought it may be helpful to jot down the issues we discussed last time and to check in with you to see what you wanted to focus on today."
   - "I listed the goals we have been discussing and thought it would be helpful to review those and see your progress."

4. Hand clients the white board or a notepad and have them write down the goals or issues they want to address in the session.

In the upcoming chapters, we discuss how you can use visually aided and multimodal communication strategies to gather information, teach therapy concepts, explain coping strategies, and collaboratively engage the client in a productive and goal-directed therapy session. The diagrams and visuals can be used in a variety of ways. In some cases, you can draw the diagram in the session, explain it, and provide the client with a handout of the diagram to use for implementing coping strategies. In other cases, you can simply display a diagram and use it to teach a coping strategy, therapy concept, or psychological principle. In other situations, you may use a diagram, such as a timeline, and fill in the information during the session. *You will find all the diagrams and worksheets in the appendices.*

We have made *display diagrams* associated with some of the more common topics that we cover. These are diagrams for you to display as needed during therapy sessions as reminders of the issues, themes, or coping strategies you have already discussed during your sessions. You can feel free to post these display diagrams on cardboard, laminate them, or simply copy them and have them visible during your therapy session. The important thing is to be flexible and to find ways to use the diagrams and other visually mediated strategies to more directly engage your clients and to keep them more focused on using coping strategies more effectively.

We also devote a chapter to illustrating how you can use visuals spontaneously in session to augment and facilitate therapist-patient communication. Additionally, we discuss ways to use visually mediated communication strategies with such populations as clients with schizophrenia, geriatric clients, and developmentally disabled clients who may not respond optimally to traditional verbal therapy. We begin the next chapter by discussing ways to use diagrams and worksheets to gather information and to identify therapy goals. For your well-established clients, you can decide which aspects of this chapter are most relevant and which information-gathering techniques will be most helpful to use with these clients. For clients you are just starting to work with or for your future clients, you may find it helpful to use a variety of these information-gathering methods.

# 4

# Using Diagrams to Gather Information and Identify Therapy Goals

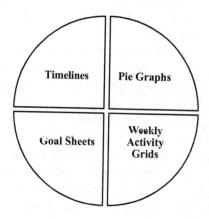

This chapter discusses ways to gather information about your clients by using various visually mediated information-gathering methods. You can use these various methods to gather different types of information, such as significant historical events, social interests, health habits, values, hobbies, philosophical and religious beliefs, goals, and typical weekly activities. Gathering relevant information about your client's mental health and social history can assist you in better understanding how certain events and experiences have affected your client's life. Clients can often share a considerable amount of information in a therapy session. These various information-gathering methods can assist your client in sharing personal and historical information in a more coherent and organized fashion.

Using these various information-gathering methods can help focus the therapy discussion, cue the client to discuss the most relevant and important topics, and facilitate the client's ability to focus on specific issues, events, goals, and concerns. In some ways these "visual methods" can help "disentangle" the most relevant information associated with certain topics and themes and by doing so can help you and your client identify the most important areas to focus on in therapy. Gathering information in a more structured manner can also facilitate your client's understanding of how certain life experiences, events, and circumstances have shaped their personality and behavior. As you gather relevant historical and personal information on your client through these various methods, you can ultimately help your client work toward the most realistic and achievable goals that can promote greater success and satisfaction with their present life circumstances.

The different information-gathering methods that we discuss in this chapter include (1) timelines. (2) pie graphs, (3) personal interest worksheets, and (4) goal-setting worksheets. *The worksheets associated with these information-gathering methods can be found in Appendix A.* When choosing a worksheet, such as a timeline or pie graph, you can use your judgment as to whether you or your client will record the information on the worksheet. For some of the information-gathering methods, there will be both an "in-session" worksheet to complete during the session and a homework worksheet that your client can complete after the session. For clients who you have been working with for a while, you may consider gathering information on topics that you have not yet explored.

For some information-gathering methods, such as timelines, it may be more helpful for you to write in the information as the client reflects on and discusses certain life events. Alternatively, when using the pie graphs, for example, it may be more effective to have your client fill in the pie graphs to enable them to more actively reflect on the specific topic covered by the pie graphs and to take more "ownership" of the information recorded on the pie graphs. Through the act of writing, clients may be inclined to more actively reflect on the topic and become more aware of how the different components and topics listed, for example, in the pie graph may apply to their lives. This may help your clients focus more on what they want to change as they visualize the issues and themes being explored through the pie graphs. We start with discussing various ways you can use timelines to gather information about significant events in your client's life.

## TIMELINES

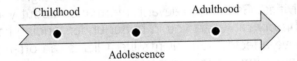

Timelines can be used in a variety of ways to gather relevant information about your client. They provide a method to systematically gather information about various events and experiences that have occurred during different time periods of your client's life. This can help you and your client identify themes and patterns to your client's experiences and behavior. It can also help you better understand how certain events may have affected or influenced the development of your client's belief systems, emotional reactions, and coping methods. Timelines have been used in various ways with specific clinical populations. For example, Berends (2011) discussed using timelines during interviews for substance use clients. She discussed how timelines can be a useful information-gathering technique by combining verbal and visual information to better understand the trajectory of historical events and substance use behaviors.

Next we discuss five ways to use timelines: (1) to gather general biographical information, (2) to identify stressful life events, (3) to identify significant positive life events, (4) to track the history of the client's clinical condition, and (5) to spontaneously record the client's social and mental health history as the client reports events and life experiences during the session. You can decide which timelines you would like to complete with your client and make copies of those timelines from Appendix A prior to your session. We start with discussing how to use timelines to gather general biographical information.

## Biographical Timeline (Adolescent and Adult Versions)

### IG Worksheets #1 and #2 in Appendix A

It can be helpful to gather a timeline of general historical and developmental events across your client's lifetime. You can use the biographical timeline to identify significant historical events, such as birth place, residential moves, school history, job history, military history, relationship history, and important social and religious events. One of the intentions of the exercise is to gather information about your client without necessarily needing to identify any particular areas to address in the therapy. Completing a timeline can help facilitate rapport building and assist you in developing a more comprehensive understanding of your client's background.

As you gather the information, you can choose to associate the event with a date (i.e., when it occurred) or with the client's age, or with both. In the following example of a biographical timeline (see Figure 4.1), we included only the client's age and no dates associated with the client's life events. Some of the information you gather will not necessarily be associated with a particular date, such as where your client grew up or how many siblings they have. For this type of information, you can simply choose to note it in the appropriate developmental section on the timeline.

Guides for Therapist

- Use *IG Worksheet #1: Biographical Timeline—Adolescent* or *IG Worksheet #2: Biographical Timeline—Adult* in Appendix A as a template. You can pick the timeline based on your client's age (note: *another option you may choose is to simply draw a timeline freestyle during the session and not use the template*). For young adult clients (i.e., ages 18–22), you can use either timeline template depending on which developmental time periods seem to be most relevant. The timeline template also allows you to record the date and age at the time of the event. You can decide whether including the dates, the age, or both is helpful as you develop the timeline with your client. Your client may have difficulty recalling the exact dates for some events. For other events—for example, a death of a family member—they may be able to recall the date versus their age at the time. Have flexibility in deciding whether to include ages or dates on the timeline. An example of a biographical timeline (using the client's age versus dates) is shown in Figure 4.1.

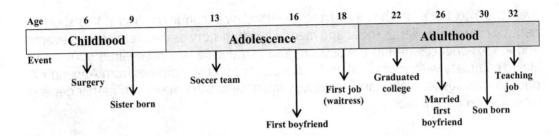

## Client Reflections

Childhood: *My first memory was being in the hospital recovering from tonsil surgery. My mom gave me an orange popsicle when I woke up. When my sister was born a few years later, I remember being excited to be the big sister.*

Adolescence: *I took well to the role of big sister and felt I started to be more of a second mom to her. I taught her a lot, and she always looked up to me. I fell in love with soccer when I made the middle school team, and to this day I love watching and playing soccer.*

Adulthood: *I was proud when I graduated from college; college was challenging, but I did well. I married the man I dated in high school. Giving birth to my son was the best day of my life. Motherhood has been challenging, especially since starting my first teaching job.*

*Figure 4.1* Example of a Biographical Timeline

- Assist your clients in identifying relevant events to include on their timelines. The following sample questions can be helpful to ask to solicit information and events for your client's biographical timeline. *Where were you born? When were your siblings born? Where did you grow up? What elementary school, middle school, and high school did you attend? What events do you most remember from your childhood? Did you attend college or graduate school? Did you join the military? When did you get your first home or apartment? What was your first job, and what other jobs have you had? Did you have a favorite job? With whom was your first romantic relationship? How many relationships have you had? Have you ever been engaged, married, or divorced? Do you have children? Are you a member of any organizations or a church? Did you ever move? What other important events would you like to put on your timeline?*
- It may be easier for you as the therapist to write in the events as your client shares their biographical information. This may allow the client more time to freely recall and reflect on their personal history.
- Invite your client to give the timeline a title. The title may reflect an underlying theme relevant to the client's life experiences.
- Invite your client to complete the reflection box at the bottom of the worksheet. These reflections can entail what your client identifies as the most significant

events during the particular time period and how they feel these events have influenced or shaped them. Your client can start the reflections in session and then finish it for homework (see Figure 4.1 for an example of a biographical timeline with sample client reflections).

## Stressful Events Timeline

### IG Worksheet #3 in Appendix A

You can gather information on significant stressful events that your client has experienced. It can assist your client in retrieving pertinent information and more actively engaging in a meaningful discussion focused on certain stressful life experiences. Drawing a timeline of these events can help you and your client review their life and gain insight into factors and events that have influenced their overall coping style, life philosophy, and decisions.

Guides for Therapist

- Use *IG Worksheet #3: Stressful Events Timeline* from Appendix A as a template, or you may choose to draw the timeline freestyle. In the following timeline example, you will notice that the time blocks are separated by 2-year intervals and the timeline covers 16 years. Listing all the dates across this period may help with your client's orientation to time and enable your client to better understand how the passage of time has influenced them. You will notice that in some of the other timeline examples discussed in this chapter, the dates are used differently. You can be flexible in how you record the time blocks. Depending on the age of your client, you may decide to use the time block differently. For example, you may choose to use 5-year time blocks for older clients to enable you to cover a longer period of time.
- Assist your client in identifying stressful life events. Examples of significant stressful events may include the following: *losing a job; a parental divorce; a family death; a significant medical diagnosis; a personal divorce; break off of an engagement; physical abuse; sexual abuse; a layoff from a job; a car accident; being a victim of a crime; being convicted of a crime; a workplace accident; witnessing a death; a natural disaster, such as a house fire or flood; a hospitalization; a physical altercation; a military trauma; or the death of a pet.*
- Discuss how certain events may have affected your client's life.
- On the bottom of the worksheet, identify themes and possible patterns in these events. Also identify coping behaviors used to manage these events. Lastly, have your client write down their "coping philosophy." You can start these reflections in session and have your client finish them for homework (see Figure 4.2 for an example of a stressful events timeline with client reflections).

45

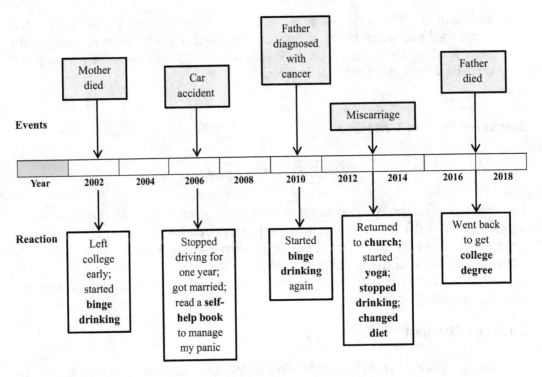

## Client Reflections

Themes: *Loss, anxiety, educational success*

Coping Behaviors: *Binge drinking, self-help, church, yoga, diet*

Coping Philosophy: *Although you may feel like giving up, if you remain optimistic and make positive lifestyle changes, you will reach your goals and feel better about yourself. Never give up.*

*Figure 4.2* Example of a Stressful Events Timeline

## Positive Events Timeline

IG Worksheet #4 in Appendix A

You can gather information on significant accomplishments and positive events that your client has experienced. It can assist your client in retrieving pertinent information and engaging in a discussion focused on your client's accomplishments, capabilities, and on how certain life events have affected your client. Drawing a timeline of these accomplishments and events can help you and your client gain insight into their self-esteem, ambitions, interests, skills, and goals.

Guides for Therapist

- Use *IG Worksheet #4: Positive Events Timeline* in Appendix A as a template, or you may choose to draw the timeline freestyle. Notice in the following example, compared to the previous timeline example, that the only years shown on the timeline are the years associated with the events.
- Assist your client in identifying positive life events. Significant accomplishments and positive events may include the following: *a first job; the birth of a child; an engagement; marriage; a high school award; an athletic achievement; an academic honor; membership in a social or religious group; a work promotion; a first pet; publishing a short story, poem, article, or book; becoming a leader of an organization; being acknowledged in a local newspaper or in the local community; inventing or patenting something; winning a contest; starting an organization, charity, or fund-raising effort; or losing weight or adhering to a regular exercise program.*
- Look for signs of your client's skills, interests, and ambitions.
- Look for signs of your client's work ethic, goals, and overall areas of accomplishment.
- Invite your client to complete the reflection box at the bottom of the worksheet. These reflections can entail what your client identifies as the most significant events and how these events have influenced their life. They can write down in the last box what their interests and skills are based on reflecting on these events. They can complete these reflections in sessions or for homework (see Figure 4.3 for an example of a positive events timeline with client reflections).

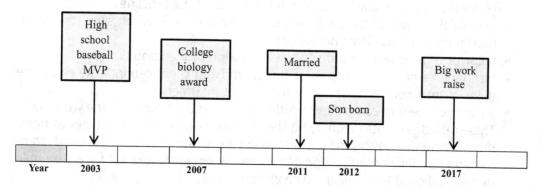

**Client Reflections**

Effect of Events: *I developed confidence in high school to be successful academically and athletically. Having a family was an important goal. I had a strong desire to pursue academic interests. Fatherhood helped me develop a stronger relationship with my own parents. After getting my work raise, I started to thrive in my career.*

Interests and Skills: *Family oriented, athletic, academically minded, creative, ambitious*

*Figure 4.3* Example of a Positive Events Timeline

## Clinical Condition Timeline

IG Worksheet #5 in Appendix A

It can be helpful to gather a timeline of your client's clinical condition. This will help you and your client understand the factors that may have contributed to the onset and maintenance of their condition. You will also learn more about your client's treatment history, triggers or precipitants to their symptoms, and how they responded to different treatment interventions. One of the intentions of developing this type of a timeline is to enable you to gather a more sequential and detailed clinical history. Additionally, constructing the timeline can help your client recall more detailed information from their past as they become cued by the events that start to appear on the timeline. This will help them more easily recall information and begin to better sequence their experiences over time.

Guides for Therapist

- You can use *IG Worksheet #5: Clinical Condition Timeline* in Appendix A as a template, or you can choose to draw the timeline freestyle during the session. You can adjust the timeline sections based on your client's age. For example, if your client is a teenager, you will write more under the childhood and adolescence sections. If your client is an older adult, you may find yourself writing mostly under the adult section. If your client is a younger adult, you may find yourself writing equally under all three sections of the timeline.
- Identify the onset of the problem and the time periods when symptoms were most prominent and least prominent.
- Look for triggers and patterns to the expression of the condition.
- Identify time periods and types of treatment (your client can indicate either the dates of treatment or their age at the time of treatment).
- Invite your client to complete the reflection box at the bottom of the worksheet. These reflections entail identifying the triggers to symptoms, the types of treatment received, and the most effective coping strategies. Your client can complete these reflections in session or for homework (see Figure 4.4 for an example of a clinical condition timeline with client reflections).

## Life Memories Timeline

IG Worksheet #6 in Appendix A

This timeline can be used to integrate many of the topics previously discussed in the various timelines. You may find that this timeline can more comprehensively and

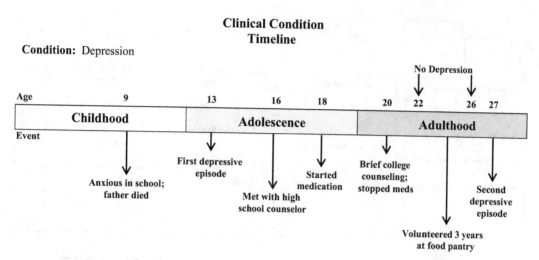

**Client Reflections**

Triggers: *Social events, social pressure, father's death*

Treatment: *Medications* (helpful in reducing some symptoms but had side effects), *self-help* (read a book on managing depression), *therapy* (brief therapy in high school and during college).

Most Effective Coping Strategies: *Exercising, self-help books, volunteering*

*Figure 4.4* Example of a Clinical Condition Timeline

easily consolidate historical information from a variety of areas instead of using multiple timelines (see Figure 4.5 for an example of a life memories timeline).

Guides for Therapist

- Use *IG Worksheet #6: Life Memories Timeline* in Appendix A to record positive and negative memories across the life areas of health, family, social, and education.
- At the bottom of the worksheet, identify the most positive and most negative memories, significant medical and mental health services, and things your client is most satisfied with in their life. Use your client's overall reflections on their life memories timeline to help identify their therapy goals.

## Using Timelines Spontaneously in Session

As your client spontaneously discusses life events, you may find it helpful to construct a timeline during the session. Developing a timeline for these events or "issues" that arise spontaneously may help your client better recall and understand how these issues and events may have affected them. We have found in our experience that as events are "visualized" and recorded on the timeline, the displayed information

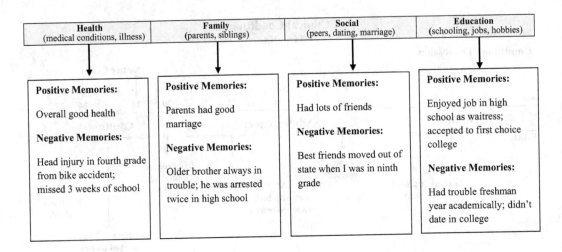

| Health (medical conditions, illness) | Family (parents, siblings) | Social (peers, dating, marriage) | Education (schooling, jobs, hobbies) |
|---|---|---|---|
| **Positive Memories:** Overall good health **Negative Memories:** Head injury in fourth grade from bike accident; missed 3 weeks of school | **Positive Memories:** Parents had good marriage **Negative Memories:** Older brother always in trouble; he was arrested twice in high school | **Positive Memories:** Had lots of friends **Negative Memories:** Best friends moved out of state when I was in ninth grade | **Positive Memories:** Enjoyed job in high school as waitress; accepted to first choice college **Negative Memories:** Had trouble freshman year academically; didn't date in college |

**Most positive memories:** Getting accepted into a college of my choice; meeting first boyfriend

**Most negative memories:** Head injury in fourth grade; best friend moving out of state when I was in ninth grade.

**Significant medical and mental health services:** Brief counseling in college for anxiety

**Things You Are Most Satisfied With in Your Life:** Currently in positive relationship with boyfriend; job is going well; have good relationship with my parents

*Figure 4.5* Example of a Life Memories Timeline

cues the client and facilitates recall of relevant associated memories. Sequencing the events can also help your client better recall how they coped with or responded to these events. The timeline serves as a sort of "memory holding space" and allows the client to discuss the event or topic in a more organized and sequential manner.

The following are three examples of ways we have used timelines spontaneously in therapy sessions (see Figure 4.6 for a work issues timelines, see Figure 4.7 for a general life events timeline, and see Figure 4.8 for a preoccupation with the past timeline). In drawing the timeline during the session, you can use a white board, notepad, or blank piece of paper.

## Case #1: Work Issue (recent dates)

You can use a timeline to track work-related events that may be causing your client stress or for which they may be required to seek counseling. You can use the timeline to track these events and to identify work stressors (e.g., people and situations) that have influenced your client's behavior. These "work stressors" can be written above the timeline. Below the timeline you can list your client's "work behaviors" that necessitated the referral to therapy. It can also be effective to identify key employees involved in your client's work environment and the role they have played. The timeline can be effective in allowing your client to reflect on performance over time and to

**Work Stressors**
Coworker
Boss
Work Conditions

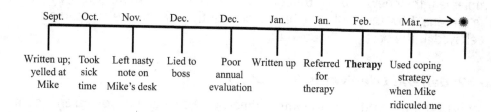

| Sept. | Oct. | Nov. | Dec. | Dec. | Jan. | Jan. | Feb. | Mar. → ☀ |
|-------|------|------|------|------|------|------|------|----------|

Written up; yelled at Mike — Took sick time — Left nasty note on Mike's desk — Lied to boss — Poor annual evaluation — Written up — Referred for therapy — **Therapy** — Used coping strategy when Mike ridiculed me

**Work Behaviors**
Yelled at Mike for messy work space
Yelled at boss for poor annual evaluation

☀ **Coping Strategies**: Ignore Mike; focus on job; foster positive relationships with other employees

*Figure 4.6* Example of a Work Issues Timeline

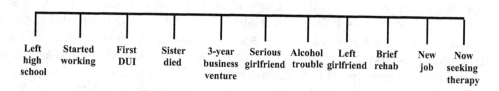

**Left high school** — **Started working** — **First DUI** — **Sister died** — **3-year business venture** — **Serious girlfriend** — **Alcohol trouble** — **Left girlfriend** — **Brief rehab** — **New job** — **Now seeking therapy**

Life themes: *loss, alcohol, relationship conflict, limited job experiences*

*Figure 4.7* Example of a General Life Events Timeline

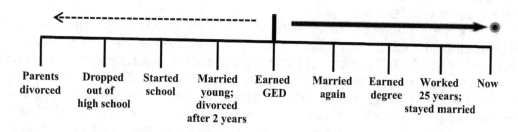

**Parents divorced** — **Dropped out of high school** — **Started school** — **Married young; divorced after 2 years** — **Earned GED** — **Married again** — **Earned degree** — **Worked 25 years; stayed married** — **Now**

*Figure 4.8* Example of a Preoccupation With the Past Timeline

become more aware of the factors that have affected work performance. The therapist and client can then discuss coping strategies to minimize the future occurrence of the problematic behaviors and use the timeline to identify new behavioral responses to similar work challenges in the future. This will help your client visualize ways they can implement their new coping strategies. They can then see more clearly, by reviewing the timeline, how they will be behaving differently in the future compared to how they behaved in the past (see figure 4.6).

## Case #2: General Life Events (no dates)

In this next example, you start to write a timeline of events that your client spontaneously discusses. Allow your client to simply talk about life events and periodically record on the timeline what they identify either implicitly or explicitly as a significant life event. You can also write in the lower corner of the timeline or on the white board the themes that are emerging. You can solicit your client's impressions of the completed timeline and discuss how life events have shaped their beliefs and behaviors. You can then discuss your client's current goals (see figure 4.7).

## Case #3: Preoccupation With the Past

In this example, the timeline is used to track time periods that your client tends to emphasize or refer to during the therapy sessions. In the example, many of the events and issues that the client discussed related to her past. In fact, you will notice that even at her current age of 60, she refers to her high school experiences. She seems to be preoccupied with events from her past. She often referred to these events, even when attempts were made to focus more on her current goals.

The client spends most of the session discussing the events in her life that occurred prior to getting her GED (illustrated by the dotted arrow). She emphasizes her non-traditional education and lack of early success and pays little attention to her accomplishments following her GED. Her affect is notably irritable. She gestures throughout, moves forward in her seat, raises her voice, and expresses dissatisfaction with how her life has turned out. As she discussed these past "negative" events, the dotted line was drawn and used to illustrate how her negative affect is generated by reflecting on these past events.

A thick line is placed on the timeline when she received her GED. Her attention is directed to the events that followed her GED. A horizontal line is then drawn to the right of the GED. The therapist and client discuss the importance of focusing on the present and moving forward by "putting the past to rest." This is symbolized by erasing the events preceding her GED and focusing now on accomplishments and the future ( ✸ An asterisk is placed at the "now" position on the timeline, which represents the present. The importance of looking forward versus backward is emphasized as a strategy to help minimize negative moods and to help reduce feelings of chronic disappointment and depression (see figure 4.8)).

## PIE GRAPHS

Pie graphs can be used in creative ways to gather information about your client and to learn more about different aspects of your client's life. Clients will find using pie graphs easy and straightforward. The pie graph can be used to identify, for example, health behaviors, social interests, values, and current weekly activities. The pie graph can display the component parts of these topics and the relative importance (e.g., size of the "slice") each component plays in the client's life. For example, in gathering information on the topic of "values," if the client places a higher value on work versus family, then the slice for work would be bigger than the slice for family. The pie graph can provide an effective "visual," which can quickly allow your client to notice the choices they are making and the relative emphasis they are placing on different areas of their life. The visual of the pie graph can quickly enable your client to notice what types of changes they may want to make in certain areas. We provide several examples of topics that you can cover with pie graphs but also encourage you to be creative in identifying other topics you would like to cover with your clients. Next we outline general guides for using pie graphs and then provide examples of four different pie graphs you could use with your clients.

## GENERAL STEPS FOR DRAWING PIE GRAPHS

- *Step 1: Identify the pie graph topic.* The first step is to establish what topic is most relevant and important to cover with your client. We provide examples for using pie graphs to gather information on the topics of values, health choices, weekly activities, and self-image. You can also choose a different topic that may be more relevant to your client.
- *Step 2: Complete pie graph #1.* Once you decide what topic you wish to cover, you can develop the first pie graph. This first pie graph, or pie graph #1,

represents the current state of your client. Your client fills in the pie graph illustrating their current situation. It is important in developing pie graph #1 to help the client determine the types and sizes of the pie slices by focusing on their current behaviors and choices.

When creating the pie graph, first develop a list of the content to include in the pie graph. On the pie graph worksheet, list the pie graph content under the heading "Content" located to the left of the pie graph. Then next to each item on the list, indicate the "relative percentage of importance" of the item. For example, if you are developing a pie graph for your client's weekly activities and your client identifies six typical weekly activities, you will develop a pie graph with six slices. If item number one is rated at 50% because your client spends 50% of their week engaged in this activity, then you know that this item will take up 50% of the pie graph. The primary goal is to work collaboratively with your client in identifying the content for the pie graph and the relative sizes of the slices by exploring how much time or interest your client devotes to the different content areas.

- *Step 3: Complete pie graph #2.* Develop pie graph #2 next by using open-ended questions to facilitate your client's self-awareness and insight into identifying desired changes in the chosen area. The goal is to look for what your client desires to change and what they can realistically change at this time. Once you determine this, you and your client construct pie graph #2. This new pie graph represents the client's desired state. The client reflects on this and shares why this new state is important to them. In developing pie graph #2, the size of some of the slices may change if your client has decided to "reduce" or "cut back" in a certain area. Also, some slices from pie graph #1 may not appear in pie graph #2 if your client has decided to eliminate certain behaviors or interests. Also, slices that did not appear in pie graph #1 may be added to pie graph #2 if your client has decided to add new behaviors or to pursue new interests.
- *Step 4: Build the bridge.* For homework you can present your client with the associated pie graph handout that depicts a bridge between pie graph #1 and pie graph #2. Your client can build their bridge by determining the steps they need to take to move from pie graph #1 to pie graph #2.

In the following example (see Figure 4.9), the client wishes to reduce time spent at work and time spent watching TV. You will notice that the TV slice has been reduced from one third of the pie (pie graph #1) to one fifth of the pie (pie graph #2). You will also notice that the client has decided to eliminate the "drinking" slice from pie graph #1 and added three new slices to pie graph #2 (family, leisure, and health). This particular client is ambitious and desires to make substantial changes. Be flexible with your client and decide with them what is most realistic and achievable. Some clients may have to only "tweak" their pie graphs to achieve their desired state. The bridge reflects the client's plan to help them move from pie graph # 1 to pie graph #2.

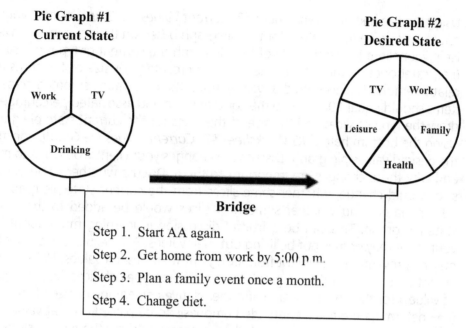

*Figure 4.9* Example of a Pie Graph

Next we discuss four pie graph topics that you could cover with your client: (1) values, (2) health choices, (3) routine weekly activities, and (4) the self. See Appendix A for copies of the pie chart worksheets and handouts.

## TYPES OF PIE GRAPHS

### Values Pie Graph

IG Worksheet #7; CS Handout #1 in Appendix A

Values help define and shape who we are. They reflect our innermost hopes, interests, beliefs, experiences, and expectations. Exploring your client's values can be helpful in learning what motivates them, where they derive meaning, and how therapy may help them live more in accord with their values. The first step in this exercise is to freely explore and identify your client's values. Using a pie graph can facilitate this process and enable you and your client to more easily identify their core values. Values may include such things as political and religious beliefs, social and personal interests, self and other expectations, and guiding life philosophies.

1. Using the top half of *IG Worksheet #7: Current Values Pie Graph*, remind your client to determine the content for this pie graph based on their current behaviors. Help your client list on the side of the pie graph the content or types of "slices" (i.e., categories of values) and the relative percentage or size of the slices (i.e., relative emphasis placed on that value) (note: the percentage summed across all items should equal 100%). Use the content listed and associated percentages to draw the type of slices and the size of the slices for the current state pie graph.

2. Using the bottom half of *IG Worksheet #7: Current Values Pie Graph*, construct the desired values pie graph. Discuss the changes your client would like to make and why these changes are important to them. Discuss whether some pie slice sizes would change, whether some slices from the current state pie graph will be eliminated, and whether some new slices would be added to the desired state pie graph. This can be a fruitful discussion in learning more about how your client may or may not be living out their values. Also, explore obstacles that may be preventing your client from living out their desired values. Help your client list on the side of the pie graph the content or types of slices (i.e., categories of values) for the new pie graph and the relative percentage or size of the slices (i.e., determine the relative intended emphasis to be placed on that value). Use the content listed and the associated percentages to draw the type of slices and the size of the slices for the desired state pie graph.

3. Use *CS Handout #1: Values Pie Graph* for homework. At the top of the handout, an example is provided to help guide your client in completing the bottom half of the handout for homework.

   a. Invite your client to copy into pie graph #1 the current state pie graph they completed with you in session. Then have your client copy into pie graph #2 the desired state pie graph they also completed with you.

   b. For homework, your client can construct a bridge from pie graph #1 to pie graph #2. This is your client's action plan to get them to their desired state. The example presented in Figure 4.10 is the same example provided on the handout in the appendix.

4. Follow-up sessions can focus on ways to implement and monitor your client's new values plan.

## Health Choices Pie Graph

**IG Worksheet #8; CS Handout #2 in Appendix A**

Our health is important to all of us and making it a priority is essential. We all know the different health choices we "should" make, but we may have difficulty implementing them. Most scientific journal articles, health magazines, and doctor's advice ends with "eat more fruits and vegetables and exercise." It is unlikely your client will need significantly more health information. What is more important is recognizing

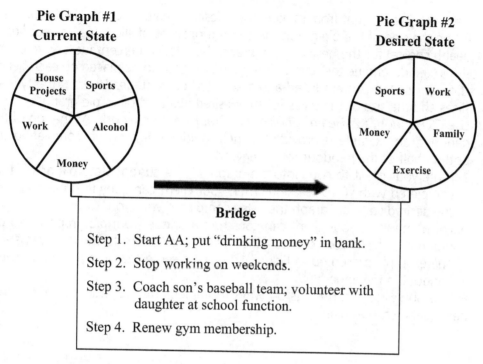

*Figure 4.10* Example of a Values Pie Graph

what health choices your client is making now, identifying what changes your client needs to make, and designing a plan to get there. You can assist your client in making these changes by using the health choices pie graph.

1. Using the top half of *IG Worksheet #8: Current Health Choices Pie Graph*, your client can include such things as the foods they tend to eat (e.g., sweets, salads, red meat, fish), their drinking habits (e.g., alcohol, caffeine), their lifestyle (watch TV, exercise, yoga), or other health-related behaviors. The pie graph can also include medical problems, such as high blood pressure, if your client wishes to address this as a health choice and maybe, for example, start a medication. Help your client list on the side of the pie graph the content or types of slices (i.e., categories of health choices) and the relative percentage or size of the slices (i.e., relative emphasis placed on that health choice) (note: the percentage summed across all items should equal 100%). Use the content listed and the associated percentages to draw the type of slices and the size of the slices for the current health choices pie graph.

2. Using the bottom half of *IG Worksheet #8: Current Health Choice Pie Graph*, discuss the changes your client would like to make. Remind your client that slices may be eliminated, added, or resized. Also, explore obstacles that may be

preventing your client from making their desired health choices. Help your client list on the side of the pie graph the content or types of slices (i.e., categories of health choice) for the new pie graph and the relative percentage or size of the slices (i.e., determine the relative intended emphasis to be placed on each health choice). Use the content listed and associated percentages to draw the type of slices and the size of the slices for the desired health choices pie graph.

3. Use *CS Handout #2: Health Choices Pie Graph* for homework. At the top of the handout, an example is provided to help guide your client in completing the bottom half of the handout for homework.

   a. Invite your client to copy into pie graph #1 the current state pie graph they completed with you in session. Then your client can copy into pie graph #2 the desired state pie graph they also completed with you.

   b. For homework, your client can construct a bridge from pie graph #1 to pie graph #2. This is your client's action plan to get them to their desired state. The example presented in Figure 4.11 is the same example provided on the handout in the appendix.

4. Follow-up sessions can focus on ways to implement and monitor your client's new health choices plan.

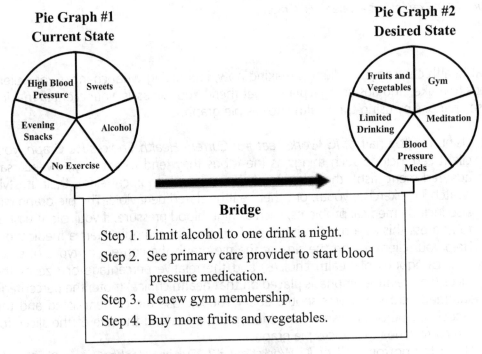

*Figure 4.11* Example of a Health Choices Pie Graph

## Weekly Activities Pie Graph

IG Worksheet #9; CS Handouts #3 and #4 in Appendix A

Activity is important to our well-being and defines and shapes who we are. Exploring your client's weekly activities can help you learn how they spend their time and what their interests are. The first step in this exercise is to freely explore what those activities are. Using a pie graph can facilitate this process and enable you and your client to identify these activities.

1. Using the top half of *IG Worksheet #9: Currently Weekly Activities Pie Graph*, your client can include such activities as work, TV, household chores, reading, social activities, computer-related activities, social media, and so on. They can size the slices based on how much time they spend on the particular activity. Their goal may be to simply reduce the amount of time they spend with a certain activity or possibly to increase the time spent in another activity. Help your client list on the side of the pie graph the content or types of slices (i.e., types of activities) and the relative percentage or size of the slices (i.e., relative time spent in that activity) (note: the percentage summed across all items should equal 100%). Use the content listed and the associated percentages to draw the type of slices and the size of the slices for the current weekly activities pie graph.

2. Using the bottom half of *IG Worksheet #9: Currently Weekly Activities Pie Graph*, your client may add some new activities, or the frequency of some current activities may be changed (i.e., reduced or increased). Discuss whether you would modify some slices, eliminate others, or add news ones to the new pie graph. Discuss why your client may want to modify, remove, or add certain activities. Help your client list on the side of the pie graph the content or types of slices (i.e., types of activities) for the new pie graph and the relative percentage or size of the slices (i.e., determine the relative intended emphasis to be placed on that activity). Use the content listed and the associated percentages to draw the type of slices and the size of the slices for the desired weekly activities pie graph.

3. Use *CS Handout #3: Weekly Activities Pie Graph* for homework. At the top of the handout, an example is provided to help guide your client in completing the bottom half of the handout for homework.

   a. Invite your client to copy into pie graph #1 the current state pie graph they completed with you in session. Then your client can copy into pie graph #2 the desired state pie graph they also completed with you.

   b. For homework, your client can construct a bridge from pie graph #1 to pie graph #2. This is your client's action plan to get them to their desired state. The example presented in Figure 4.12 is the same example provided on the handout in the appendix.

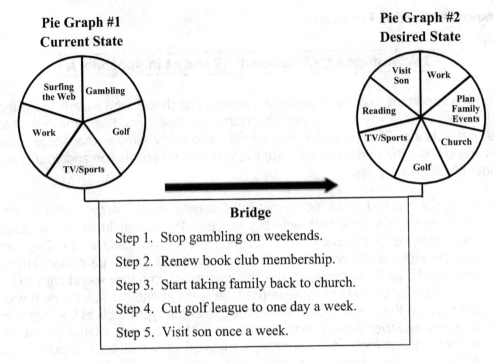

Pie Graph #1
Current State

Pie Graph #2
Desired State

Bridge

Step 1. Stop gambling on weekends.

Step 2. Renew book club membership.

Step 3. Start taking family back to church.

Step 4. Cut golf league to one day a week.

Step 5. Visit son once a week.

*Figure 4.12* Example of a Weekly Activities Pie Graph

4. Using *CS Handout #4: Weekly Schedule*, help your client schedule in desired activities for the upcoming weeks. They can start filling in the weekly grid during the session.

5. Follow-up sessions can focus on ways to implement and monitor your client's new weekly activities.

## The Self Pie Graph

**IG Worksheet #10; CS Handout #5 in Appendix A**

We can sometimes struggle with certain personality characteristics or behaviors, such as anger or perfectionism, that can negatively influence our relationships. We may also desire to strengthen certain behaviors that can improve our relationships, such as becoming a better listener. You can develop this "self" pie graph by assisting your client in reflecting on those personality characteristics they may want to modify to improve their self-esteem and relationships. For example, maybe your client identifies certain family members, friends, or colleague who may perceive them in a certain way or may have "complaints" about some of their behaviors. For instance, maybe their family members perceive them as having a bad temper or their boss believes they are a poor listener. With this pie graph, you can help your client determine their "current self" and create their "desired self."

1. Using the top half of *IG Worksheet #10: Current Self Pie Graph*, assist your client in identifying the characteristics or lifelong "traits" that may be positive or negative. Your client can include such traits as angry, good listener, impatient, caring, pessimistic, critical, generous, optimistic, and so on. In this exercise the client is focusing on change, so your client can identify traits that they desire to change or traits they desire to enhance. Therefore, it is important to include both positive and negative traits. Help your client list on the side of the pie graph the content or types of slices (i.e., types of traits) and the relative percentage or size of the slices (i.e., relative strength of that trait) (note: the percentage summed across all items should equal 100%). Use the content listed and the associated percentages to draw the type of slices and the size of the slices for the current self pie graph.

2. Using the bottom half of *IG Worksheet #10: Current Self Pie Graph*, work with your client to identify the characteristics of the desired self. Think of positive traits that your client desires to increase and negative traits that your client desires to decrease. Discuss why your client may want to modify or reduce certain traits or behaviors. Help your client list on the side of the pie graph the content or types of slices (i.e., types of traits) for the new pie graph and the relative percentage or size of the slices (i.e., determine the relative intended emphasis on that trait). Use the content listed and the associated percentages to draw the type of slices and the size of the slices for the desired self pie graph.

3. Use *CS Handout #5: The Self Pie Graph* for homework. At the top of the handout, an example is provided to help guide your client in completing the bottom half of the handout for homework.

   a. Invite your client to copy into pie graph #1 the current state pie graph they completed with you in session. Then your client can copy into pie graph #2 the desired state pie graph they also completed with you.

   b. For homework, your client can construct a bridge from pie graph #1 to pie graph #2. This is your client's action plan to get them to their desired state. The example presented in Figure 4.13 is the same example provided on the handout in the appendix.

4. Follow-up sessions can focus on ways to implement and monitor your client's new self plan.

## PERSONAL INTERESTS

**IG Worksheet #11 in Appendix A**

Using *IG Worksheet #11: Personal Interests Worksheet*, invite your client to list their personal interests. This will enable you to learn more about your client's interests,

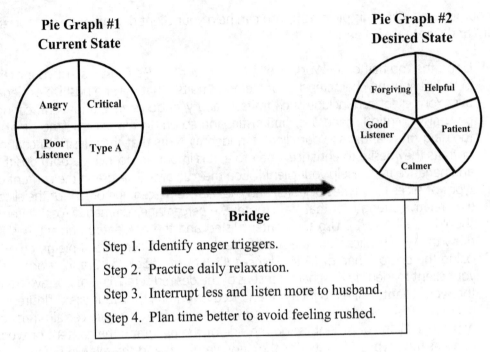

**Pie Graph #1**
**Current State**

Angry | Critical
Poor Listener | Type A

**Pie Graph #2**
**Desired State**

Forgiving | Helpful
Good Listener | Patient
Calmer

**Bridge**

Step 1. Identify anger triggers.

Step 2. Practice daily relaxation.

Step 3. Interrupt less and listen more to husband.

Step 4. Plan time better to avoid feeling rushed.

*Figure 4.13* Example of a Self Pie Graph

values, and social activities. It may be easiest to give your client the worksheet for homework so that they have enough time to reflect on their interests and complete it more thoroughly. Identifying personal interests can build rapport and enable you to get to know different facets of your client's life that are not always easily discovered or identified during traditional therapy sessions. This is a quick way to learn a lot about different aspects of your client's experience and interests, which may help increase your understanding of your client and help you formulate more meaningful and relevant treatment goals. Some of the treatment goals may be focused on fostering and developing these interests. Completing the worksheet can allow your client the opportunity to discuss topics that are less emotionally laden and focused more on positive aspects of their life and experiences. You can be flexible and creative in how you use the worksheet.

Here is an example of how you could introduce the worksheet: *"Here's a worksheet that I have found helpful to use with my clients. It helps me to get to know you a little better and explore how we may use our sessions to help you pursue your interests and to find more satisfaction in your life."*

Here are a few examples of different ways you could use your client's answers from their personal interests worksheet:

- Ask your client to share what they feel is most important from the worksheet.
- Ask your client what their answers may say about them and if they noticed any particular themes to their answers.

- Pick three to four topics from the worksheet and have your client discuss them. For example, you could have your client discuss their favorite hobby, favorite book, favorite movie, and their best friend. You can explore why these are their favorites and what it may say about their interest, values, and experiences.
- Have your client discuss in detail their ideal day. What makes it ideal? What does it say about what your client values and how they derive meaning in their life?
- Ask your client to describe their most supportive family members. Explore why these relationship are important. What support has your client received from these family members, and how do they provide support to them? This may help you learn more about your client's coping skills, needs, and ways they sustain meaningful relationships in their life.

## GOAL SETTING

Identifying goals is a cornerstone to psychotherapy. Clients in many ways seek therapy to identify and work toward meaningful goals. Therapy can effectively assist clients in making better decisions and in working toward goals that can enhance their well-being, productivity, and relationships. You can explore various types of goals with your clients in therapy. For example, you may want to explore ways to work on reducing certain symptoms and developing better coping skills. Alternatively, you may want to focus on enhancing positive attributes and capabilities and assisting your clients in reaching their potential in certain life areas, such as health, finances, and work. Next we discuss two ways to use goal-setting worksheets.

### Therapy Goals

> **IG Worksheets #12 and #13; CS Handout #6 in Appendix A**

This worksheet entails identifying the problems your client is experiencing that have caused them to seek therapy. You can assist your client in identifying these problems and then prioritizing them. Lastly, you can assist your client in formulating therapy goals aimed at alleviating these symptoms or problem areas. The worksheet can be used to address common therapy problem areas your client would like to address and can include such goals as reducing certain symptoms and developing more effective coping skills.

Use *IG worksheet #12: Therapy Problem Areas* to identify your client's problem areas. Listed in alphabetical order on the worksheet are more than 20 different problem areas that are commonly addressed in therapy. Encourage your client to circle all that apply. Then help your client prioritize these problems by listing which ones (up to four) are the most important to work on. For each problem your client can indicate the severity and duration of the problem as well as their confidence in resolving the problem. You may choose to start with the problems that your client has the most confidence in resolving. Next you can assist your client in identifying three therapy goals. Help your client be as descriptive and specific as possible. What is it that they hope therapy will accomplish for them? What changes would they like to see?

Using *CS Handout #6: Goal Planning*, you and your client can then develop an initial plan to address their three therapy goals. You may find that your client may want to work on just one or two goals. Discuss with your client what goals seem to be most realistic and practical to address in therapy. Your client can next write out the steps they need to take to reach these goal, and indicate the "estimated completion time." You and your client can develop these steps during the upcoming therapy sessions as you both explore ways to reach your client's goals. You can then monitor your client's progress in working toward these goals in follow-up sessions.

*IG Worksheet #13: Goal-Setting Chart* will assist your client in discussing their goals and developing a plan to reach their goals. You can use the chart to gather information on your client's current level of functioning and relevant life circumstances that are affecting their functioning. This may include certain stressors, symptoms, people, or situational factors that are influencing their functioning. After gathering this information in section A, you can then identify your client's therapy goals in section C. You can discuss both short- and longer-term goals and then in section B identify the steps to reach these goals. Finally, you can identify barriers to your client reaching their goals and list these in section D. These barriers may be current obstacles, chronic problems, or things in the past that have been obstacles to your client achieving their goals.

You can point out that the barriers listed in section D do not lead to goals. There is no arrow that goes from the barriers to the goals. Bringing attention to this visually on the chart will help reinforce this concept with your client. It will help call attention to the importance of focusing on productive steps versus becoming distracted by barriers or obstacles to their goals. You can indicate that the sequence for success is to move from section A to section B to section C (path 1). That is, your client moves from their current life circumstances (A) to practicing the steps to reach their goals (B), which leads to achieving their goals (C) (see Figure 4.14 for an example of a completed goal-setting chart).

You can highlight visually that following path 1 leads to success and following path 2 leads to barriers. For some clients you may choose to use the computer screen to complete the goal-setting chart as you do the typing and the client follows the visual screen and collaborates with you in reviewing and editing the information. Some clients with typing facility may want to do the typing as the two of you coalborate on what information to include in the chart. This process of collaborative dialogue with visual aids allows the client to more actively engage in the therapy discussion. If you choose to use the computer-facilitated method, it will also be helpful to have a template available through, for example, your computer's word processing program and if possible to present the goal chart on the computer screen prior to the start of the session. If the computer is used to complete the chart, then the chart can be printed out at the end of the session and given to the client to help them remember their therapy goals and the action steps needed to reach these goals. In Chapter 8 we

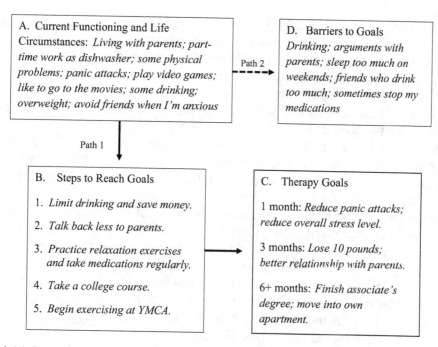

*Figure 4.14* Example of a Completed Goal-Setting Chart

discuss ways we have used this method of computer-facilitated therapy with certain clinical populations (Ahmed, 2016; Ahmed & Boisvert, 2006, 2013; Ahmed, 1998).

In talking about their personal problems and issues in relation to their goals, some of your clients may find themselves ruminating on path 2 and not being able to move in the direction of path 1. They may be able to express their goals but have difficulty recognizing and articulating that achieving their goals requires a new path (path 1). Using the goal-setting chart can help your clients see more easily how taking new steps (box B) will allow them to move from their current functioning to their goals.

## General Life Goals

**IG Worksheet #14; CS Handouts #7, #8, and #9 in Appendix A**

These worksheets entail brainstorming general life goals in various areas of your client's life, such as work, health, relationships, and finances. These worksheets can be used when the focus in therapy is more "growth-promoting" and aimed at enhancing certain life skills and capabilities. These goals will be less problem-focused and more "strengths-focused."

Use *IG Worksheet #14: Brainstorming Life Goals* to identify your client's general life goals in various areas. Encourage your client to think of their life goals across the categories of career, finances, health, relationships, social, and spiritual. For this exercise, encourage your client to think in a flexible and "unrestricted" way about these goals. Then work with your client in categorizing these goals at the bottom of the page. If your client finds that some categories do not have any goals, encourage them to think of at least one goal for that category.

Lastly, use *CS Handouts #7, #8, and #9: Life Goals Plan* to develop a plan with your client to address their life goals across the six domains: health and relationships (CS Handout #7), financial and career (CS Handout #8), and social and spiritual (CS Handout #9).

For each category encourage your client to think of breaking down their goals across time. Have your client think of goals across time (i.e., 1–4 weeks, 1–3 months, 3–6 months, and 1 year). The goals could entail attaining some "objective" outcome, such as losing 15 pounds (health goal), or participating in some activity, such as volunteering at a homeless shelter (social goal). The goals should follow some sort of sequential order where they build on one another. Lastly, invite your client to write down the steps they need to take to achieve the identified goals (see Figure 4.15 for an example of a completed health goal chart).

You can use follow-up sessions to monitor your client's progress in reaching these goals. In working toward the goals, your client may develop new goals and may begin to implement other steps that were not previously listed on the goal sheet. It is important to be flexible in using the goals sheets and to keep in mind that the primary aim is to keep your client moving toward their goals and experiencing an ongoing sense of accomplishment.

| Category | | 1–4 Weeks | 1–3 months | 3–6 months | 1 Year |
|---|---|---|---|---|---|
| Health | Goals | Reduce drinking | Reach sobriety; start diet; reduce blood pressure medications; get AA sponsor | Remain sober; lose 20 pounds; stop blood pressure medication | Becoming AA sponsor; maintain sobriety; achieve normal blood pressure; reach healthy weight |
| | Steps | | | | |
| | 1. Stop drinking on weekdays and start diet this month. | | | | |
| | 2. Renew gym membership in the spring. | | | | |
| | 3. Join AA and get sponsor. | | | | |
| | 4. Discuss with doctor a plan to reduce medications. | | | | |
| | 5. Eliminate fast food from diet. | | | | |

*Figure 4.15* Example of a Completed Health Goal Chart

66

## MAPPING THE MIND

### IG Worksheet #15; CS Handout #10 in Appendix A

It can be helpful to gather information on the topics, ideas, beliefs, philosophies, and attitudes that "occupy your client's mind." This can be particularly helpful for clients who are psychologically minded, reflective, and insight-oriented. This activity entails exploring what "bounces around" in your client's head, what thoughts and beliefs are most easily accessible, and what they tend to spend their time thinking about.

1. Using *IG Worksheet #15: Mapping the Mind*, invite your client to rate the topics listed by placing a check mark in the column that reflects how frequently they think about the particular topic. After completing the worksheet, your client can circle from the list of descriptors at the bottom of the page all the words that describe their mind and then give themselves a "mind state" rating from 1–10 (see Figure 4.16 for a sample completed worksheet).
2. Use *CS Handout #10: Remapping the Mind*.
   a. Use CS Handout #10 to first map the "current mind" of your client. They can do this by placing in the large circle all the topics listed as a 2 (Sometimes) or a

| Topics | Rarely (1) | Sometimes (2) | Often (3) |
|---|---|---|---|
| Mistakes | | X | |
| Work | | | X |
| Finances | | | X |
| Health | | X | |
| Politics | X | | |
| Sports | | | X |

The way I would describe my mind (circle all that apply—sample answers are *italicized* for the example): *noisy*, calm, positive, negative, critical, supportive, reflective, *detail-oriented, task-oriented, practical*, rigid, flexible)

Mind State Rating: [ 7 ]    1--------------10
                            Calm       Noisy

*Figure 4.16* Sample Completed Worksheet

3 (Often). Your client can draw smaller circles around the topics rated a 2 and larger circles around the topics rated a 3 (see Figure 4.17 for an example).

b. At the bottom of CS Handout #10, your client can map their "new mind" by "resizing" topics and indicating what their ideal mind would look like to achieve a more peaceful and calmer "mind state." The goal is to ultimately change the mind rating from a higher to a lower score by remapping the mind. You can periodically assess your client's mind state rating in follow-up sessions. You and your client can discuss how to maintain this new mind state by using some of the strategies discussed in this book, such as mindfulness and redirection strategies.

Figure 4.18 provides an example of a new mind handout. You will notice that some new topics have been added to the new mind that were not part of the current mind, and some topics from the current mind have been eliminated from the new mind.

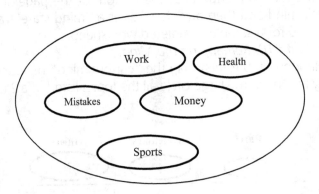

*Figure 4.17* Example of a Current Mind

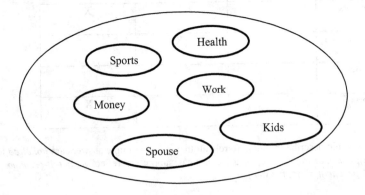

*Figure 4.18* Example of a New Mind

| Summary of Tools | | |
|---|---|---|
| **Information-Gathering Tools**<br>*Information-Gathering (IG) Worksheets*<br>*Coping Strategy (CS) Handouts* | | |
| **Method** | **Diagram** | **Appendix A** |
| Timelines | Biographical Timeline—Adolescent<br>Biographical Timeline—Adult<br>Stressful Events Timeline<br>Positive Events Timeline<br>Clinical Condition Timeline<br>Life Memories Timeline | IG Worksheet #1<br>IG Worksheet #2<br>IG Worksheet #3<br>IG Worksheet #4<br>IG Worksheet #5<br>IG Worksheet #6 |
| | | |
| Pie Graphs | Current Values Pie Graph<br>Values Pie Graph<br>Current Health Choices Pie Graph<br>Health Choices Pie Graph<br>Current Weekly Activities Pie Graph<br>Weekly Activities Pie Graph<br>Weekly Schedule<br>Current Self Pie Graph<br>The Self Pie Graph | IG Worksheet #7<br>CS Handout #1<br>IG Worksheet #8<br>CS Handout #2<br>IG Worksheet #9<br>CS Handout #3<br>CS Handout #4<br>IG Worksheet #10<br>CS Handout #5 |
| | | |
| Personal Interests Worksheet | Personal Interests Worksheet | IG Worksheet #11 |
| | | |
| Goal-Setting Worksheets | Therapy Problem Areas<br>Goal Planning<br>Goal-Setting Chart<br>Brainstorming Life Goals<br>Life Goals Plan (Health/Relationships)<br>Life Goals Plan (Career/Financial)<br>Life Goals Plan (Spiritual/Social) | IG Worksheet #12<br>CS Handout #6<br>IG Worksheet #13<br>IG Worksheet #14<br>CS Handout #7<br>CS Handout #8<br>CS Handout # 9 |
| | | |
| Mind Maps | Mapping the Mind<br>Remapping the Mind | IG Worksheet #15<br>CS Handout #10 |

# 5

# Using Diagrams to Explain Universal Therapy Topics

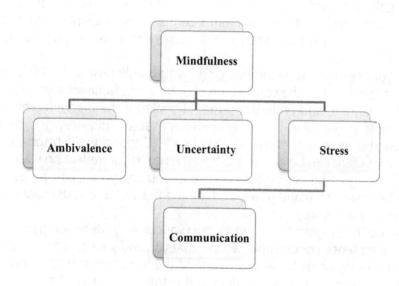

This chapter covers five universal therapy topics that will likely be relevant to the work you are doing with many of your clients, despite their clinical diagnosis or problem. These topics speak to universal themes, shared experiences, and common challenges that we all experience as we navigate through our day and attempt to cope with situations, people, thoughts, feelings, and personal life circumstances. These universal experiences and challenges include (1) trying to focus on and function in the present moment while being distracted by reflections on our past or thoughts about our future (*mindfulness*); (2) making important decisions among the various choices and options available to us in our current life circumstances (*ambivalence*); (3) managing the "probabilistic world of events" whereby we try to plan for our future and navigate through time in a world where nothing is absolutely certain and the outcome of actions and events vary based on "degrees of probability" (*uncertainty*); (4) trying to cope with change and manage the demands and expectations that we put on ourselves or that are imposed on us (*stress*); and (5) trying to maintain meaningful relationships with others through communicating our personal and shared beliefs, thoughts, feelings, experiences, and opinions (*communication*).

We present various diagrams to help you address these topics more effectively with your clients and to assist your clients in learning more effective coping strategies. You should find the diagrams useful for clients you are just starting to work with or with your already established clients. In both cases, the diagrams can provide a new method for interacting and communicating with your clients and enable you to address facets and elements of these topics that may not be ordinarily discussed or explored in more traditional verbal therapy. You can draw these diagrams on an easel, legal pad, plain white paper, white board, blackboard, or use, for example, a computer or media screen. The diagrams and drawing techniques can be used at any time during your therapy sessions once a therapeutic relationship has been established using the standard "conversational mode of therapy." As you discuss the topics of interest with your clients, the diagrams can assist your clients in more effectively collaborating with you in the therapeutic dialogue via the multimodal communication format that is created.

Prior to your session, we recommend that you briefly review the topic so that you can become familiar with the core features of the topic, familiarize yourself with how to draw the diagram, and understand the rationale for the diagram. This will enable you to be more prepared to introduce the topic, successfully draw the diagram, and discuss how the topic applies to your client's life. Choosing which topic will be best suited for your client can be determined in advance as you reflect on your knowledge of your client's style and needs, the topics that you and your client believe best align with their treatment plan and goals, and the themes you and your client have already been discussing in therapy.

You can use the diagrams and handouts in various ways depending on the status of your particular clients. For example, a topic that you and your client have already been discussing in therapy may be similar to one of the topics presented in this chapter. In this situation, you can continue to discuss this topic (e.g., stress) but now augment the discussion by incorporating a multimodal method of interaction, which includes using various teaching strategies and visual methods (e.g., diagrams and handouts) to augment the therapy discussion that has occurred up to this point. In other situations, you may decide to directly introduce one of the topics in an upcoming session after reflecting on your client's needs, goals, and problem areas. You can use the main teaching points for the particular topic as a guide and discuss your rationale for addressing the topic with your client. You can then follow the instructions for drawing the diagram and incorporate the associated worksheets and handouts. In other cases, you may find that during a session you and your client start to spontaneously discuss one of the topics addressed in this chapter (e.g., uncertainty). In this case, you may elect to more formally discuss this topic in follow-up sessions by introducing the teaching points of the topic, drawing the diagram, and completing the associated worksheets and handouts.

Next we discuss the "DRAW" technique, which describes the format for introducing these different topics in the therapy session. After describing the DRAW technique, we discuss each topic in more detail, present the main teaching points, outline the specific diagram drawing instructions, and provide detailed directions for using the in-session worksheets and coping strategies handouts. *When you know you will be addressing a particular topic with your client for an upcoming session, prior to your session we recommend that you make copies of all the in-session worksheets and coping strategy handouts you will need for the topic. Appendix B contains the in-session worksheets and coping strategy handouts for the topics covered in this chapter.*

For each topic we provide various *teaching points* for you to review prior to drawing or displaying the diagram. These main teaching points will help your clients better understand the nature of the topic and how it may apply to their lives. After reviewing the teaching points, you can use the diagram drawing techniques to *draw the diagram*, or you may choose to display the diagram by using the display diagram handout from the appendix. After drawing or displaying the diagram, and discussing the identified problem area, you can use an in-session worksheet to assist your clients in applying the topic to their lives. Finally, at the end of the session, you can provide your clients with the coping strategy handout, which they can use for homework to help them practice new coping strategies.

## THE DRAW TECHNIQUE

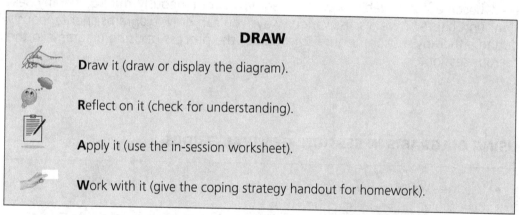

### DRAW

**D**raw it (draw or display the diagram).

**R**eflect on it (check for understanding).

**A**pply it (use the in-session worksheet).

**W**ork with it (give the coping strategy handout for homework).

For each topic you will find a display diagram. This is the diagram that you will be drawing (or displaying) to illustrate the topic covered in the session and that you can display in follow-up sessions to help reinforce the strategies you are teaching your client. As we introduce each topic, we discuss the nature of the topic and provide a picture of the diagram you will be drawing to help familiarize you with the nature of the diagram. You may initially be more comfortable teaching the concept by displaying, rather than drawing, the diagram. As you become more accustomed to writing and using diagrams during your sessions, you will become more comfortable drawing diagrams during therapy sessions. For the more detailed diagrams, it will be easier to display the diagram rather than to draw the diagram during the session. For these particular diagrams, it will be recommended in the instructions to display rather than to draw the diagram.

For each topic discussed in this chapter, we provide directions for drawing the associated diagram. All the diagrams are designed to enhance your client's understanding of the topic and to make it easier for your client to remember the core concepts and themes associated with the topic. Your client should be able to recall the diagram after the session and as a result more easily recall the therapy discussion that accompanied the diagram. It can be particularly effective if your client observes you drawing the diagram in the session. This drawing "action" or physical activity displayed in the session provides a "salient" multimodal communication method that can facilitate your client's memory of the themes and concepts discussed during the session.

After you have discussed the diagram in session, you can later use the display diagram in follow-up sessions to facilitate your client's ability to recall prior therapy discussions associated with the diagram. You do not have to necessarily refer to the diagram in every session, but by simply placing the diagram within the client's visual field, it may help trigger the client's memory of the topics and issues discussed. Having the diagram visible during follow-up sessions can also help the client remain focused on important therapy topics and goals. After a while you will even become comfortable drawing diagrams spontaneously during therapy sessions (in Chapter 7 we discuss various ways you can draw diagrams spontaneously during a therapy session). Figure 5.1 outlines the process of using diagrams in the therapy session.

## USING DIAGRAMS IN SESSION: GENERAL GUIDES

- Use the *DRAW technique* as a guide.
- Be flexible.
- Introduce the topic by first covering the **main teaching points**.
- **Draw** or use the **display diagram** to further explain the topic.
- Use the **in-session worksheet** to apply the topic to your client's life.
- Use the **coping strategies handout** for homework to help your client practice new coping strategies associated with the topic.
- You don't have to write during the entire session.
- You don't have to write in every session.
- Post the display diagrams in future sessions as needed.

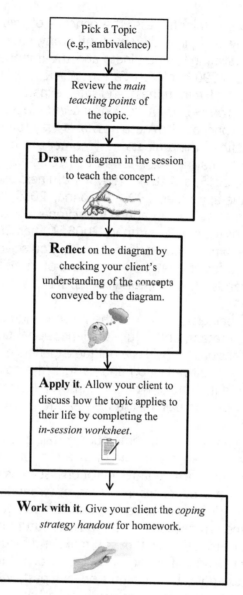

Figure 5.1 The Steps of the DRAW Technique

## MINDFULNESS

The first topic we cover is mindfulness. The concept of *mindfulness* has become a central concept in many fields, including psychotherapy, education, and business. We hear today about "cultivating" mindfulness and the importance of "staying in the present." In his famous 1990 book *Full Catastrophic Living*, Jon Kabat-Zinn formally introduced the concept of mindfulness and later expanded on the concept in his 1994 book, *Wherever You Go, There You Are: Mindfulness Meditation in Everyday Life*. He discussed the concept of mindfulness as a way to become more connected to the present. He defined mindfulness as "moment-to-moment, non-judgmental awareness, cultivated by paying attention in a specific way, that is, in the present moment" (Kabat-Zinn, 2015, p. 1481). Today mindfulness exercises are readily incorporated into psychotherapy (Baer, 2003; Didonna, 2009; Mace, 2008) and have been shown to enhance well-being and self-awareness (Brown & Ryan, 2003) and to decrease ruminations (Coffey & Hartman, 2008; Kumar, 2010). Today the practice of mindfulness has become commonplace. Teaching ourselves to stay in the present moment is important to foster one's well-being and one's ability to cope with current life stressors and demands. However, for all of us, staying in the present can be quite challenging.

As conscious living beings, we exist in the present momentary existence of time characterized by past, present, and future unidimensional time direction. This "existence across time dimensions" provides a unique experience to human beings in that we have the capacity for self-reflection and as such the ability to remove ourselves from the present moment. That is, we can "jump time zones" and place ourselves in a moment of time (i.e., the past or the future) outside of our present moment of existence.

This ability to "reimagine," or to remember certain past experiences or imagine certain future experiences can create within us a sort of "emotional vulnerability." For example, we can experience negative emotions, such as regret, anger, or guilt, if we reflect on certain past experiences, mistakes, or wrongdoings. We can also experience worry or anxiety if we imagine certain unfortunate, dangerous, or threatening future experiences. These reflections on the past or future can cause "distractions" and negative emotional experiences that can make it difficult for us to focus on the present. On the other hand, reflecting on our past or future may at times serve a useful purpose. For example, by reflecting on our past, we may gain insight into our behavior, learn from past decisions, and make better decisions in the future. By reflecting on our future and what may lie ahead, we may arrive at solutions to problems and learn how to be better prepared when certain situations arise. In these cases, a positive goal is achieved by temporarily visiting a "time zone" outside of the present moment.

This first diagram we present is the time circles diagram. This diagram can be used to teach mindfulness as well as a variety of related concepts. In our experience, clients are able to easily understand the concept of mindfulness by using the time circles diagram. The time circles diagram provides a framework for clients to begin to "visualize" their thought processes and the emotions that are associated with visiting different "time dimensions." After presenting the time circles diagram in sessions, clients have often responded with the following: "*Yes, I remember those circles . . . I think I was dwelling on the past . . . I think at that time I was in the 'zone of the past' and felt guilty again . . . I tried to get myself refocused on the present and back to the middle circle like we discussed.*" You will find that most, if not all, of your clients will readily relate to, easily understand, and remember the time circles diagram. I (Charles Boisvert) have used this diagram with almost all my clients and display a copy of it on the table in my therapy office.

The time circles diagram illustrates our ability to remove ourselves from the present moment and to reflect on our past experiences or imagine our future. Visually presenting the three time circles, or time zones, helps clients recognize how much time they may spend in these different time zones and how staying in a particular zone may influence their present behavior and mood. It helps to raise your client's awareness of how negative moods, such as depression, may be due in part to remaining too long in the circle of the past and how anxiety may be due in part to remaining too long in the circle of the future. The goal is to reduce your client's negative feelings by teaching them strategies to return to the present.

---

### Mindfulness Diagrams

a. *DD #1: The Time Circles*
b. *IS Worksheet #1: Visiting the Time Circles*
c. *CS Handout #1: Coping With the Time Circles*
d. *CS Handout #2: Staying in the Present*

---

*Make copies of all the time circle diagrams, worksheets, and handouts prior to your session.*

---

### Main Teaching Points

1. Humans are unique in that they can mentally remove themselves from the present and put themselves in different time zones. For example, we can remove ourselves from the present moment simply by thinking about our past. We can reflect on past experiences, mistakes, accomplishments, or wrongdoings. We can also remove ourselves from the present by focusing on the future and worrying. For example, we may worry about an event, think about something that might happen to a loved one, envision ourselves successfully solving a problem, acquiring an illness, losing our job, or winning an award.

2. Thinking about the past and future is not necessarily problematic and at times can be helpful. For example, thinking about the past may lead to insight and help us learn from our experiences. Thinking about the future may lead to successful planning and problem-solving.

3. Thinking too much about the past and future, however, may be unhelpful and ultimately cause stress. For example, dwelling on the past may lead to guilt, regret, anger, or feelings of depression. Dwelling on the future may lead to worry and feelings of anxiety.

4. Learning to more consistently focus on the present moment can help reduce feelings of depression and anxiety.

A. **Draw the following diagram.**

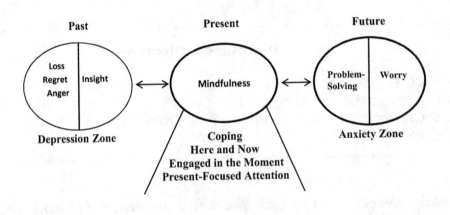

STEPS:

*Step 1:* **Draw a circle and write the word "present" above it**. *You and I are here in the present moment. This circle represents the "here and now" and the "immediate moment," which we are experiencing at this time. We will call this the present time zone. When we are in the present, we are aware of the*

*immediate moment and are focusing our attention on what we are doing in the here and now. We are engaged in the present moment and not worrying about the future or thinking about the past. Some call this a state of mindfulness.* **Write the word "mindfulness" in the middle.**

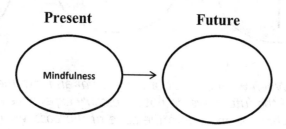

Present            Future

Mindfulness

*Step 2:* **Draw an arrow exiting the circle of the present and then draw the circle of the future to the right of it.** *In addition to the present time zone, we can think about our future and envision ourselves exisiting in a time that is different from the present time. Throughout the day, our mind can travel to the future. For example, we can consciously direct ourselves to the future zone (e.g., we can sit down and plan a summer vacation). When doing this, we are leaving the present and directing our thoughts ahead to plan something. Sometimes we may even think about something happening to us in the future and will dwell on it awhile.*

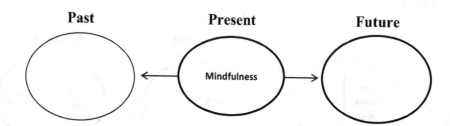

Past         Present        Future

Mindfulness

*Step 3:* **Draw an arrow exiting the circle of the present and then draw the circle of the past to the left of it.** *Alternatively, we can leave the present and think of our past. For example, we may see a child playing baseball and think back to when we played baseball. We can visit the past for different reasons and reflect on things that have happened to us. We could think of an accomplishment, a job we had, a death of a family member, or a specific event that happened to us in the past. The percentage of time we spend in each of these zones can be influnced by, for example, current life stressors, a particular thinking style we have developed, or the particular mood we may be experiencing at the moment.*

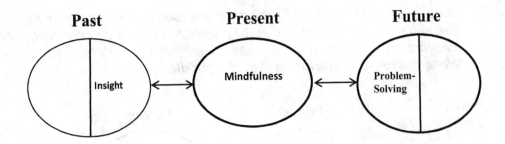

Step 4: When we move out of the present and into the zone of the past or the zone of the future, we do not necessarily experience a negative mood. For example, when we move into the zone of the past. we may gain insight and learn something about ourselves. **Draw a line separating the circles of the future and past into two even halves. Write the word "insight" in the right half of the circle of the past**. After visiting the past, we then direct ourselves back to the present. **Draw the arrow as bidirectional, now going to and from the circles of the past and present**. When we move into the zone of the future, we may be planning and working toward goals. **Write the word "problem-solving" in the left half of the circle of the future**. Then we return to the present after we have figured out what we need to do. **Draw the arrow as bidirectional, now going to and from the circles of the future and present**. The important thing to notice is whether moving out of the present is serving to promote a positive mood or whether it is promoting a negative mood.

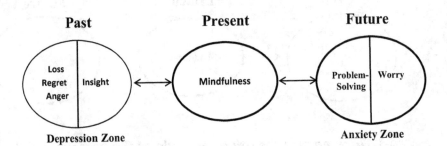

Step 5: However, when we move out of the present and move into the zone of the past or the zone of the future, we can experience a negative mood. For example, the zone of the past can become a "depression zone" if we start to dwell on past mistakes, regrets, others' actions, or our failings. **Write the words "loss," "regret," and "anger" in the left half of the past circle and the words "depression zone" underneath the circle of the past**. Alternatively, the zone of the future can become an "anxiety zone" if we start to worry about things we cannot control or that we cannot resolve. **Write the word "worry" in the right half of the future circle and the words "anxiety**

**zone" underneath the circle of the future**. *Notice that the negative emotions and themes are at the far ends of the circles and are experienced when we are reaching deep into those zones and reflecting on things that are further and further removed from the present.*

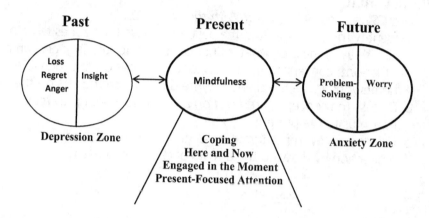

*Step 6: Even though we may be able to move into another time zone, such as the time zone of the past, we can stop ourselves from dwelling on the past by directing our attention back to the present time zone. We can do this, for example, by focusing on a current activity. When we remain in the present, we are in a state of mindfulness. Our attention is focused on the present, and we are in the here and now, not worrying about our future and not dwelling on our past.* **Finish by writing the words that are listed below the circle of the present.**

B. **Reflect on it.** Check for understanding. Determine if the client understands the diagram and the concept of mindfulness. After soliciting the client's feedback, move to the "Apply it" step.

C. **Apply it.** Use *IS Worksheet #1: Visiting the Times Circles*.

1. Review the concept of *emotional vulnerability* (anxiety and depression) when we leave the present circle—that is, we can become emotionally vulnerable when we focus away from the present. Depression and anxiety can be coped with more effectively when we recognize that we have jumped time zones and when we take steps to actively redirect ourselves back to the *present*.

2. Ask your client how the time zones may relate to their life and thinking style. Ask them how much time they may spend in the different zones throughout the day. Using IS Worksheet #1, discuss the client's time circle *percentages* (i.e., determine how much time the client estimates they spend in each circle). Write these percentages above the associated circle. The percentages should equal 100%.

3. Identify typical *content* in the circles (e.g., the past circle may have themes from childhood or past relationships, such as loss, death, regret; the future circle may have themes of poor health, death, danger, or financial instability).

81

4. Discuss the client's intended *purpose* of visiting the circles. Emphasize that when visiting the circles, one may not be able to resolve anything, and one may not be able to achieve any specific goal. Visiting the circle may simply reinforce negative thinking and lead to negative emotions.

D. **Work with it.**

1. Use *CS Handout #1: Coping With the Times Circles*.

a. Identify triggers to visiting the past and future time zones to help raise your client's awareness of what influences their moods. Triggers can be people, situations, conversations, events, or even times of day, such as evening. For homework, invite the client to write down these triggers on their handout.

b. Discuss the concept of *redirection* as a central coping strategy, which helps return us to the present.

c. Use the following diagram as a guide to discuss redirection. Emphasize redirection by drawing the arrows back to the present.

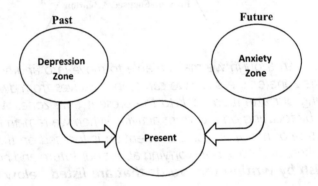

d. Using CS Handout #1, invite your client to practice various redirection strategies for homework and record these at the bottom of the handout.

2. Use *CS Handout #2: Staying in the Present*.

a. Review the concept of *mindfulness* as a strategy to stay in the present time zone.

b. Assist your client in identifying various mindfulness strategies they can practice for homework to help them remain in the present.

3. Post *DD #1: The Time Circles* in follow-up sessions as a visual reminder to your client to practice different mindfulness strategies.

## AMBIVALENCE

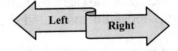

We can all experience *ambivalence*, whether it is over a relationship, a job, a particular decision, or pursuing certain life goals. Ambivalence often involves having conflicting feelings about a person, situation, object, or action. For example, we may have ambivalent feelings about someone (e.g., feel both positive and negative feelings toward this person) or ambivalent feelings about a situation (e.g., feel both excited and anxious about attending a social gathering). We may also experience ambivalence about making a certain decision, such as whether to say something to someone, take a new work position, leave a relationship, start a medication, apply for a job, or stop drinking. We can also experience ambivalence about a personal belief or feeling. For example, we may be ambivalent about resolving something from our past or ambivalent about changing a certain personality feature, such as deciding to become more assertive.

Ambivalence can create a state of tension and unease as we try to decide what to do. When we are in a state of ambivalence, we can be stuck between deciding among options or courses of action. In certain ambivalent situations, we often consider the pros and cons to each decision and try to determine which decision may have more advantages. In these situations we are often deciding among two "equally attractive options." For example, we may need to decide between exercising and watching TV. In attempting to make this decision, we may consider such things as how easy, stressful, healthy, time consuming, or enjoyable the activity is. However, despite reflecting on the nature of our different options, we can sometimes still be unsure about what decision to make. In other situations, we may be deciding whether to take action, such as whether to say something to someone or whether to volunteer, for example, at a local senior center. In these situations, we are deciding between *acting* and *not acting*.

The goal in any ambivalent situation is to move out of the stuck state and to decide on a given course of action. The decision could be to simply accept the given circumstances or in other situations to choose a certain course of action. In either case a decision is made and there is resolution to the ambivalence. We provide worksheets for managing these two different ambivalence scenarios. One worksheet (*CS Handout #4: Decision-Making: Pros and Cons*) is designed to help your clients identify the pros and cons to certain options. The other worksheet (*CS Handout #3: Resolving Ambivalence: The 2As*) is designed to help your clients decide whether to take action or to accept a certain situation.

---

### Ambivalence Diagrams

a. *DD #2: Ambivalence*
b. *IS Worksheet #2: Decision-Making: The T-Path*
c. *CS Handout #3: Resolving Ambivalence: The 2As*
d. *CS Handout #4: Decision-Making: Pros and Cons*

---

*Make copies of all the ambivalence diagrams, worksheets, and handouts prior to your session.*

| Main Teaching Points |
|---|

1. Ambivalence is a normal part of life and can create stress and tension as we reflect on two seemingly equally attractive options that both have advantages and disadvantages.
2. Emphasize that many decisions do not need to be made immediately.
3. Emphasize that few decisions are permanent and can often be reevaluated when circumstances change.
4. Ambivalent feelings are a sign that a decision must be made. The decision we need to make can sometimes require us to choose between two alternatives, both of which require us to change (e.g., choosing between two job offers). Other times the decision we need to make requires us to either act or not act (e.g., deciding whether to start a diet).

A. **Draw the following diagram.**

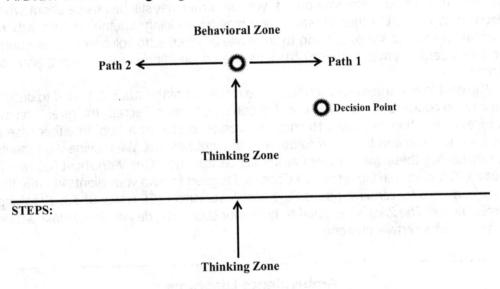

*Step 1:* **Write the words "thinking zone" at the bottom of the page and draw an arrow upward from it.** *We are moving along and reflecting on what to do. This can be considered a time of reflection, contemplation, and consideration of our options. We may be in the thinking zone for just a few minutes or for many days depending on what we are trying to decide and how much time is needed. For example, if we are considering a new job, we may have some time to reflect on this before deciding. However, in other cases the*

*decision may be more urgent, such as whether to say something to someone in the moment.*

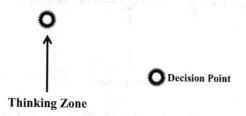

Step 2: **Draw the circle at the top of the arrow.** *Explain that this is the "decision point." This is the "fork in the road" where you decide what to do and choose the path to take. Here you make a decision to turn right or to turn left.* **In the bottom right-hand corner, place a small dot and next to it write the words "decision point."**

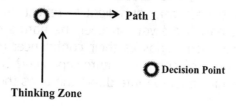

Step 3: *Before stepping onto your chosen path, you may be considering such factors as which path is easier and less stressful to travel or what the consequences will be of traveling the chosen path.* **Draw an arrow to the right of the circle and label this "path 1."** *For example, you may think of the advantages of taking path 1. Maybe this is the path you typically take and you are familiar with it. You may consider it less stressful, more predictable, and easier.*

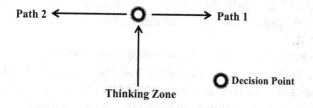

Step 4: **Draw an arrow to the left of the circle and label this "path 2."** *On the other hand, you may think of the advantages of taking path 2. Maybe this is the path you really want to take, yet it is less familiar to you but possibly has more advantages and positive consequences. However, it may be the more difficult path because you are unsure of exactly how to travel it.*

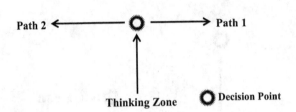

*Step 5:* **Finish by writing the words "behavioral zone" at the top of the diagram. Emphasize that this is the behavioral zone where you engage in the behaviors associated with your decision. In making a decision, it is important to think of the behaviors associated with each decision.**

B. **Reflect on it.** Check for understanding. Determine if the client understands the diagram and the concept of ambivalence. After soliciting the client's feedback, move to the "Apply it" step.

C. **Apply it.** Use *IS Worksheet #2: Decision-Making: The T-Path*.

1. Using IS Worksheet #2, ask your client to reflect on ways they have made decisions in the past. Here you uncover the nature of their thinking zone. Do they consider such things as their confidence, resources, outcomes of decisions, influence on others, or future capability? Under the thinking zone section, invite your clients to write down the ways they have made decisions in the past.

2. Discuss the current decisions that your client must make. At the bottom of the worksheet under the types of decisions section, invite your client to list the "categories" or types of decisions they need to make, and then next to each decision, invite your client to describe the specific decision they need to make. Two examples are provided. In the relationship example, the decision is to act or not act (e.g., deciding whether to say something to someone); in the work example, the decision is choosing between two actions (e.g., work weekends or evenings).

3. Decide what type of decision your client would like to work on for homework and use the appropriate handout described next.

D. **Work with it.**

1. Use *CS Handout #3: Resolving Ambivalence: The 2As*.

   a. Use CS Handout #3 for decisions that may not require changing your current behavior. That is, the situation doesn't necessarily require you to take action. This may include such situations as deciding whether to communicate something to your partner or a family member, becoming more assertive, applying for a new job, or confronting your boss or neighbor.

   b. Draw the following diagram to explain the 2As strategy, which shows how to resolve ambivalence by taking *action* (doing something different) or reaching *acceptance* (deciding to accept the current circumstances). Either option leads to resolution of the ambivalence.

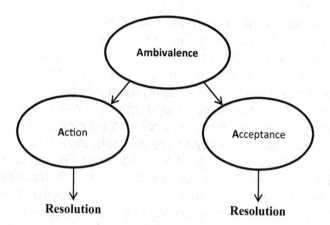

a. For homework, your client can develop an action or acceptance plan depending on which option they choose.

2. Use *CS Handout #4: Decision-Making: Pros and Cons.*

a. Use CS Handout #4 in situations where your client has decided to change their current behavior and they need to choose among different options. This may entail such situations as choosing certain work hours, deciding among treatment options, or choosing a certain diet program.

b. For homework, your client can write down in the middle of the page the decision they need to make. Then under the behavioral zone section, your client can list the pros and cons of each decision and end by evaluating the pros and cons of each choice to help them choose the best path to take.

c. At the bottom of the handout, your client can write down which path they believe they will choose.

3. Post *DD #2: Ambivalence* in follow-up sessions to remind your client to discuss how they are managing their ambivalence.

## UNCERTAINTY

We are all challenged to cope with uncertainty in our lives. Managing the uncertainty of life is difficult and can be a source of anxiety. We can experience uncertainty about our future, the future of others, or the outcome of certain events. Although we may be able to sometimes "accurately predict" some events based on our past experiences, "hunches," and "redundancy" (events that appear to happen with the same experiential features), we cannot predict the future with absolute certainty. This is due in part to the process of "change" that occurs across time. Due to change, we cannot know for sure the future of our health, the future of our job, the future of the weather, the future behavior of those around us, or the exact moment of our death.

We try to manage the experience of uncertainty by discerning what is known, unknown, or unknowable. The *knowns* are available to us based on our personal, social, cultural, and educational experiences. For example, we know what rituals, foods, and social events are part of our ethnic and religious traditions. We also can know certain things that are occurring in our immediate experience. For example, we can know what the weather is like by looking outside. We also experience *unknowns*, which are things that we do not know but that we have the possibility of knowing (e.g., we may not know the intentions of another but could discover this by asking the person; we may not know the nature of the tumor in our stomach but could find this out by getting an MRI). Lastly, we also experience *unknowables*, which are things that we cannot know for sure and are unlikely to ever know. These are things that we may not be able to experience or things for which our human mind cannot fully understand or explain. Things in the unknowable category may include determining whether a deceased family member ever really loved us, understanding the root causes of a medical or psychiatric problem, or predicting when someone is going to be born, when one will die, how and where one will die, or what it will be like after one's death. To address some of these unknowables, many of us use our individual beliefs, social supports, personal coping strategies, and spiritual faith.

The experience of uncertainty can prompt clients to ask *why* questions. For example, some of your clients may find that they frequently ask such questions as "Why did my partner do that?" "Why did my boss say that?" "Why did my neighbor put up a fence?" "Why did the town start the project now?" "Why did my taxes go up?" "Why did my dog die young?" "Why does my car keep breaking down?" "Why didn't I get a raise?" These *why* questions will be important to the extent that they are answerable. However, many *why* questions lead to only speculative answers and often will be unanswerable and generate unresolved stress for clients.

In this section we discuss ways to understand the concept of uncertainty across the three dimensions of knowing (knowns, unknowns, and unknowables). We discuss ways to cope with these dimensions of uncertainty as well as ways to better manage the different types of questions your clients may ask to try to resolve their uncertainty.

---

### Uncertainty Diagrams

a. *DD #3: Uncertainty*
b. *IS Worksheet #3: Shining the Light of Certainty*
c. *CS Handout #5: Adjusting the Light of Certainty*

---

*Make copies of all the uncertainty diagrams, worksheets, and handouts prior to your session.*

---

### Main Teaching Points

1. Emphasize the importance of becoming more comfortable with ambiguity and uncertainty and resisting efforts to seek absolute certainty in life.
2. Discuss the ongoing presence of uncertainty and the importance of accepting limitations in our human capacity for knowledge to resolve the uncertainties in life.
3. Discuss the universal appeal of various faith-based practices among billions of people to help them cope with existential uncertainties and "meaning of life" questions.
4. Introduce the idea of minimizing *why* questions, as these questions are often unanswerable, generate stress, and often lead only to speculative answers.

---

A. **Display Figure 5.2 (see Appendix B).**

Using the diagram, discuss the following with your client:

1. Identify the three spheres of knowing:
   a. White = knowns (what we can be certain about)
   b. Grey = unknowns (what is potentially knowable)
   c. Black = unknowables (what we cannot know)
2. Discuss the four examples in the diagram. These questions are rated 1, 2, 3, and 4 to help your client distinguish between "shades" of knowing. Discuss how these questions all differ in the degree to which the question is knowable or answerable.
3. Discuss that we are often moving around in the grey circle of uncertainty and unsure of what is exactly happening, why it is happening, and whether something will happen. As a result, we are often compelled to seek answers to these unknowns. For example, we may be uncertain of the following: *what our spouse or significant other meant by a comment or gesture, how our day will go, whether our back pain will act up, or whether we will ever find happiness.* These events or reflections can cause us to ask certain questions in an effort to predict the future, understand certain events, understand the behavior of others, or seek resolution to philosophical questions.
4. Discuss that a way to manage uncertainty in life is to consider questions that are more answerable, or knowable, and to minimize efforts to consider questions that are less answerable and therefore less knowable.

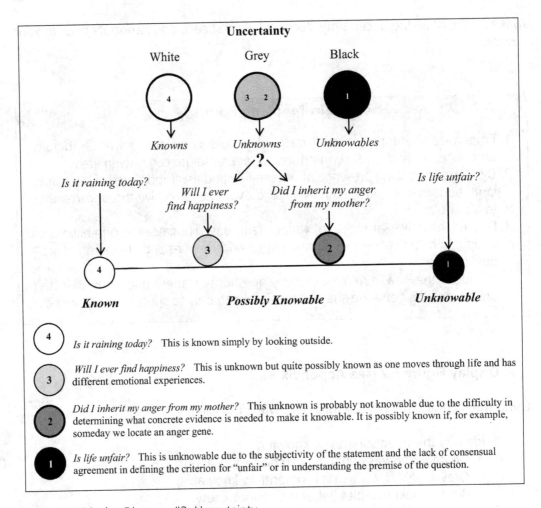

**Uncertainty**

White     Grey     Black

*Knowns*    *Unknowns*    *Unknowables*

*Is it raining today?*

*Will I ever find happiness?*

*Did I inherit my anger from my mother?*

*Is life unfair?*

**Known**     **Possibly Knowable**     **Unknowable**

(4) *Is it raining today?* This is known simply by looking outside.

(3) *Will I ever find happiness?* This is unknown but quite possibly known as one moves through life and has different emotional experiences.

(2) *Did I inherit my anger from my mother?* This unknown is probably not knowable due to the difficulty in determining what concrete evidence is needed to make it knowable. It is possibly known if, for example, someday we locate an anger gene.

(1) *Is life unfair?* This is unknowable due to the subjectivity of the statement and the lack of consensual agreement in defining the criterion for "unfair" or in understanding the premise of the question.

*Figure 5.2* Display Diagram #3: Uncertainty

5. You may also be comfortable discussing the concept of *existential mystery* with some clients. Many people, such as those who practice a spiritual faith or those who are naturalists, may use such phrases as "God willing" or "That's nature's call" when trying to predict future events. Such expressions may be used as a positive redirection strategy to manage "unnecessary worries" or to reduce "existential anxiety." In some ways, using the term *existential mystery* equalizes all of us, independent of our differences in social status, religion, acquired knowledge, or living circumstances, as it reflect something all human beings grapple with. The use of this concept may become particularly helpful if you are working with clients facing end-of-life issues, clients with physical disabilities residing in nursing homes or in supervised residences, or clients who tend to frequently grapple with philosophical questions.

B. **Reflect on it.** Check for understanding. Determine if the client understands the diagram and the concept of uncertainty. After soliciting the client's feedback, proceed to the "Apply it" step.

C. **Apply it.** Use *IS Worksheet #3: Shining the Light of Certainty*.

   1. Identify what topics, events, situations, ideas, or issues are the cause for your client's uncertainty or for which your client is trying to achieve some certainty. These would be called the unknowns.

   2. List these topics in the form of a question in the box entitled "Unknowns" and then rate them to see where they may fall on the "Possibly Knowable" scale. Remind your client that higher-rated items are more useful to consider as they are more likely to be answerable.

D. **Work with it.** Use *CS Handout #5: Adjusting the Light of Certainty*.

   1. Invite your client to categorize the questions they listed on IS Worksheet #3 into two categories: *More Knowable* (questions rated 3) and *Less Knowable* (questions rated 2).

   2. Discuss and list strategies that your client can use to help them possibly answer the *More Knowable* questions. An example is provided on the handout.

   3. Discuss and list strategies that your client can use to "settle" the *Less Knowable* questions. An example is provided.

   4. Post *DD #3: Uncertainty* in follow-up sessions as needed as a reminder to discuss how your client is managing life's uncertainties.

## STRESS

Stress can be defined as a demand to cope with change. A change can occur in any area of our life (e.g., relationship, finances, health, job) and this can place a "demand" on us to cope and adjust to the change. We can experience different types of stressors, such as acute stressors (e.g., traffic, bills), chronic stress (e.g., poor health, family conflict), or distant stressors (e.g., past abuse or trauma). Stress alerts us to something that requires our attention and that often requires us to take action to manage the stressor. Our particular reaction to stress will be influenced by various factors, such as our belief systems, our past experiences, our perceived social supports, our current stress levels, and our biological predispositions.

Brief stress can mobilize us into action and promote certain functions, such as memory, immune system functioning, and bodily strength—all initiated to promote our survival and ability to adapt to the situation. These bodily changes help us better manage the stress over the short term. Even though short-term stress can temporarily enhance our functioning and motivate us to perform a given task and cope with a particular event or situation, prolonged stress may cause physical and psychological problems, such as degraded memory, depression, and compromised immune system functioning. Long-term stress can ultimately interfere with our ability to cope successfully with life's demands and can lead to chronic health problems (Sapolsky, 2004). The worksheets for this topic can assist your clients in identifying their stress triggers and developing strategies to more effectively manage stress.

---

## Stress Diagrams

a. *DD #4: Stress Monitoring*
b. *IS Worksheet #4: Stress Meter*
c. *CS Handout #6: Stress Monitoring Form*
d. *CS Handout #7: Stress Management Strategies*

---

*Make copies of all the stress diagrams, worksheets, and handouts prior to your session.*

---

## Main Teaching Points

1. Stress is a demand placed on us to respond to a change. The change can be positive (e.g., marriage) or negative (e.g., loss of job).
2. Stress is a biopsychological experience that affects our psychological functioning as well as our physical functioning.
3. Short-term stress can have positive effects. Long-term stress can have negative effects.
4. The higher one's stress level, the more difficult it is to control.
5. It can be helpful to monitor our stress level and to notice what causes our stress level to increase. When we begin to notice that our stress level is increasing, this is the best time to intervene and to use a strategy to reduce our stress and to prevent it from further increasing.

## A. Draw the following diagram.

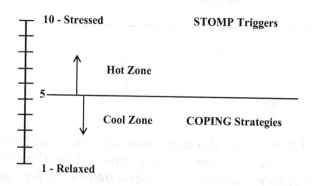

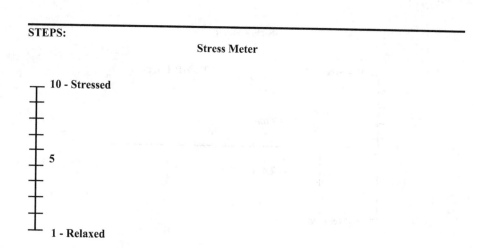

STEPS:

*Step 1:* **Start by writing the words "stress meter" at the top of the page. Draw the stress meter with the numbers 1, 5, and 10, as shown. Draw hash marks to represent increments along the way. Label the top of the meter next to the number 10 with the word "stressed" and indicate that this would be our highest level of stress. Label the lowest part of the meter next to the number 1 with the word "relaxed." This would be the most relaxed you could be.** *Discuss how our level of stress can move up and down on this meter throughout the day based on what we are doing or thinking.*

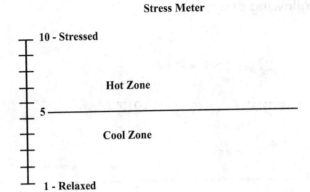

***Step 2:* Draw a line across the page and indicate that there are two stress zones we may be in at any given moment. Label the zone above the line as the "hot zone" and label the zone below the line as the "cool zone."**

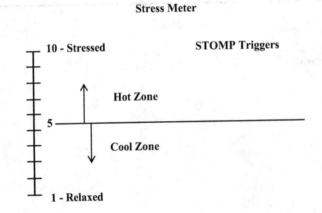

## STOMP Triggers

**S**ituations: "I hate going to this place; it's always so loud."

**T**houghts: "I never have anything interesting to say."

**O**verall Stress: "My chronic health problems always seem to stress me out."

**M**emories: "Why did my father always tell me what to say when I was a kid?"

**P**eople: "My aunt talks about politics all the time. She always thinks she's right."

*Step 3:* **Draw an arrow moving up from the midline at number 5 and ascending into the hot zone**. *Discusss that our level of stress can slowly rise based on different events, thoughts, and demands that we experience during the day.* **Then write the words "STOMP triggers" at the top right corner of the diagram**. *Explain that this is an acronym for various factors that can raise our level of stress and move us up the scale. See the earlier decription of the STOMP triggers. An example is provided for each, which you can review with your client. Your client can remember these by reminding themselves that when they get upset, they start "stomping" their feet and moving up the scale!*

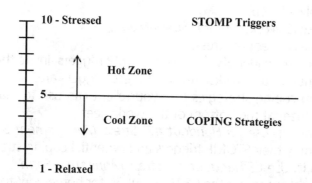

**Stress Meter**

10 - Stressed          STOMP Triggers

Hot Zone

5——————————————————

Cool Zone          COPING Strategies

1 - Relaxed

*Step 4:* **Draw a line starting at the midline at number 5 and descending into the cool zone**. *Discuss how we can lower our level of stress by taking direct action to cope with our stress. Practicing coping strategies will help keep us in this zone, minimize movement up the scale, or help us move down the scale.* **Write the words "coping strategies" in the cool zone to emphasize that coping strategies help keep us in this zone**. *Then discuss various coping strategies your client can practice. See the following descriptions of COPING strategies. These strategies can be remembered by using the acronym COPING. These are available on one of the stress handouts you can give your client.*

## COPING Strategies

**C**ount:     Count to 10 slowly to center yourself.

**O**rder:     Order your priorities by deciding what is most important to do at this very moment to calm yourself down. What would you order or put at the top of the list?

**P**ause:     Pause and slow down. Move more slowly. This will reduce stress in your body and will slow down your thoughts.

| | |
|---|---|
| **I**magine: | Imagine your future. How will it be affected by what is happening right now? Is this event or situation critical, important, significant, or just a passing nuisance? |
| **N**otice: | Notice what you are thinking. Try to think of the situation in a different way. |
| **G**uess: | Guess or estimate your level of stress. Try to do something to move the number down one notch on the stress meter. |

B. **Reflect on it.** Check for understanding. Determine if the client understands the diagram and the concept of stress. After soliciting the client's feedback, move to the "Apply it" step.

C. **Apply it.** Use *IS Worksheet #4: Stress Meter.*
1. Review the concept of stress.
2. Ask your client to identify their own STOMP triggers. Invite them to be specific and to write on the worksheet what these triggers are.
3. Brainstorm coping strategies that your client can use to manage these triggers. List them at the bottom of the worksheet.
4. Your client can use *CS Handout #7: Stress Management Strategies* to help them identify their STOMP triggers and potential coping strategies.

D. **Work with it.** Use *CS Handout #6: Stress Monitoring Form.*
1. Invite your client to use the CS Handout #6 for homework to help them monitor their stress triggers and to implement coping strategies to better manage these stressors.
2. Discuss ways your client can navigate the stress zones and use coping strategies to prevent their stress meter from rising. Emphasize the importance of monitoring small incremental changes on the scale that may not be immediately noticeable but that may be easier to manage compared to numbers higher on the scale.
3. Post *DD #4: Stress Monitoring* in follow-up sessions as a visual reminder to your client to review how they are doing monitoring their stress level.

## COMMUNICATION

Sustaining positive relationships requires good communication skills and an awareness of ways to adjust our communication when needed based on the current context and circumstances in which we are communicating. It can be a challenge to sustain and achieve effective communication with others. Our general style of communication can be shaped by such factors as our experiences, expectations, personality, and learning history. We can adjust our communication in different ways, such as by modifying our tone, changing our words, altering our nonverbal behavior, or adjusting the balance between listening and speaking. Our communication in any given moment can also be influenced by the context of the situation, our perceived intentions of the other, our immediate goals, our current stress level, and the communication style of the other. Sometimes our typical communication style can add stress to a situation, which can often be unintentional due to the particular habits of communication we have developed over the years.

Communicating with others can serve various goals depending on the context, the people who are communicating, and the needs of those communicating. Some of the goals we may aim to achieve in our communication include to be understood or supported; to show we are right or correct about something; to ask for something or to make a request; to direct someone to do something; to convey a feeling, such as love; or to gather information. The communication diagrams in this section are designed to assist your client in better understanding the various components of communication, gaining insight into the nature of their personal communication style, and learning more effective ways to communicate with others.

---

**Communication Diagrams**

a. *DD #5: The Song of Communication*
b. *IS Worksheet #5: Tuning the 2Ts of Communication*
c. *CS Handout #8: Playing a New Station: The 3Ls*
d. *CS Handout #9: Communication Ambiguity*

---

*Make copies of all the communication diagrams, worksheets, and handouts prior to your session.*

---

**Main Teaching Points**

1. Good communication is achieved by finding the right balance between speaking and listening and learning how to best adjust our tone and our words for any given conversation.
2. Deciding how to adjust our communication style can be determined by identifying our immediate communication goals and understanding the communication goals of the other.

3. Communication can often be ambiguous, and we can sometimes misinterpret the intended message of the other.
4. Think of communication as a "song" composed of:
   a. Lyrics—the words (*what* we communicate)
   b. Music—the tone (*how* we communicate)
   c. The lyrics are the words the person hears and the music is the tone the person hears. The words are "heard through our thoughts," and the tone is "heard through our feelings." Sometimes we respond more to the music than to the lyrics. Think of a favorite song. We may like the song more for its music than for its lyrics, or conversely we may like the song more for its lyrics than for its music.

A. **Draw the following diagram.** You will notice that the display diagram has more information on it compared to the following diagram that you can draw. You may prefer to use the display diagram instead of drawing the diagram.

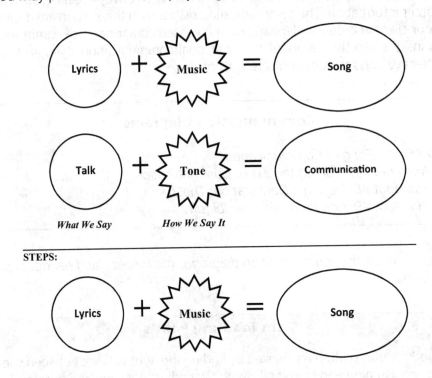

STEPS:

*Step 1:* **Draw the previous diagram and explain that a song is made up of both lyrics and music**. *Make the "lyrics" and "music" circles different shapes to emphasize that they are separate and different components of a song. You may choose to make them different colors instead of different shapes.* **Explain**

**that the lyrics involve the words and that the music involves the tone**. *They combine to produce the song. Sometimes we listen more to the words; sometimes we listen more to the tone.*

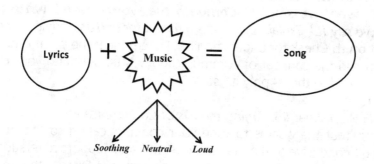

*Step 2:* **Draw three arrows exiting the word "music." After each arrow write the corresponding word**. *Emphaisize that the tone can have a significant influence on what we hear.*

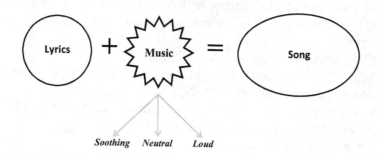

*Step 3:* **Erase the arrows and the three words underneath the word "music."**

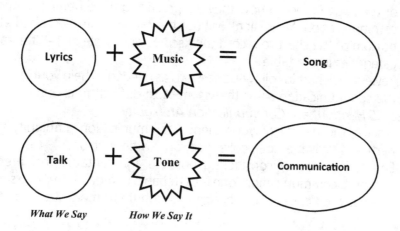

*Step 4:* **Finish by drawing the corresponding shapes below the original diagram. Inside the new shapes, write the new words "talk" and "tone."** Introduce this as the 2Ts of communication. **Then write the word "communication" in the third circle. Next, underneath the word "talk," write the phrase "what we say." Underneath the word "tone," write the phrase "how we say it."** Explain that this is a model for understanding communication.

B. **Reflect on it.** Check for understanding. Determine if the client understands the diagram and the concept of communication. After soliciting your client's feedback, proceed to the "Apply it" step.

C. **Apply it.**
1. Use *IS Worksheet #5: Tuning the 2Ts of Communication.*
2. Discuss that the goal is to tune your communication so that it produces a "song" conducive to maintaining effective and supportive relationships.
3. Discuss the 2Ts of communication: *tone* and *talk.* Discuss the importance of controlling both the volume (tone) and the channel (talk).
4. Using the middle of the worksheet, invite your client to classify their communication style by circling all the descriptors that apply. They will classify both the tone and the talk of their communication style. Then invite your client to write in the box at the bottom of the worksheet the desired changes they would like to make to the tone and talk of their communication.

D. **Work with it.**
1. Use *CS Handout #8: Playing a New Station: The 3Ls.*
   a. Discuss the importance of ultimately developing a communication style that promotes positive relationships.
   b. Use the handout to emphasize the following components to communication and the importance of practicing these:
      i. Listening-speaking balance
      ii. The 3Ls: *look* (good eye contact), *listen* (focused attention), and *learn* (understanding the message)
   c. Invite your client to practice these components with four different people (or four times with the same person) and to use the chart at the bottom of the page to record how they did practicing the different components of communication. Your client will use the rating scales described at the very bottom of the chart to record their scores on a scale of 1–5 for each of the categories in the table.
   d. Review the chart in follow-up sessions as needed to help your client improve the communication areas that seem most difficult to change.
2. Use *CS Handout #9: Communication Ambiguity.*
   a. Discuss the nature of your client's communication ambiguity with their partner, family member, colleague, or another person.
   b. Emphasize that by considering possible and tentative interpretations of another's communication, one is better able to reduce stress. Assuming that one has the "correct answer" can contribute to more stress, particularly if

the interpretation is negative. Brighter or "higher-rated" interpretations are more likely to promote the well-being of the relationship and lead to more positive interactions.

c. Invite your client to use CS Handout #9 to practice arriving at new interpretations of communication in one of their relationships. Your client can think of two ambiguous communication behaviors or patterns in one of their relationships. They can then think of the different ways they have chosen to interpret this communication. Lastly, your client can choose an interpretation that is "brightest" and leads to more positive emotions and thoughts about the relationship. Invite your client to practice the exercise for patterns of communication, which historically have been unclear in the relationship.

3. Post *DD #5: The Song of Communication* in follow-up sessions as a visual reminder to your client to discuss how they are doing modifying their communication style.

| Summary of Diagrams | | |
|---|---|---|
| **Universal Therapy Topics** *Display Diagrams (DD)* *In-Session (IS) Worksheets* *Coping Strategies (CS) Handouts* | | |
| **Therapy Topic** | **Diagram** | **Appendix B** |
| Mindfulness | The Time Circles Visiting the Time Circles Coping With the Time Circles Staying in the Present | DD #1 IS Worksheet #1 CS Handout #1 CS Handout #2 |
| | | |
| Ambivalence | Ambivalence Decision-Making: The T-Path Resolving Ambivalence: The 2As Decision-Making: Pros and Cons | DD #2 IS Worksheet #2 CS Handout #3 CS Handout #4 |
| | | |
| Uncertainty | Uncertainty Shining the Light of Certainty Adjusting the Light of Certainty | DD #3 IS Worksheet #3 CS Handout #5 |

(Continued)

(Continued)

| Summary of Diagrams | | |
|---|---|---|
| Stress | Stress Monitoring<br>Stress Meter<br>Stress Monitoring Form<br>Stress Management Strategies | DD #4<br>IS Worksheet #4<br>CS Handout #6<br>CS Handout #7 |
| | | |
| Communication | The Song of Communication<br>Tuning the 2Ts of Communication<br>Playing a New Station: The 3Ls<br>Communication Ambiguity | DD #5<br>IS Worksheet #5<br>CS Handout #8<br>CS Handout #9 |

# 6

# Using Diagrams to Build Coping Strategies for Common Clinical Problems

In this chapter we discuss ways to use diagrams to address common problems that can be part of ordinary human experience but that can sometimes create significant impairment and problematic symptoms for which clients may seek professional help. You will most likely be familiar with many of the topics discussed, and you may already be addressing some of these topics with your clients. For example, you may be working with a client diagnosed with generalized anxiety disorder and working on ways to assist this client in managing *worry*. You may, in other cases, be working with a depressed client and assisting this client in developing *mood regulation* strategies or possibly helping this client increase *motivation*. Some of the other topics we cover may not be associated with a specific clinical condition per se but rather may be a more generalized problem, such as *pain*, *low self-esteem*, or *disorganization*. You can choose the topics that are most appropriate for your clients. We encourage you to be flexible in the ways that you use the handouts and diagrams to address these topics. The worksheets and handouts for these topics are available in Appendix C. The topics covered in this chapter are listed in the box that follows:

**Worry**
**Pain**
**Rumination**
**Mood Regulation**
**Motivation**
**Self-Esteem**
**Panic**
**Urges**

For each of the eight areas we cover, we begin by briefly discussing the nature of the particular problem and then provide the *main teaching points*. These main teaching points can be used as guides to explain the nature of the problem and to help your clients reflect on and better understand the various characteristics of the problem. Then we provide directions for drawing or displaying a diagram that "visually" illustrates the different "features" of the problem and can help your clients better understand the nature of the problem. The teaching points can also be emphasized as you draw or display the diagram during the session. For each problem area, we also provide an in-session worksheet, which you can use after drawing the diagram to assist your clients in recognizing how they experience the problem in their lives. Finally, we also provide a coping strategy handout that you can give your clients to help them develop new coping skills. For example, if you are addressing the topic of pain, you can first review the main teaching points of pain with your client and then draw the diagram. After drawing the diagram, you can use the in-session worksheet to explore how the topic of pain applies to your client's life. Lastly, you can help your client develop coping strategies to better manage their pain by providing your client with the coping strategy handout for homework. We start by discussing the topic of worry.

## WORRY

Worry is a very common problem addressed in therapy and is associated with virtually every anxiety disorder (Leahy, 2006). It is also a characteristic of other conditions, such as depression, somatic symptom disorders, and various other clinical conditions (APA, 2013). Worry is a universal characteristic of human nature due in part to our ability to envision our future and to predict outcomes to life events or consequences to our behavior. Worry in and of itself is not maladaptive and can serve various functions. Worry can help us solve problems, formulate goals, and better prepare us for certain events and situations we will encounter. However, worry can also impair our functioning and ultimately be maladaptive if the focus of our worry does not lend itself to the resolution of a problem or if the worry itself becomes the primary source of our anxiety. You are most likely addressing the topic of worry with some of your clients and may be familiar with various approaches to helping your clients manage worry.

The **worry diagrams** *are designed to enable your clients to better distinguish between "productive" worry, which leads to solutions, and "unproductive" worry, which leads to more worry. The visuals can help create a mental image of these two "zones of worry" and help your clients better notice and "visualize" which worry zone they may find themselves in. The visuals will also provide your clients with easy-to-remember coping strategies to help them reduce their worry.*

---

### Worry Diagrams

a. *DD #1: The Worry Zones*
b. *IS Worksheet #1: My Worry Zones*
c. *CS Handout #1: Coping With the Worry Zones*
d. *CS Handout #2: Managing Worry: The 2Rs*

---

*Make copies of all the worry diagrams, worksheets, and handouts prior to your session.*

---

### Main Teaching Points

1. Worry can be adaptive or maladaptive. In either case, worry often surfaces in the form of certain thoughts and visual images in our mind.
2. Adaptive worry is problem-focused and resolvable. It is tied to thoughts and visual images that can lead to "solvable actions" and a solution. Such worries can motivate us to solve problems that preoccupy our mind.
3. Maladaptive worry is free-floating and unresolvable. It is tied to thoughts and visual images that cannot lead to any "resolvable actions" or solutions. Such worries can produce more distress by producing a repetitive pattern of thinking that has no targeted goal and that interferes with our daily functioning. Maladaptive worry can be reinforced by bringing us reassurance that we are thinking about a "problem" and trying to "solve" it, despite the absence of a real problem or specific method of resolution.
4. During problem-focused worry, attention is primarily directed outward. In directing attention outward, one actively uses input from one's physical and social surroundings to evaluate the problem and to formulate steps to resolve the problem. This leads to resolution of the worry and promotes one's adaptive functioning.
5. During free-floating worry, attention is directed inward. In directing attention inward, one becomes more self-absorbed in thoughts and images that are self-created and not formulated by input from one's physical and social surroundings. These thoughts and images do not lead to an actionable plan. One can become more fixated on the worry, ultimately creating more impairment in one's everyday functioning.
6. Discuss the concept of whether the "object" of one's worry exists in "space and time." Introduce the idea that some of our worries are abstract and may be focused on events or happenings that do not exist in reality. These worries may also be characterized by images, thoughts, and predictions that have a low probability of occurrence (e.g., "I might die in a plane crash").

A. **Draw the following diagram.** Note that the display diagram in Appendix C has more information than the following diagram that you will draw.

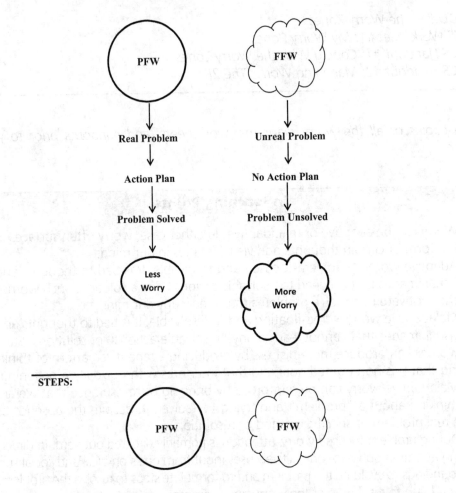

**STEPS:**

*Step 1: **Draw the two circles first to introduce the idea of the "two zones of worry."** Explain that worry zones represent different facets of the phenomenon of worry and are used to help you distinguish between problem-focused worry (PFW; the circle) and free-floating worry (FFW; the cloud). Presenting the two different circles will help your client recognize which zone they may be in during a worry episode and then determine how to best cope.*

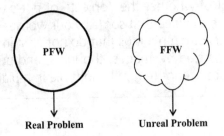

*Step 2:* **Draw the arrows exiting the circles and write the words "real problem" underneath the PFW circle and the words "unreal problem" underneath the FFW cloud.** *Explain that a real problem exists with problem-focused worries and that no real problem exists with free-floating worries.*

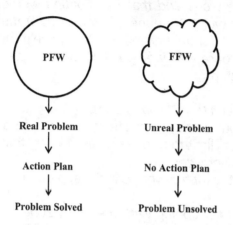

*Step 3:* **Draw an arrow exiting the phrase "real problem," write the words "action plan" and then draw an arrow exiting "action plan" and write the words "problem solved." Draw an arrow exiting the words "unreal problem," write the words "no action plan" and then draw an arrow exiting "no action plan" and write the words "problem unsolved."** *Explain that some worries are resolvable and others are not. We want to consider worries that can generate an action plan and lead to a resolution.*

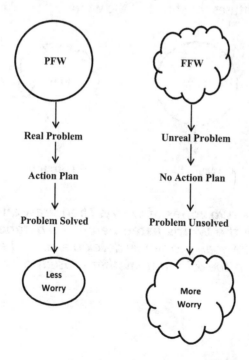

*Step 4:* ***Finish by drawing an arrow exiting the words "problem solved" and draw a small circle with the words "less worry." Then draw an arrow exiting the words "problem unsolved" and draw a large cloud with the words "more worry."*** *Explain that problem-focused worries lead to a resolution that reduces worry and that free-floating worries are unresolvable and often lead to more worry. Note the different sizes of the circles.*

B. **Reflect on it.** Check for understanding. Determine if the client understands the diagram and the concept of worry. After soliciting the client's feedback, move to the "Apply it" step.

C. **Apply it.**
   1. Use *IS Worksheet #1: My Worry Zones.*
   2. Determine if your client can relate the worry zones to the nature of their worry. Invite your client to give examples of worry that reflect their experience with these two worry zones.
   3. Invite your client to list the worries in the appropriate zones on the worksheet.

D. **Work with it.**
   1. Use *CS Handout #1: Coping With the Worry Zones.*
      a. Draw the following diagram to explain the 2Rs strategy. First, review the steps so that you feel prepared to draw the entire diagram during the session. Explain the following concepts.
      b. Problem-focused worry is coped with by developing a plan to resolve the problem. Free-floating worry is coped with by using the 2Rs strategy (*redirection* or *reassurance*).
      c. Redirection diverts attention outward to a concrete task so that the worry is no longer a preoccupation. Reassurance entails developing a coping statement that diffuses the threat of the worry.

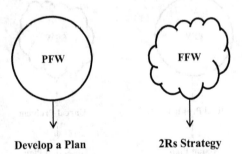

Develop a Plan          2Rs Strategy

*Step 1:* ***Draw the two zones of worry. Then draw an arrow exiting each zone and write the words listed below each zone.*** *During a problem-focused worry, the goal is to simply develop a plan. The rest of the drawing will now focus on the 2Rs strategy that is used to cope with free-floating worries.*

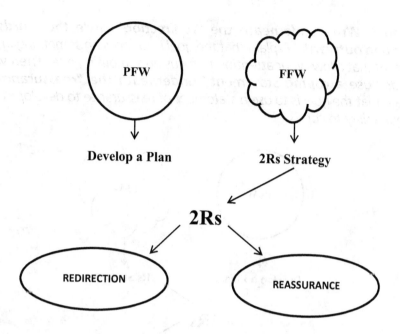

*Step 2:* **Write "2Rs" and then draw arrows going to the words "redi-rection" and "reassurance." Explain each one. Emphasize that both are used to achieve the goal of less worry**. *This allows your client to consider two different ways to respond to worry. In some situations redirection will be more effective while in other situations reassurance will be more effective.*

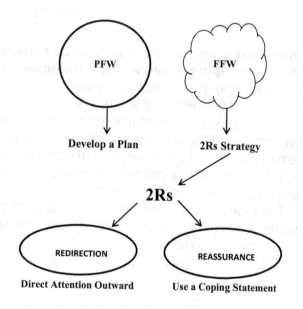

*Step 3:* **Write underneath the "redirection" circle the words "direct attention outward."** *Explain that the goal is to focus on something in the environment that allows your attention to focus on something else.* **Then write the words "use a coping statement" underneath the "reassurance" circle.** *Explain that the goal is to use a statement of reassurance to develop confidence in your ability to cope.*

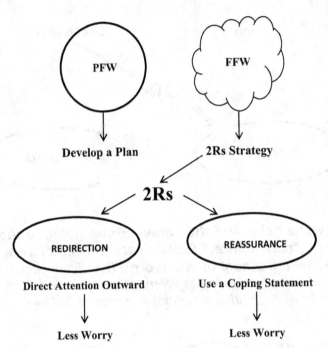

*Step 4:* **Finish by drawing a line exiting each statement and ending with the words "less worry" below each statement.** *Explain that each strategy achieves the same goal of reducing worry.*

2. Use *CS Handout #2: Managing Worry: The 2Rs.*
   a. Give the handout to your client to practice for homework.
   b. Your client can record three of their worries at the top of the worksheet. Invite them to choose one of the worries listed and to then, on the bottom of the worksheet, identify various redirection and reassurance coping strategies they can practice to help manage this worry.
3. Post *DD #1: The Worry Zones* at the next session as a reminder of ways your client can better cope with worry and to visually cue your client to discussing their progress in managing their worries.

## PAIN

Pain is the body and mind's way of communicating to us that an "injury" has occurred. For example, physical pain communicates to us that a "bodily injury" has occurred and causes us to focus attention on our body. In a similar way, psychological pain communicates to us that a "psychological injury" has occurred and causes us to focus attention on our psyche. The perception of pain also provokes a "defense reaction" to motivate us to alleviate or manage the pain. For example, if we experience physical pain, we may try to alleviate the pain by sitting down or taking a "painkiller." If we experience psychological pain, we may try to alleviate the pain by thinking about something else or "suppressing" it. Whether we experience physical or psychological pain, we may be able to better manage our pain by using either physical or psychological interventions, or both.

Managing pain may be an important therapy goal for some of your clients. Your client's pain can have physical and psychological origins and thus influence both their physical and their emotional well-being. Their pain can generate a biological response that makes them feel physically uncomfortable. Their pain may also generate a psychological response that makes them feel stressed and frustrated due to their chronic pain. This frustration and stress can in turn worsen their pain. In her book *Managing Pain Before It Manages You*, Caudill (2016) describes the mind-body connection in pain and the significant role that thoughts and mental activity play in influencing our pain. For example, when your client feels pain, they may be reminded of how the pain started, or they may imagine the event that caused it. Your client may reflect on the limitations it has caused them and the modifications they had to make in their life because of the pain. Your client may think of their future and envision themselves never resolving their pain. They may even think of their doctors and their inability to cure them of their pain.

Pain can often be a contributing factor to a client's psychiatric symptoms and can be a risk factor for increased depression, substance use, anger, and anxiety. Pain can be a reason a client quits a job, loses a relationship, starts using painkillers, or begins isolating from others. It can become a focal point to a client's existence where the client can become accustomed to "consulting" their pain prior to making any decision. Similarly, a client can be accustomed to defining their existence and overall well-being based on how much pain they are experiencing.

The **pain diagrams** are designed to help your clients rethink their pain experience and to develop a new relationship with their pain—a relationship focused on managing versus eliminating their pain. The aim is to help your clients develop strategies to respond differently to their pain and to learn ways to manage their pain without feeling overwhelmed or unduly debilitated by their pain. You will notice that the diagrams are also designed to help clients appreciate the "psychological" component of pain.

---

### Pain Diagrams

a. *DD #2: The Pain Circuits*
b. *IS Worksheet #2: My Pain Circuits*
c. *CS Handout #3: Rewiring My Pain Circuits*

---

*Make copies of all the pain diagrams, worksheets, and handouts prior to your session.*

## Main Teaching Points

1. Pain is a biopsychological experience that is influenced by both our body and our thoughts. The management of pain may require both biological and psychological interventions.
2. In some cases the most important goal is to manage the pain ("pain management") rather than to eliminate the pain. The elimination of pain in certain cases may be unrealistic.
3. It is important to identify "triggers," or factors that initiate our pain or activate our "pain circuit." Triggers to pain can include certain physical activities, thoughts, times of day, the weather or barometric pressure, or various social and psychological factors.
4. Developing new pain management coping strategies can help us become less reactive to our pain and enable us to develop a "different relationship" to our pain.
5. Time can be an important part of the pain healing process. It is important to manage one's expectations and to avoid actions that attempt to accelerate or interfere with the healing process (e.g., taking too much medication, overexerting oneself, talking too much about our pain, or chronically experiencing anger, which can increase the circulation of the body's stress hormones and increase our pain).

A. **Draw the following diagram.** Note that the display diagram in Appendix C has more information than the diagram you will draw.

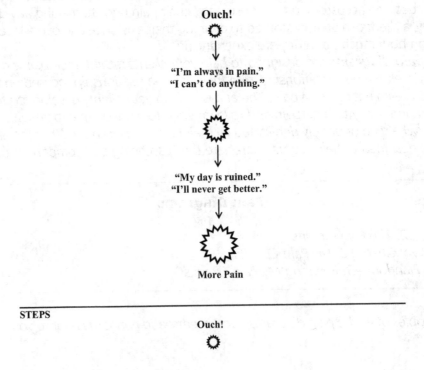

Ouch!

"I'm always in pain."
"I can't do anything."

"My day is ruined."
"I'll never get better."

More Pain

STEPS

Ouch!

*Step 1:* **Write the word "ouch." Then draw a starburst underneath the word "ouch"** *(note: if easier, you can draw an asterisk, a circle, or an X instead of a starburst). Explain that a noticeable biological sensation usually starts the pain cycle, but a negative thought about one's pain may also start the cycle.*

*Step 2:* **Draw an arrow exiting the word "ouch"** *and emphasize that the pain can trigger a "mental response." Give an example of this by writing these possible responses after the arrow:* **"I'm always in pain"** *and* **"I can't do anything."** *Explain that these may be automatic responses that you may be unaware of at the immediate moment.*

*Step 3:* **Draw an arrow exiting the words.** *Explain that these words or "interpretations" of the pain can influence our experience of the pain. These words send a message to the brain. Explain that the brain believes what we tell it and then responds in kind.* **After the arrow, draw a larger starburst.** *Explain that our interpretation of the pain in this example suggests that the pain is extremely debilitating and has almost completely immobilized us (which may be an "overinterpretation"). As a result, our pain can actually increase, which may be the result of our brain reminding us that this is a serious and almost life-threatening situation where we have lost almost all our functioning and "cannot do anything." As illustrated by the visuals of the starbursts, explain that the result is an increase in our pain.*

Ouch!

"I'm always in pain."
"I can't do anything."

"My day is ruined."
"I'll never get better."

*Step 4:* **Draw an arrow exiting the starburst**. *Explain that the increase in pain sends a message to our brain.* **Then write the words "my day is ruined" and "I'll never get better."** *Explain that due to the increase in the pain, we begin to think these negative thoughts. Explain that our interpretation of the pain continues to suggest that the pain is extremely debilitating and has permanently disabled us.*

Ouch!

"I'm always in pain."
"I can't do anything."

"My day is ruined."
"I'll never get better."

More Pain

*Step 5:* **Draw an arrow exiting the words.** *Explain that these words or "interpretations" of the pain can continue to influence our experience of the pain. These words send another message to the brain confirming the nature of the pain. Explain that the brain continues to believe what we are telling it.* **After the arrow, draw a larger starburst and write the words "more pain" underneath it.** *Explain that our pain now continues to increase, which may be the result of our brain continuing to remind us of this "life-debilitating" and "life-destroying" situation.*

B. **Reflect on it.** Check for understanding. Determine if the client understands the diagram and the concept of pain. After soliciting the client's feedback, move to the "Apply it" step.

C. **Apply it.** Use *IS Worksheet #2: My Pain Circuits.*
   1. Invite your client to use the worksheet to discuss their experience of pain by describing their pain circuit.
   2. Start by having your client identify common thoughts they have in response to their pain. Your client can write these thoughts in the "thought" boxes. Explain that these thoughts lead to an increase in the pain (direct your client's attention to the now bigger starburst).
   3. Invite your client to then describe what emotional and behavioral reactions occur in response to their pain. For example, does your client get angry, worried, sad, throw things, lie down, yell at someone, or take pain medication?
   4. Finish by having your client describe their "relationship" to their pain. Invite your client to describe this in as much detail as possible by reflecting on the thoughts, emotions, and behaviors that are triggered in response to their pain (an example is provided on the worksheet).

D. **Work with it.**
   1. Use *CS Handout #3: Rewiring My Pain Circuits.*
   2. For homework, have your client practice "rewiring" their pain circuit by responding to the pain with new thoughts, emotions, and behaviors. These new reactions will help your client develop a new relationship to their pain.
   3. Invite your client to identify two new thoughts they can practice in response to their pain. Then have them record what new emotional and behavioral reactions they may have experienced in response to their pain. New emotional reactions may include feeling calmer and less angry. New behavioral reactions may include keeping focused on the task at hand despite the pain or going for a short walk rather than lying down and dwelling on the pain.
   4. At the bottom of the sheet, have your client write down their new relationship to their pain in as much detail as possible.
   5. Lastly, to sustain this new relationship to their pain, have your client practice ways to manage the triggers to their pain. Triggers can include times of day (such as simply waking up in the morning), certain physical moments, stress, sitting too long, working too long, and sometimes random biological events. A few examples of ways to manage pain triggers are listed on the handout.

6. Post *DD #2: The Pain Circuits* at the next session or as needed in follow-up sessions as a visual reminder to discuss your client's progress in managing their pain.

## RUMINATION

Rumination can be defined as repetitive thinking and reflection whereby one focuses on the internal world of images, thoughts, and memories (Watkins, 2016). Rumination is a natural human tendency driven by our inherent self-reflective capacities. Ruminating or repetitive thinking momentarily removes us from the present moment and can serve some useful purposes. For example, rumination can stimulate creativity, insight, and problem-solving. It can also contribute to emotional relief by allowing us to momentarily escape from a stressful situation, avoid an unpleasant reality, or relieve boredom. It can also allow us time to identify and anticipate future consequences to our behavior and motivate us to take action. Over time "adaptive rumination tendencies" can be reinforced by bringing us reassurance and generating solutions to our problems.

Rumination, however, can also become maladaptive when the repetition of an idea, belief, or thought has no end point, no final goal, and no productive resolution. For example, rumination can be a problem when it serves as a substitute for engaging in the present moment or when it prevents us from engaging in goal-directed thinking and actions. In this context, rumination becomes an end in and of itself and a "maladaptive thinking habit" when it interferes with one's ability to function. That is, it can become a habit of "dwelling without resolution or purpose," which can create distress and interfere with one's ability to focus on daily tasks. When rumination becomes a maladaptive habit with no specific "practical" purpose, the ability to redirect oneself back to the present moment can be lost. It is this incapacity for redirection that can contribute to rumination becoming a maladaptive habit.

When rumination becomes maladaptive, it can lead to chronic worry or negative feelings. It can also result from such negative feelings as anxiety, depression, or anger. This "emotional cycle" of rumination can be easily reinforced. For example, you may ruminate over a past wrongdoing by a family member and as a result feel chronically angry toward this family member. As you experience this anger, it can serve to trigger more ruminating thoughts. These ruminating thoughts can then in turn create more anger. Many psychiatric conditions or symptoms can be characterized by some feature of rumination, which can fuel the negative emotions that are characteristic of these conditions. Given that one's emotional reactions are often influenced by one's attentional and thought processes, rumination could be considered a "necessary condition" for many chronic psychiatric conditions.

*The* **rumination diagrams** *are designed to assist your client in "visualizing" the mental processes that characterize rumination, such as how a single thought can take over the mind and become the sole focus of attention. Rumination is visualized in one* *of the diagrams as a hamster wheel—something that is constantly moving but not getting anywhere. The diagrams also highlight such strategies as "redirection" that your clients can use to better manage rumination.*

---

## Rumination Diagrams

a. *DD #3: Rumination*
b. *IS Worksheet #3: The Hamster Wheel*
c. *CS Handout #4: Managing Rumination: The 3Ds*

---

*Make copies of all the rumination diagrams, worksheets, and handouts prior to your session.*

---

### Main Teaching Points

1. Rumination is repetition of thoughts, images, or ideas. It can differ from worry in that rumination may not necessarily involve a particular worry. For example, your client may ruminate about having few friends, not achieving career goals, or being neglected as a child. These ruminations may or may not lead to the experience of worry.
2. Explaining rumination using the metaphor of a hamster on a wheel can be effective in emphasizing that rumination is characterized by expending endless "thinking energy" that does not lead anywhere. Like the hamster running on the wheel, rumination leads to no "finish line." Just like the hamster gets physically stronger by continuously spinning on the wheel, ruminating thoughts that continuously spin in our head get "mentally" stronger.
3. Rumination can be adaptive by helping us focus on a problem and generate potential solutions to a problem.
4. Rumination can be maladaptive by generating chronic anxiety, depression, and anger without leading to any resolution.
5. Repeatedly talking about our problems can establish and reinforce a habit of maladaptive rumination.
6. It is important to notice triggers to rumination, such as certain people, being alone, certain times of day, or when under stress. This will allow us to more easily "break the cycle" of rumination and to eventually weaken the habit by employing redirection strategies.

A. **Display Figure 6.1.**

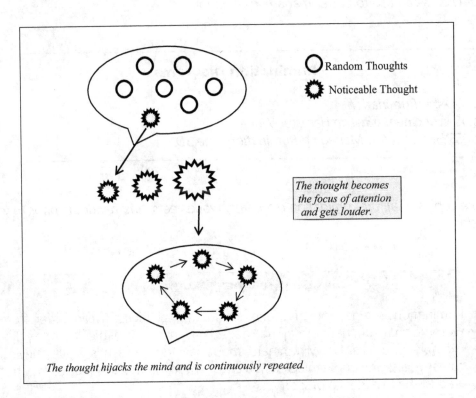

*Figure 6.1* Display Diagram #3: Rumination

Explain the process of rumination by highlighting the following points illustrated in the diagram:

1. Multiple thoughts circulate throughout our mind during the day. This is depicted in the diagram by the many circles moving around inside the image of our mind.
2. We tend to notice those thoughts that show up more frequently than others. They begin to simply become more noticeable. Point out in the diagram that one particular thought appears to be "sharper" and more noticeable than the others. This thought becomes the focus of attention.
3. This noticeable thought is then "extracted" from the others. It becomes the primary focus of attention and becomes "louder," as illustrated in the diagram by the thought being separated from the others and gradually increasing in size.

4. As we begin to repeat the thought, it eventually "hijacks" or takes over our other thoughts, as illustrated in the final image depicting the mind now being full of just this one thought. We then repeat this thought over and over again in our mind, which illustrates the phenomenon of rumination.

B. **Reflect on it.** Check for understanding. Determine if your client understands the diagram and the concept of rumination. After soliciting your client's feedback, move to the "Apply it" step.

C. **Apply it.** Use *IS Worksheet #3: The Hamster Wheel*.

1. In the session help your client identify two thoughts they tend to ruminate over.

2. For each thought, invite your client to write the specific thought on the "rumination thought" line on the worksheet. To "motorically" illustrate the phenomenon of rumination, have your client write the thought in the five boxes on the wheel. This will help them "visually experience" the phenomenon of rumination that occurs in their mind. The act of repetitive writing will also help your client experience the phenomenon of "repetition," which characterizes rumination. An example is provided next.

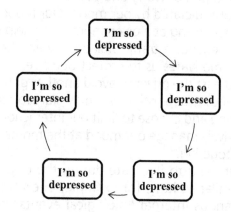

D. **Work with it.**

1. Use *CS Handout #4: Managing Rumination: The 3Ds*.

2. For homework, invite your client to practice managing rumination by using the 3D strategy (detect, decide, dismiss). To manage rumination, your client will first have to *detect* the ruminating thought, then *decide* to stop ruminating, and finally *dismiss* the thought by redirecting their attention.

3. Invite your client to practice this with one of the two thoughts identified on the in-session worksheet or with any other ruminating thought.

4. Your client can use the chart at the bottom of the handout to record how they did managing the thought across three different episodes. For the different columns, you can instruct your client to complete them as follows: detect (record the exact thought that you noticed); decide (record what you said,

such as "I need to stop ruminating"); and dismiss (record what you did, such as refocused on a work task or engaged in an activity).

5. In each episode box, your client can indicate where they were when they first noticed they were ruminating. This may help them identify triggers to their rumination, such as being around certain people (e.g., a boss) or being in certain situations (e.g., being alone).

6. Post *DD #3: Rumination* at the next session to visually remind your client of ways they can better cope with rumination and to cue your client to discuss how they did practicing the strategies to reduce rumination.

## MOOD REGULATION

Managing our mood is essential to our well-being. The three primary moods we tend to address with our clients are anger, anxiety, and depression. This section on mood regulation focuses on managing anger and depression. We address anxiety elsewhere in this chapter under the topics of worry and panic.

Generally, our behavior is dictated by our mood. Our mood often reflects a particular response we are experiencing at a given moment to help us adapt to a situation. For example, we may experience a traffic violation by another driver and as a result experience anger, which motivates us to protect ourselves. We may pull over to the side of the road or speed past the driver to avoid another potentially dangerous interaction. If we are experiencing depression, we may start to feel overwhelmed at, for example, a social gathering and choose to limit our interactions with others. This may enable us to more effectively manage our mood at the moment and to possibly avoid leaving the gathering altogether.

Our moods, however, tend to fluctuate during the day in response to internal and external events, similar to how, for example, one's blood pressure may fluctuate in response to various internal "biological events" and external "environmental events." It is important to notice the subtle mood changes that can occur during the day in response to different events. By noticing these changes, we can become increasingly proactive in learning how to more effectively manage our mood. Additionally, by avoiding specific triggers to negative mood states and engaging in certain behaviors that maintain a more stable mood, we can achieve improved mood regulation. This may be analogous to staying away from certain foods to avoid elevations in blood pressure and eating certain foods to sustain normal blood pressure.

*The* **mood regulation diagrams** *are designed to help your clients better monitor changes in their mood, identify triggers to their mood changes, and learn how to better manage their mood. The diagrams also illustrate through, for example, the image of a "wave" how our mood fluctuates throughout the day in response to both internal ("mental") and external ("social") events.*

## Mood Regulation Diagrams

a. *DD #4: The Mood Wave*
b. *IS Worksheet #4: Watching the Wave*
c. *CS Handout #5: Depression Ditches and Joy Jolts*
d. *CS Handout #6: Launching the Anger Arrows*
e. *CS Handout #7: Resetting the Anger Arrows*

*Make copies of all the mood regulation diagrams, worksheets, and handouts prior to your session.*

## Main Teaching Points

1. Moods fluctuate throughout the day like blood pressure. Think of your mood like a "wave in motion" throughout the day. Our moods are dynamic throughout the day and respond in different degrees of intensity and duration to internal and external events.
2. Some mood changes are fleeting while other mood changes persist.
3. Anger and frustration are related to one's expectation of change or what one believes should and shouldn't happen. Depression can lead to prolonged anger and frustration experiences that can overuse our "emotional energy."
4. Anger and depression are biological adaptive modes of communicating to others what is happening to us and what our expectations are of ourselves and others. At times, expressing these emotions can be an effective way to change the behavior of others to meet our immediate needs. However, the way we communicate anger and depression can sometimes be misunderstood or can negatively influence the reactions of others and their understanding of us.
5. In many situations other people or external events can be difficult to change, despite repeatedly communicating anger or frustration aimed at changing the circumstances. It is important to evaluate the reality of one's expectations for change, taking into account what is possible in any given situation.
6. Mood management improves when we become "better students of our experience" and have an awareness of those factors that tend to influence our moods.
7. We can be both proactive and reactive in managing our mood. For example, we can notice a change in our mood and do something to prevent it from getting worse, or we can be proactive and develop a coping style that enables us to keep our mood more stable during the day.

## A. **Draw the following diagram.**

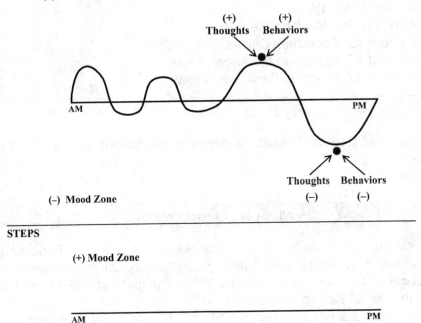

(+) Mood Zone

(+)       (+)
Thoughts  Behaviors

AM                    PM

Thoughts  Behaviors
(–)       (–)

(–) Mood Zone

**STEPS**

(+) Mood Zone

AM                    PM

(–) Mood Zone

*Step 1:* **Draw a horizontal line and the letters "AM" to the far left end and the letters "PM" to the far right end.** *Explain that this is the line of mood stability or a "neutral mood state." Then explain that sometimes during the day our mood is positive and rises above the line.* **In the upper left corner of the diagram, draw the symbol (+) and the words "mood zone" next to it to indicate that this is our positive mood zone.** *Explain that sometimes our moods are negative and go below the line.* **In the lower left corner of the diagram, draw the symbol (–) and the words "mood zone" next to it to indicate that this is our negative mood zone.**

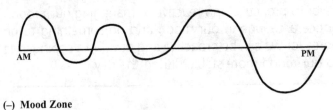

(+) Mood Zone

AM                    PM

(–) Mood Zone

*Step 2:* **Draw the wave across the mood line**. *Explain that the wave depicts changes in our mood throughout the day. Explain that some of the changes in the size of the wave are small and indicate subtle changes in our mood, and other changes are big and indicate more obvious and noticeable changes in our mood. Also explain how some mood changes are sustained as indicated by more "flattened" wave peaks and others are more fleeting as depicted by more "pointed" wave peaks.*

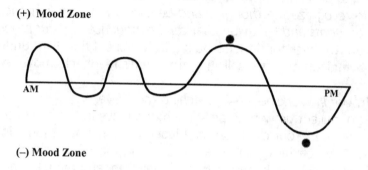

*Step 3:* **Draw the two dots as indicated in the diagram**. *Explain that these dots represent the different thoughts and behaviors that may be associated with positive or negative moods. These thoughts and behaviors could trigger mood changes or they could be the result of mood changes.*

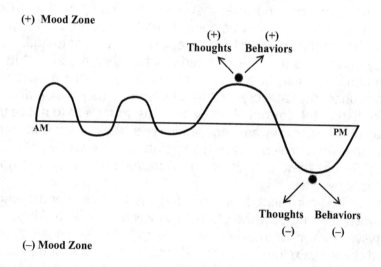

*Step 4:* **Draw two arrows exiting each of the dots and the words "thoughts" and "behaviors" and their corresponding signs (+) or (–).** *Explain that our mood changes can be caused by internal events, such as having certain thoughts, or external events, such as engaging in certain behaviors or experiencing certain events. Our mood changes may also lead to changes in our*

*thoughts and behaviors. For example, an internal trigger could be a negative thought (e.g., "I'll never feel better"). In this case the internal trigger is likely to decrease our mood. Other triggers can be external, such as getting a call that you just got a job. In this case the external trigger is likely to improve our mood. Additionally, when we find ourselves in a positive or negative mood, we may notice that we start to think or do certain things as a result of this mood. For example, if we feel depressed, we may isolate ourselves and think that we are all alone and unworthy of other people. To regulate our mood better, it can be helpful to recognize the thoughts and behaviors that can influence our mood and the thoughts and behaviors that can be influenced by our mood.*

B. **Reflect on it.** Check for understanding. Determine if the client understands the mood wave diagram. After soliciting the client's feedback, move to the "Apply it" step.

C. **Apply it.** Use *IS Worksheet #4: Watching the Wave.*

1. Invite your client draw their personal mood wave in the box in the middle of the worksheet. Your client can first label the horizontal mood line with their typical daily activities. In the example at the top of the sheet, the activities listed are e-mail, work, gym, news, dinner, free, and read. Listing daily activities will help your client determine how much their mood may fluctuate based on where they are and what they are doing.

2. Have your client draw their typical daily mood wave across the horizontal line, reflecting on their typical day and the various ways their mood may fluctuate across their day. This will give you and your client a better idea of how much their mood changes and what they may be doing when their mood is at its highest and what they may be doing when their mood is at its lowest.

3. In the chart at the bottom of the page, invite your client to notice those times of day or activities they are engaged in when their mood is at its lowest on the graph. There may be a few low points along the graph. Record these low periods under the category "Vulnerable Periods" (depression ditches).

4. In the chart at the bottom of the page, invite your client to notice those times of day or activities they are engaged in when their mood is at its highest on the graph. There may be a few high points or more stable periods along the graph. Record these periods on the worksheet under the category "Stable Periods" (joy jolts).

5. Lastly, invite your client to identify triggers to their mood changes, noticing when their mood wave starts to descend or ascend. These changes in the wave's movement may serve as clues to potential triggers to your client's mood changes. Explore both internal triggers, such as thoughts or memories, and external triggers, such as events, settings, and people. For example, your client's mood may decline when they dwell on the past during periods of free time, or their mood may improve if they go for a walk after work. Record these events on the worksheet under the category "Triggers." Next to each trigger listed in the table, label it as (+) or (–) depending on whether it has a positive or negative effect on the mood.

D. **Work with it.**
  1. Use *CS Handout #5: Depression Ditches and Joy Jolts*.
      a. Use this handout for clients who are trying to better manage their depression. For homework, have your client practice monitoring their mood over three different days. Using the top half of the worksheet, invite your client to draw their mood waves for each of these three days. Emphasize that even though they may feel a more persistent level of depression, it is likely that they have moments or brief episodes when their mood is more elevated and more positive. They may need practice in learning how to identify and notice these periods, even if the periods are fleeting.
      b. Invite your client to review the three days and to identify two episodes of a low mood (depression ditches) and two episodes of a positive mood (joy jolts). Your client can use the chart at the bottom of the page to record the two episodes of depression and the two episodes of joy. An example is provided. For each episode, your client can record the direction of change on a 1–10 scale. In general, use the number 5 as the neutral reference point. Your client can record the duration of the change as well as the internal and external triggers that seemed to initiate the change (these can be either positive or negative triggers). Emphasize the importance of noticing small mood changes and identifying those factors that initiated those changes.
      c. Lastly, invite your client to identify at the bottom of the page a list of "mood elevating strategies" they can practice to help them sustain a positive mood. This list can be generated by reviewing both the joy jolts and depression ditches on the graph and may include such strategies as positive self-talk, limiting time in situations that worsen mood, and engaging in activities that promote a positive mood, such as exercise, reading, meditating, or socializing with others.
  2. Use *CS Handout #6: Launching the Anger Arrows*.
      a. Use this handout to assist your client in identifying the triggers to their anger. Invite your client to think of these triggers as events that "launch anger arrows" (i.e., sharp, piercing behaviors that cause "injury"). The longer the arrow, the stronger the anger response. The example at the top of the handout illustrates different triggers with different-size arrows.
      b. In the middle of the handout, your client can identify their anger arrows and the triggers that launch these arrows.
      c. Using the chart at the bottom of the handout, invite your client to monitor their anger over the week and to record the times when they launched their anger arrows. Invite your client to identify the triggers, the strength of the arrow, and the thoughts and behaviors they experienced related to the event.
  3. Use *CS Handout #7: Resetting the Anger Arrows*.
      a. You can use this handout to list the primary triggers to your client's anger and the associated behaviors, which your client previously identified in the

table at the bottom of CS Handout #6. For this new handout, the triggers would be listed in the top left portion of the handout under the heading "Triggers" and would be placed on the scale proportional to the recorded rating. In the example, traffic is placed at an 8 on the scale as that was the rating recorded in the example from the table in CS Handout #6. In the top right portion of the handout, your client records the behavior that is associated with traffic. In the example, the behavior recorded is "hit steering wheel."

    b. Using the bottom of the handout, your client can list their primary triggers again but this time identify a coping strategy they can use to reduce their anger response. The coping strategies can be recorded across from the associated trigger.

4. Post *DD #4: The Mood Wave* as needed in follow-up sessions to visually facilitate discussing ways that your client is managing their mood.

## MOTIVATION

Motivation is a common topic addressed in therapy, particularly when working with depressed clients. Low motivation can lead to depression and depression can lead to low motivation. In some ways this is a cycle where depression can be the cause and effect of low motivation. Often we wait to feel better before we do things. We sometimes "wait" for our feelings to change so that this can give us the motivation to do something. In some ways, feeling better can provide the fuel to mobilize us into action. However, research suggests that waiting to feel better may prolong depression and can reinforce low motivation. Deciding to engage in activities despite feeling depressed often improves our depression and promotes increased motivation. By taking action first, we are not waiting for our mood to change, but rather we are engaging in an activity, which then changes our mood.

Research has shown that engaging in such activities as exercise can alleviate some forms of depression and subsequently improve motivation (Dunn, Trivedi, Kampert, Clark, & Chambliss, 2005). In some ways, one "becomes motivated" by deciding to engage in an activity or complete a task, which then leads to a mood change and subsequent increased motivation. In their book *Behavioral Activation for Depression*, Martell, Dimidjian, and Herman-Dunn (2010) call this acting from the "outside-in." This is a process whereby one directs attention to the "outside" environment by taking action first and initiating certain behaviors. This in turn leads to changes in one's "inner" environment or mood state.

*The **motivation diagrams** are designed to help your clients structure their day better, identify their immediate goals, prioritize these goals, and develop a plan to accomplish these goals. Focusing on immediate goals will help your clients feel less overwhelmed. Using the weekly schedule grid can help your clients schedule exactly when they will get tasks done. This will allow them to follow "a plan" rather than "a mood" in deciding what to do.*

---

### Motivation Diagrams

a. *DD #5: Motivation Movement*
b. *IS Worksheet #5: Goal Sheet*
c. *IS Worksheet #6: Weekly Chart*
d. *CS Handout #8: Immediate Goals: Plan*

---

*Make copies of all the motivation diagrams, handouts, and worksheets prior to your session.*

## Main Teaching Points

1. Motivation is both a cause and an effect of our mood. Our mood can influence our level of motivation and our level of motivation can influence our mood.
2. Motivation is more of an "action" than a "feeling." It can sometimes be thought of as a by-product of action. For example, we do a task and as a result we feel better; we then decide to do another task. Our motivation increases due to engaging in tasks.
3. Improving motivation is often best achieved by following a plan versus following a mood.

## A. Draw the following diagram.

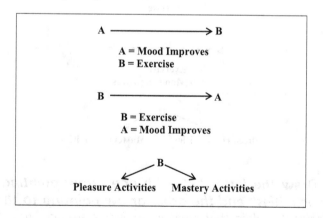

STEPS

A ————————→ B

A = Mood Improves
B = Exercise

*Step 1:* **Draw the letter "A" and then an arrow leading to the letter "B."** *Explain that A represents "waiting for our mood to improve," and B represents the behavior that results from our mood change. In this case the behavior is exercise.* **Below the A-B arrow, write "A = mood improves" and "B = exercise."** *Explain that A has to happen first, and then B occurs.*

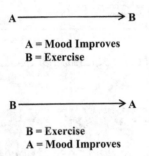

*Step 2:* **Draw the letter "B" and then an arrow leading to the letter "A."** *Explain that the letters on the arrow have shifted. B represents exercising, and A represents what results from exercising. In this case what results from exercising is an improved mood.* **Below the B-A arrow, write "B = exercise" and "A = mood improves."** *Explain that exercising happens first, and then the mood improves. Explain that to improve motivation we will now be using the B-A model versus the A-B model.*

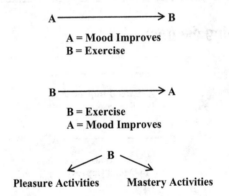

*Step 3:* **Draw the letter "B" with one arrow pointing to the words "pleasure activities" and the other arrow pointing to the words "mastery activities."** *Explain that pleasure activities are activities that bring enjoyment, such as reading, cooking, or going to the movies. Explain that mastery activities are activities or tasks that you need to accomplish, such as doing the dishes, balancing the checkbook, or applying for a job. Explain the importance of engaging in these two types of activities to help us improve our moods.*

B. **Reflect on it.** Check for understanding. Determine if the client understands the diagram and the concept. After soliciting the client's feedback, move to the "Apply it" step.

C. **Apply it.** Use *IS Worksheet #5: Goal Sheet* and *IS Worksheet #6: Weekly Chart* together.

 1. Invite your client to use IS Worksheet #5 to identify up to eight immediate goals or tasks they need to accomplish. Focus on tasks that must be done in the next week or two.

 2. After identifying these goals, use the bottom half of the worksheet to priorotize these goals. Order them based on which ones need to be accomplished first. Then in the two side columns in the chart, indicate a projected date by which to complete the goal and estimate the amount of time it will take to accomplish the goal.

 3. Then use IS Worksheet #6 to schedule when the goals will be completed based on the projected day identified on the goal sheet. Also use the appropriate number of time slots to cover the estimated time needed to complete the task based on the estimated time on the goal sheet. If some of the goals extend beyond a week's time period, you can use two weekly charts to enable your client to cover all the goals.

D. **Work with it.**

 1. Use *CS Handout #8: Immediate Goals: Plan.*

 2. For homework, your client can use CS Handout #8 to write down the steps required to accomplish each goal and to record the completion date in the right-hand column.

 3. At the next session, review the weekly chart to assess how your client did in accomplishing their weekly goals. Use additional handouts and weekly charts as needed to continue to identify goals with your client and to improve their overall motivation.

## SELF-ESTEEM

Therapy often focuses on ways to enhance clients' self-esteem and to assist them in developing a more positive self-image. Clients who experience depression or anxiety can frequently experience low self-esteem. Their low self-esteem may be a by-product of their depression or anxiety or a personality characteristic that has contributed to the development of their depression or anxiety. One's self-esteem can be influenced by various factors, such as cultural upbringing, parental influences, habits of self-talk, personal experiences and expectations, and other factors.

The **self-esteem diagrams** are designed to help your clients visualize how low self-esteem reflects a type of biased or "imbalanced" thinking and can persist due to dwelling on certain characteristics (e.g., being single) and negative self-impressions ("I'm a failure"). The diagrams also illustrate how positive self-esteem is fostered by "shifting" the balance of one's thinking to more positive characteristics (e.g., "I'm well educated") and positive self-impressions ("I'm sincere").

---

**Self-Esteem Diagrams**

a. *DD #6: Self-Esteem*
b. *IS Worksheet #7: Shifting the Balance*
c. *CS Handout #9: Self-Talk*

---

*Make copies of all the self-esteem diagrams, worksheets, and handouts prior to your session.*

---

**Main Teaching Points**

1. Discuss the idea that self-esteem can be influenced by our identification with a life vocation, purpose, and role.
2. Self-esteem is also influenced by the extent to which we feel capable of reaching our goals or achieving life satisfaction.
3. We can raise our self-esteem by identifying our psychological assets, vocational goals, and personal goals as well as by identifying our natural strengths and skills.
4. It is important to focus more on our behaviors versus our thoughts when "evaluating ourselves."
5. It is important to minimize comparisons with others and to limit time spent on social media, such as Facebook, Instagram, Snapchat, and other social media sites.
6. Our selfhood and self-image in many ways are influenced by and change in response to new experiences. As new experiences and memories are formed, they are superimposed on our old memories. Therapy can help clients consciously identify with new memories and develop new experiences that promote a more positive self-image. This can help free clients from negative thinking and negative memories from the past. This may be particularly helpful to clients with past histories of "trauma" or clients coping with residual symptoms of persistent mental illness.

## A. Display Figure 6.2.

*Figure 6.2* Display Diagram #6: Self-Esteem

Using the diagram, discuss the following:

1. Explain that low self-esteem is like biased thinking. You tend to look only at negative aspects of yourself. You tend to define your self-worth based on limited characteristics (e.g., being married, having an ideal body weight) or specific conditions (e.g., making so much money, having so many friends, having lots of hobbies, being popular).

2. Explain how one's thinking can be biased or "negatively skewed" and as a result contributes to a negative self-image and low self-esteem. The top half of the diagram displays a negative way of thinking about the self. Notice in

the diagram that the word "SELF" is used as a mnemonic to highlight these negative characteristics.

3. Using the bottom half of the diagram, discuss how positive self-esteem can be fostered by focusing on other features and aspects of the self. The "balance" of thinking has shifted. Notice again in the diagram that SELF is used as a mnemonic to highlight positive characteristics.

B. **Reflect on it.** Check for understanding. Determine if the client understands the concept of *biased thinking*. After soliciting the client's feedback, move to the "Apply it" step.

C. **Apply it.** Use *IS Worksheet #7: Shifting the Balance*.

1. Invite your client to use the top half of the worksheet ("Old Self") and to use the four open boxes in the diagram to write in four negative characteristics that have contributed to low self-esteem.

2. Invite your client to use the bottom half of the worksheet ("New Self") and to use the four open boxes to write in four positive characteristics that can contribute to improved self-esteem.

3. Use follow-up sessions to monitor your client's self-talk and to work on promoting improved self-esteem by continuing to shift the "thinking balance" from negative to positive.

D. **Work with it.**

1. Use *CS Handout #9: Self-Talk*.

2. For homework, have your client spontaneously practice rehearsing positive self-statements and practice using positive self-statements to replace negative self-statements that they may find themselves rehearing simply out of habit. Your client can write down eight positive self-statements on the handout.

3. At the very bottom of the handout, your client can write down their "go-to" positive self-statement.

4. Post *DD #6: Self-Esteem* at the next session as a reminder of ways your client can increase their self-esteem.


## PANIC

Panic symptoms or panic attacks can be part of any anxiety condition, such as social anxiety, panic disorder, obsessive-compulsive disorder, or post-traumatic stress disorder. Panic symptoms can also be associated with certain medical conditions, such as thyroid disease or cardiac disease, or can occur for no apparent reason and from no apparent cause. Panic often provokes a cascade of physical symptoms that can cause a feeling of loss of control over one's body, creating a sense of impending doom. These symptoms may become so distressing that one may experience an imminent sense of death or a degree of fear more profound than any fear one has ever experienced. Finding ways to effectively manage panic is important in the overall management of one's anxiety.

Using a learning model, panic can in part be conceptualized as a "conditioned reaction" to accumulating stress experiences that have not been directly evaluated or reflected on. As such, one may be conditioned to panic by associating certain thoughts to certain panic symptoms. Talking through the stress and soliciting new coping thoughts can help "desensitize" clients to their panic symptoms. As a result, over time the panic symptoms can become associated with more adaptive thoughts and the symptoms that surface in the future are likely to be associated with a more adaptive response.

The **panic diagrams** are designed to help your clients learn more about the psychobiology of panic attacks and to appreciate how the symptoms are biological events designed to promote survival in the event of a real danger. The diagrams are also intended to help clients learn how to respond differently to their panic symptoms so that ultimately the symptoms are experienced as harmless biological events. The diagrams depict the human body encircled by a "wave" to illustrate how panic can often feel like a wave that "surrounds the body."

---

### Panic Diagrams

a. *DD #7: The Wave of Panic*
b. *IS Worksheet #8: Mapping Panic: The Body Mines*
c. *CS Handout #10: Managing Panic: The Body Minds*
d. *CS Handout # 11: The Changing Wave of Panic*

---

*Make copies of all the panic diagrams, handouts, and worksheets prior to your session.*

---

### Main Teaching Points

1. Panic is a *psychobiological experience*. Panic is influenced by the interaction between our thoughts and our body. The physical symptoms alone do not produce panic, as can be seen in the example of exercise. Exercise can produce biological changes that are similar to the changes experienced in panic, yet the physical sensations produced by exercise (e.g., racing heart, shortness of breath) do not typically generate anxiety or fear. For the symptoms to produce fear, a cognitive or "thinking" component needs to exist, which interprets the physical symptoms as dangerous.
2. Discuss the *thought-body panic cycle*. Biological symptoms can lead to an anxious thought, which in turn can intensify the biological symptoms (see the following diagram). Alternatively, an anxious thought can lead to biological symptoms, which in turn can intensify the anxious thought.

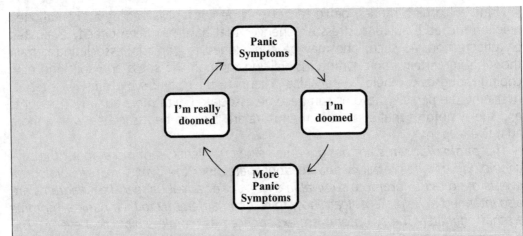

3. A primary goal in managing panic is to convince yourself that the biological symptoms are benign events—events that are not dangerous and that are in many ways very similar to the biological events one experiences when exercising.
4. The *fear of death* or *fear of loss of control* can exist in someone who experiences panic symptoms. Discussing this phenomenon may help "normalize" the experience of panic as your client learns that they are not the only ones who have experienced the thought of death during a panic attack.

A. **Display Figure 6.3.**

Using the diagram, discuss the following:

1. The biological symptoms experienced in panic can be intentionally generated by the body in response to a danger signal produced by our thoughts. The body mobilizes resources and initiates a cascade of biological symptoms to protect us from the danger, unaware that no real danger exists.
2. Discuss how the combination of all these symptoms can be experienced as a wave of panic circulating the body. Bring your client's attention to the "wave figures" at the bottom of the diagram and how our thoughts can contribute to the increasing intensity of the wave.

B. **Reflect on it.** Check for understanding. Determine if the client understands the diagram and the psychobiological concept of panic. After soliciting the client's feedback, move to the "Apply it" step.

C. **Apply it.** Use *IS Worksheet # 8: Mapping Panic: The Body Mines.*

1. Discuss the concept of *body mines*. Invite your client to identify their body mines, which are the places in their body where your client experiences panic. These are bodily areas they have learned to fear and continuously monitor,

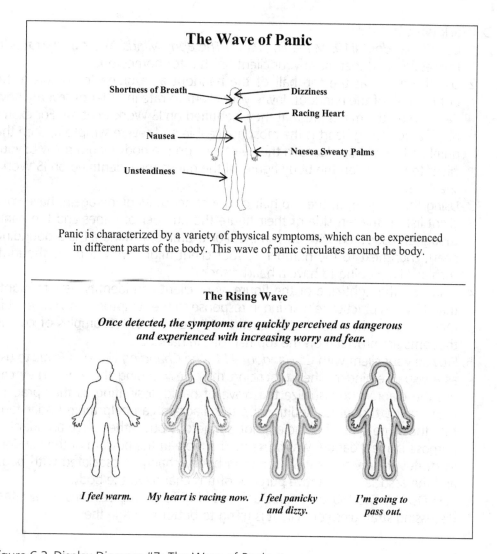

**The Wave of Panic**

Shortness of Breath

Dizziness

Racing Heart

Nausea

Naesea Sweaty Palms

Unsteadiness

Panic is characterized by a variety of physical symptoms, which can be experienced in different parts of the body. This wave of panic circulates around the body.

**The Rising Wave**

*Once detected, the symptoms are quickly perceived as dangerous and experienced with increasing worry and fear.*

*I feel warm.*   *My heart is racing now.*   *I feel panicky and dizzy.*   *I'm going to pass out.*

*Figure 6.3* Display Diagram #7: The Wave of Panic

hoping that the "mine" does not get "activated." You can assist your client in identifying these body mines by first inviting them to use the list provided in the second half of the worksheet to circle the panic symptoms they experience.

2. Using the second half of the worksheet, invite your client to indicate on the body map their most active body mines. They can indicate where these mines are located by drawing an arrow to the body part (they can use the figure at the top of the worksheet as a guide). Next to the arrow, your client can describe the symptom (e.g., pounding heart, palpitations, dizziness, shortness of breath).

D. **Work with it.**

1. Use *CS Handout #10: Managing Panic: The Body Minds*. You can start this in the session and then have your client finish it for homework.

2. Use the figure at the top half of the handout as a guide to complete the bottom half of the handout. Invite your client to rate in order of severity how "explosive" the mines are that they identified on IS Worksheet #8. For example, if a pounding heart is the most noticeable and severe symptom, then the number 1 would be placed in the heart area on the body diagram. Invite your client to number on the body figure all the mines they identified on IS Worksheet #8.

3. Using the diagram at the top half of the handout as guide again, have your client list on the left side of their figure the number of mines and the panic thoughts associated with each mine. For example, if mine #1 is a pounding heart, then next to the number 1, your client might write a panic thought, such as "I am going to have a heart attack."

4. Lastly, on the right side of the figure, your client can identify new thoughts that they can practice rehearsing in response to the symptom. This will enable them to use "their mind" to deactivate "their mines." Examples of coping thoughts are provided on the top half of the handout.

5. Provide your client with *CS Handout #11: The Changing Wave of Panic* to use as a visual reminder when practicing their new coping thoughts. They can use the diagram to visualize the wave of panic dissipating as they practice their coping thoughts. Additionally, the diagram can help them understand that the symptoms of panic are not dangerous but rather serve an adaptive purpose if a real danger was present. The table at the bottom of the handout illustrates this by presenting common bodily changes associated with panic and the associated adaptive purpose of this change in the body.

6. Post *DD #7: The Wave of Panic* as needed in follow-up sessions to facilitate discussing strategies your client is using to better manage their panic.

## URGES

Urges can be associated with a variety of clinical problems, such as addictions (e.g., alcohol, drugs, gambling, or pornography), anger, perfectionism, impulse control disorders, OCD-spectrum conditions, mania, and eating disorders. These different clinical conditions are often characterized by problematic behavioral habits, impulses, compulsions, and cravings. Conceptualizing these clinical conditions as being driven or "motivated" by urges can assist your clients in learning ways to reduce and better manage these problematic or maladaptive behaviors. The urges associated with these different clinical conditions can manifest in a variety of ways, such as the urge to yell or swear, criticize, physically harm oneself or another, wash one's hands, pull one's hair, pick one's skin, check one's surroundings, order or clean one's environment, spend money, watch pornography, overeat, purge food, drink too much alcohol, ingest or administer a nonprescribed drug, or gamble.

To successfully moderate one's behavior, one needs to find ways to better manage one's urges and identify those triggers or factors that influence the onset and intensity of one's urges. For example, the urge to drink may be triggered by any number of factors, such as driving by a favorite bar, experiencing work stress, the approaching weekend, anticipating watching a sporting event, watching a commercial about alcohol, or receiving an invitation from a friend to go drinking. There may also be subsequent urges once one begins to engage in the behavior. For example, if one decides to start drinking, one will likely have urges to continue to drink. Directly implementing certain coping strategies can assist us in successfully managing urges and ultimately moderating our behavior. These strategies can help us sometimes even avoid the initial urge or better manage the urge once we experience it. The strategies may also help us better manage our behavior once we give in to the urge (e.g., by using certain strategies, we may be able to drink moderately versus excessively).

*The **urges diagrams** are designed to assist your clients in better understanding and monitoring the different "stages" of an urge by depicting how an urge can be visualized like a wave, where the urge slowly rises in intensity, reaches a peak, and then slowly subsides. The wave or stages of an urge occur whether we give in to the urge or simply let it pass. The diagrams should assist your clients in noticing the subtle progression of their urges and developing ways to better manage these urges. Practicing "urge management strategies" can assist your clients in ultimately reducing their maladaptive behaviors (e.g., drinking, drug use, gambling, anger outbursts, compulsions) that are driven by certain urges.*

---

### Urges Diagrams

a. *DD #8: The Hunger Urge*
b. *IS Worksheet #9: Detecting Urge Triggers*
c. *CS Handout #12: Surfing the Urge*

---

*Make copies of all the urges diagrams, worksheets, and handouts prior to your session.*

### Main Teaching Points

1. Urges create tension and stress.
2. Urges surface more in the face of stress and "high-risk situations."
3. Discuss these features of urges:
   a. Urges are like waves in the ocean. They come and go in intensity.
   b. Urges will eventually go away on their own whether or not you give in to them. An example is the hunger urge.
   c. The more you continue to give in to the urge, the stronger and more frequent it becomes.
   d. Each time an urge is resisted, it becomes less frequent and less intense.

A. **Display Figure 6.4.**

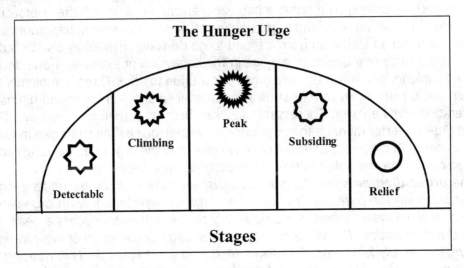

Figure 6.4 Display Diagram #8: The Hunger Urge

Explain the wave of an urge by using the hunger urge as an example. Discuss the five stages illustrated in the diagram.

1. *Detectable*: Hunger pains are first detected by noticing that our stomach is rumbling or that we are experiencing slight twinges in our stomach. We are slightly distracted by the onset of the hunger urge and begin to think of how we may satisfy the urge. However, at this point we are not overwhelmed by or overly focused on it.

2. *Climbing*: The hunger urge slowly starts to rise and become more noticeable. We can become distracted and more inclined to focus on the tension created by the growing urge. As the hunger urge becomes stronger, we feel hungrier and experience thoughts and images about food, such as envisioning a McDonald's sign or a dinner plate with steak and potatoes on it. As the hunger urge climbs, we become more and more inclined to satisfy the urge. This is where attention becomes more focused on what we need to do to satisfy the urge.

3. *Peak*: During this stage we experience the hunger urge at its strongest. The hunger pains are experienced intensely, and we become our most motivated to satisfy the urge. We may pull into a drive through to order lunch.

4. *Subsiding*: The hunger urge soon starts to subside as we engage in eating. The pain and tension are gradually reduced. We begin to feel more relaxed and slowly start to feel satisfied. Attention slowly starts to be directed to other activities.

5. *Relief*: We no longer experience the hunger urge. The urge has been satisfied. We may experience different feelings at this stage, such as content-
   ment or even guilt if, for example, we feel we ate too much. Attention is
   no longer focused on eating but is now focused on other activities.

B. **Reflect on it.** Check for understanding. Determine if your client understands
   the diagram, the nature of urges, and the different stages. After soliciting your
   client's feedback, move to the "Apply it" step.

C. **Apply it.** Use *IS Worksheet #9: Detecting Urge Triggers*.

   1. In the first part of the worksheet, invite your client to identify the types of
      urges they have struggled with. List these under the section entitled "My
      Urges." Several examples are given.
   2. In the next part of the worksheet, under the section entitled "My Urge Trig-
      gers," invite your client to identify the general triggers to their urges. Trig-
      gers can include, for example, certain people, a favorite dessert, a weekend
      afternoon, certain websites, local pubs, a dirty kitchen floor, books out of
      alignment on the bookshelf, stress, or boredom.
   3. In the last part of the worksheet, entitled "High-Risk Situations," discuss with
      your client their specific high-risk situations and the urge that is triggered by
      these situations. In this section your client can be more detailed in describing
      specific situations that can increase their chances of succumbing to a certain
      urge (e.g., sitting home alone bored on a Saturday night presents a high-risk
      situation to drink; getting a demanding e-mail from the boss at the end of
      the week triggers the urge to throw objects and to send a critical e-mail;
      experiencing stress due to your partner's drinking triggers the urge to yell and
      curse).

D. **Work with it.**

   1. Use *CS Handout #12: Surfing the Urge*.
   2. For homework, have your client practice managing urges and record three
      episodes using the table at the bottom of the handout.
   3. Discuss the following three intervention strategies to assist your client in
      learning how to use these strategies:
      a. *Distract the urge*. This is the "first-line" intervention as soon as "tension"
         is experienced. The urge may surface as a thought, such as "I'd like to get
         something to eat," "I'd like a drink right now," or "I'd like to buy a lottery
         ticket." It may also be a feeling, such as experiencing a slight twinge of
         hunger. Distraction can work in this stage. Refocus yourself on your activ-
         ity; redirect yourself back to the task at hand.
      b. *Delaying the urge*. In stage 2, the urge is now rising, and you will become
         increasingly inclined to act on the urge. Postpone your behavior for a min-
         ute before giving in to the urge. Keep postponing for as long as you can.
         For example, don't go wash your hands right away, don't order the dessert
         right away, don't send the negative e-mail right away, don't say the critical
         comment right away. As you delay, the urge may become stronger, but
         keep delaying it if possible; the urge will eventually start to weaken.

      c. *Surf the urge*. This is the final stage where the urge is at its greatest and will be the most difficult to resist. We are acutely sensitive to the urge. Surf the urge like a wave by riding it and noticing it. Simply notice it and tell yourself that it will soon pass. You can remind yourself that the urge will eventually go away, even if you don't do anything about it. Using cognitive strategies can be useful here. You can use coping statements, such as "I'm on a diet and I'm trying to lose weight," "I'll feel better if I don't eat dessert," and "I can do this . . . it's not impossible . . . I've done it before."

      d. *Reward yourself* for resisting an urge. You can, for example, buy a new book, go to the movies, or go out to eat as a result of not giving in to the urge.

4. Post *DD #8: The Hunger Urge* in follow-up sessions to remind your client of ways they can better understand and manage their urges. Posting the diagram will also help cue the client to discuss how they are doing in practicing strategies to manage their urges.

| Summary of Diagrams | | |
|---|---|---|
| **Common Clinical Problems**<br>*Display Diagrams (DD)*<br>*In-Session (IS) Worksheets*<br>*Coping Strategies (CS) Handouts* | | |
| **Therapy Topic** | **Diagram** | **Appendix C** |
| Worry | The Worry Zones<br>My Worry Zones<br>Coping With the Worry Zones<br>Managing Worry: The 2Rs | DD #1<br>IS Worksheet #1<br>CS Handout #1<br>CS Handout #2 |
| | | |
| Pain | The Pain Circuits<br>My Pain Circuits<br>Rewiring My Pain Circuits | DD #2<br>IS Worksheet #2<br>CS Handout #3 |
| | | |
| Rumination | Rumination<br>The Hamster Wheel<br>Managing Rumination: The 3Ds | DD #3<br>IS Worksheet #3<br>CS Handout #4 |

| Summary of Diagrams | | |
|---|---|---|
| Mood Regulation | The Mood Wave<br>Watching the Wave<br>Depression Ditches and Joy Jolts<br>Launching the Anger Arrows<br>Resetting the Anger Arrows | DD #4<br>IS Worksheet #4<br>CS Handout #5<br>CS Handout #6<br>CS Handout #7 |
| | | |
| Motivation | Motivation Movement<br>Goal Sheet<br>Weekly Chart<br>Immediate Goals: Plan | DD #5<br>IS Worksheet #5<br>IS Worksheet #6<br>CS Handout #8 |
| | | |
| Self-Esteem | Self-Esteem<br>Shifting the Balance<br>Self-Talk | DD #6<br>IS Worksheet #7<br>CS Handout #9 |
| | | |
| Panic | The Wave of Panic<br>Mapping Panic: The Body Mines<br>Managing Panic: The Body Minds<br>The Changing Wave of Panic | DD #7<br>IS Worksheet #8<br>CS Handout #10<br>CS Handout #11 |
| | | |
| Urges | The Hunger Urge<br>Detecting Urge Triggers<br>Surfing the Urge | DD #8<br>IS Worksheet #9<br>CS Handout #12 |

# Using Diagrams Creatively and Spontaneously in Session

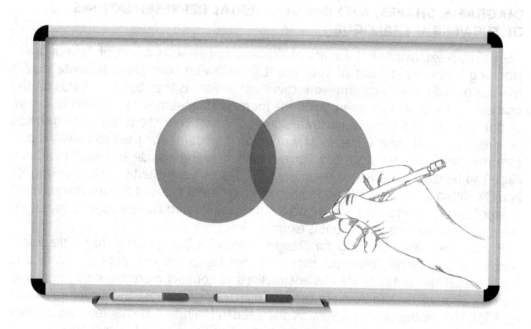 Writing Tips and Drawing Pics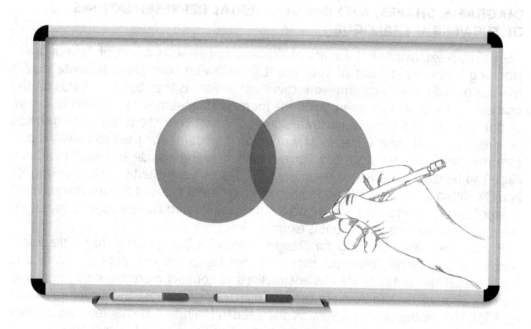

*The palest of ink is more reliable than the most powerful memory.*

—Confucius

In addition to using drawings and diagrams in a planful and deliberate way to address universal therapy themes and clinical problems, you can use diagrams, shapes, images, and other visually mediated strategies spontaneously during a therapy session. As you become accustomed to using visuals, you will find that you will be able to more easily visualize what your client is saying and as a result you will feel more comfortable spontaneously drawing a diagram or image during the therapy session. You may also find yourself periodically presenting any of the numerous display diagrams found in the appendices as a way to reinforce or better illustrate a theme or issue being addressed in the therapy. The multiple diagrams in the appendix can also be used as guides to help create your own diagrams or images. As you equip your therapy station with different visual materials, you will be more inclined to access and incorporate visual materials into your therapy sessions. For example, displaying the white board in the office or keeping other materials, such as a notepad, easel, or paper, accessible to both you and your client will help remind you to visually represent concepts and themes as needed during therapy sessions. You may also find it helpful to use various other visual aids, such as the computer or a smartphone, to visually engage your client during therapy sessions.

## DIAGRAMS, SHAPES, AND IMAGES: VISUAL REPRESENTATIONS OF THE VERBAL DIALOGUE

Ware (2008) explained that the act of drawing can serve as a sort of "visual brainstorming." Writing in front of your client (or allowing your client to write during the session) will quickly capture your client's attention as they begin to focus on the images, words, or shapes emerging in the moment. Sometimes a simple circle, arrow, or dot can convey a point or illustrate something that your client has just expressed or verbalized. Additionally, the act of writing can sometimes be used to visually represent the client's mental processes. For example, drawing a circle and words within a circle can be used to represent themes and topics on your client's mind; drawing X's and O's within a circle can be used to represent different types of thoughts your client is experiencing; or drawing a wave across the white board can be used to represent the mood fluctuations your client is experiencing.

In his book *Visual Thinking for Design*, Ware (2008) explained that a diagram's purpose is to "express concepts that need not be spatial in nature . . . lines and other spatial elements are used as abstractions to connect more basic concepts into concept structures. Diagrams are used to plan, design things, and structure ideas" (p. 155). The various display diagrams discussed in the previous chapters can be used as visual reminders to both you and your client of the clinical issues, concepts, and coping strategies discussed in prior sessions.

Ware (2008) discussed how circles and arrows represent universal communication symbols and trigger multiple information processing systems in the brain. He indicated that

*arrows are interesting because of the way they allow the application of the powerful pattern finding mechanisms of the visual system to be combined with a measure of abstract meaning. They can express . . . abstract conceptual relationships of various types, including causal relationships, sequences, and taxonomic hierarchies.*

(pp. 155–156)

During the therapy session, you can, for example, use arrows to illustrate the "directionality" or "degree" of something, such as your client's mood or stress level, to direct your client's attention to a theme or to illustrate various processes, such as goal-directed movement.

Circles are also quite effective in communicating information, ideas, and concepts. Circles have a sort of "universal appeal" and through their shape can convey completeness, containment, wholeness, and security. Circles are not only the universal design of many heavenly bodies (e.g., sun, moon, and planets) and the general shape of many common objects, such as clocks, balls, tires, flowers, and faces, but also have been used as universal symbols throughout history. For example, many important cultural symbols are circular, such as mandalas, dream catchers, the yin-yang, peace signs, Venn diagrams, and even the modern-day "smiley face" emoji. In this chapter we discuss how using images and certain shapes, such as dots, arrows, and circles, can facilitate the expression of ideas, feelings, and thoughts during therapy sessions.

The "motor act" of writing during the session can also be effective in conveying information or illustrating various themes during the therapy session. Certain *motoric writing actions* can help illustrate or represent a mental process that the client is experiencing or a particular coping strategy that may assist the client. For example, drawing dots and then erasing them may illustrate the process of removing certain thoughts or ideas from the client's mind; drawing a word, erasing it, and replacing it with a new word can represent cognitive restructuring or can illustrate the process of "developing a new thought"; or repeatedly drawing over a certain part of a diagram or repeatedly drawing over a certain shape, such as a circle, may help to emphasize a particular point you are trying to make or may serve to visually represent a repetitive process the client engages in, such as ruminative thinking.

In this chapter we provide several examples of ways you can use diagrams, writing exercises, and handouts to better engage your clients in therapy. Some of the examples illustrate ways to use the client's own act of writing to facilitate communication and engagement during the session. This may entail, for example, having your client fill out a worksheet, draw an aspect of a diagram, use the white board to express a thought, or write down a list of goals. We start with a list of drawing tips describing ways you can use basic shapes (e.g., arrows, dots, and circles) and common images (e.g., Venn diagram, tree diagram, and barometer) in therapy sessions.

### Diagram Drawing Tips

- Use *size* to emphasize importance, priority, or severity.
- Use **color** to distinguish between concepts and ideas or for visual aesthetics.
- Use **arrows** to connect ideas, show relationships, indicate directionality or degree, and show goal-directed movement.

- Use **dots** for thoughts, themes, and behaviors.
- Use **circles** to convey separate but related facets of the same concept (e.g., types of worry); represent the mind or brain of the client and what thoughts may "reside" inside the brain; represent family members or members of a group; and represent different time dimensions, such as the past, present, and future.
- Use **X's and O's** (or +'s and –'s) to distinguish adaptive from maladaptive thoughts, distinguish positive self-talk from negative self-talk, and represent desired versus undesired behaviors.
- Use the **tree diagram** to represent the themes of busyness, distractibility, and worry.
- Use the **barometer** to measure and monitor mood and to scale certain behaviors.
- Use the **Venn diagram** to illustrate communication processes and for comparing and contrasting certain themes, concepts, or ideas.

Next we describe various ways to use the tree diagram, Venn diagram, and barometer (these diagrams are available in Appendix D).

## THE TREE DIAGRAM

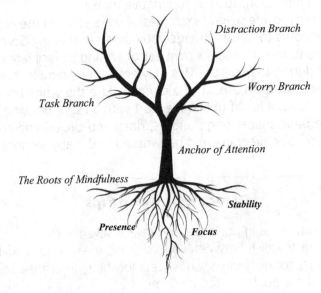

---

### The Tree Diagram can be used to illustrate the following:

a. **Busyness** (*task branches*): The branches represent tasks to accomplish.
b. **Distractibility** (*distraction branches*): The branches represent typical distractions.
c. **Worry** (*worry branches*): The branches represent worry themes.
d. The **trunk** can represent the *anchor of attention*.
e. The **roots** can be considered one's *mindful foundation* characterized by presence, focus, and stability.

---

*Drawing the tree diagram.* You can use the tree diagram to illustrate the concepts of *busyness, distractibility,* and *worry* (your client can circle the name of their tree on IS Worksheet #1). The tree diagram may be helpful to use for clients with ADHD, concentration difficulties, significant worry, busyness, and perfectionistic or obsessive tendencies. You can free draw a tree diagram or display the tree diagram available in Appendix D (*note: it may be more effective to initially free draw the tree diagram as this will capture your client's attention quickly. You can then display the tree diagram from Appendix D in follow-up sessions as a reminder of the concepts you covered in prior sessions*). Once you decide on the topic you would like to cover (i.e., busyness, distractibility, or worry), follow these steps:

1. *Draw the roots.* Explain that the three roots are our "mindful foundation," which enables us to maintain our focus and stay present in the moment and promotes our overall stability. Collectively these characteristics enable us to sustain our concentration and attention, accomplish tasks, minimize feeling overwhelmed, and help us organize ourselves so that we are less likely to succumb to stress and distraction.
2. *Draw the trunk.* Explain that the trunk is our "anchor of attention," which is the core of the tree. It controls the tree and promotes its stability.
3. *Draw the branches.* Explain that at different times throughout our day, we can start to move farther away from the trunk or lose focus and attention. As we start to branch off and move farther and farther from the trunk or core, the tree loses strength and our stability weakens. These branches can represent our distractions, worries, or tasks we try to accomplish.
4. *Discuss the following concepts:*
   - *Branching out:* This is the phenomenon of leaving the trunk of attention and beginning to branch out along the tree. This can be caused by certain triggers or stressors that cause your client to lose focus and begin to feel overwhelmed or stressed.

- *Returning to the trunk:* This is achieved by using strategies to help your client return to the trunk and to regain attention, focus, and organization.
- *Staying anchored:* This is achieved by using strategies that promote mindfulness and enable your client to cultivate more focused attention and "presence."
- You can also use such phrases as "monitoring the 'tree of the mind';" "watching for 'branching out' and getting too busy, distracted or worried;" "going out on a limb and forgetting what you are doing;" and "getting distracted by moving from branch to branch without any direction."
- The image of the tree should be useful in assisting your client in monitoring their thoughts and attention and becoming more aware of when they are becoming too busy, distracted, or worried.

5. *Use IS Worksheet #1: The Tree of My Mind).* You can use this worksheet to do the following:
   - *Label the type of one's tree.* Use the labels of busyness, worry, or distractibility.
   - *Identify the types of tree branches* associated with the type of tree. You can label some of the branches with your client's *distraction themes* (e.g., the Internet, cell phone, details, certain people), *worry themes* (i.e., work, health, finances, children), or *usual tasks* (i.e., work tasks, household tasks, child-rearing tasks, miscellaneous tasks).
   - *Identify the triggers to branching.* These would be things that cause your client to begin to worry, become distracted, or become too busy. To help identify your client's triggers, you can ask your client, for example, "What tends to make you worried, to make you distracted, to make you feel too busy?" Branching can cause your client to lose focus and experience more stress. Examples of triggers to branching may include boredom, being alone, certain times of day, certain settings or situations, spontaneous memories, thoughts of the past, thoughts of the future, expectations from others, or certain people.

6. *Use IS Worksheet #2: The Tree: Anchoring Strategies.* You can use this worksheet to do the following:
   - *Identify anchoring strategies.* These are strategies that can help redirect your client back to the trunk or anchor of the tree. These strategies can be thought of as "reactive strategies" that are deployed when your client notices that they are branching out and becoming more worried, distracted, or too busy. These could include brief breathing exercises, spontaneous writing or brief journaling, redirecting oneself to a certain task, or rehearsing coping statements, such as "I need to finish this first," "I'll be okay," "I can get through this," and "I don't have to do everything today."
   - *Identify mindfulness strategies.* These are strategies that can help to proactively maintain your client's focus and attention and to reduce susceptibility to branching. These strategies may include such things as practicing a daily meditation, prayer, or reflection exercise; journaling; being more planful about

one's day and how to spend one's time; writing out one's goals; and rehearing positive coping statements.

- Post *DD #1: The Tree* in follow-up sessions as needed to discuss ways that your client is managing their worry, distractibility, or busyness.

## THE BAROMETER

---

**The Barometer can be used to illustrate the following:**

a. **The degree of one's emotional state** (e.g., rate on a scale of 1–10 the degree of one's anger, anxiety, depression, or stress)

b. **The strength of certain characteristics** (e.g., rate on a scale of 1–10 the degree of one's motivation, patience, hope, or confidence)

c. **Your client's current mood rating** (e.g., rate on a scale of 1–10 the degree of one's current overall mood or sense of well-being)

---

Follow these guides:

1. *Display the barometer.* Explain that the barometer can be used as a gauge for one's mood or to measure certain characteristics, such as motivation or confidence. For some clients you may just display the barometer and use it periodically to get a "reading" on any changes that the two of you are monitoring, such as confidence, motivation, or overall mood level.

Some helpful questions to ask when using the barometer to measure change include the following:

- *What makes the barometer move up a notch?*
- *What makes the barometer move down a notch?*
- *What can you do more of to move the barometer in a positive direction?*
- *What can you do more of to prevent the barometer from moving in a negative direction?*

Note that how you interpret movement on the scale will vary depending on what is being measured. For example, if one is measuring depression, then lower numbers could indicate going "lower in mood" and thus a worsening of depression; if one is measuring anger, then higher numbers could indicate "getting angrier" and thus indicate a worsening of anger.

2. *Discuss the numbers.* Explain that our mood rises and falls based on various factors, such as time of day, thoughts, people, and situations. Changes in the reading of the barometer can be subtle and hardly noticeable but can initiate a process of a progressively worsening mood or an increasingly improving mood. For example, a simple negative thought could move our mood down a notch and then we become more stressed and potentially vulnerable to a worsening mood.

3. *Discuss monitoring the barometer.* Discuss the importance of noticing small changes in our barometer and taking immediate action when these changes occur. This requires your client to be more aware of how they are responding to the "weather" and what they may be anticipating in certain situations. For example, if your client pays attention to the small weather changes around them, such as the clouds moving in, then they may bring an umbrella to protect themselves from the weather changes and continue to function well in anticipation of these "environmental changes." In the same way, your client can prepare for anticipated changes in their moods based on their past experiences and take action early when they notice subtle mood or "barometric" shifts. The following image, which also appears in *DD #2: The Barometer* in Appendix D, can be used to discuss factors that influence fluctuations in your client's mood states.

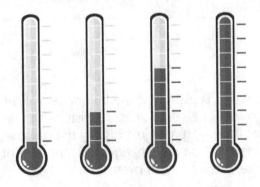

4. *Use IS Worksheet #3: My Barometer.* You can use the worksheet to do the following:
   a. Give the barometer a title: (e.g., *Anger, Depression, Confidence*).
   b. Identify triggers that move your client's barometer.
   c. Identify strategies that will assist your client in moving their barometer in a positive direction and strategies that will assist them in preventing their barometer from moving in a negative direction.
   d. Post the barometer in follow-up sessions as needed to discuss ways that your client is practicing strategies to best manage "fluctuations" in their mood or in any other behaviors they are monitoring.

## THE VENN DIAGRAM

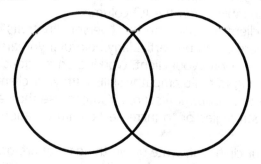

**The Venn Diagram can be used to illustrate the following:**

a. **Compare and contrast** two concepts, people, or ideas
b. Represent the communication platform between two people to help them identify **mutually agreeable conversation topics**
c. Represent **independent and mutual goals** or interests between two people

The Venn diagram will have broad appeal and can be used in multiple ways in therapy sessions. Be flexible and creative in using the Venn diagram. Suggested guides are provided next.

1. *Draw the diagram.* Draw the Venn diagram freestyle or display the sample Venn diagram (*DD #3: The Venn Diagram*). Explain that each circle has separate or *independent* parts as well as overlapping or *shared* parts. Explain that the Venn diagram can be used in therapy to explore such topics as comparing and contrasting, communication, or identifying mutual goals. Next you can choose the topic you wish to cover with your client.

2. *Use IS Worksheet # 4: Comparing and Contrasting.* You can use the Venn diagram to compare certain characteristics or themes between two people. For example, you could use the Venn diagram to compare goals, interests, behaviors, and personality traits between your client and another person (e.g., significant other, family member, coworker). This may help your client gain insight into this particular relationship and better understand how differences and similarities influence the relationship.
   - In circle A, your client can identify their characteristics and list them in the table under the A column.
   - In circle B, your client can identify their partner's characteristics and list those in the table under the B column.
   - In the overlapping circle AB, your client can identify related characteristics or similarities across the topic, feature, or characteristic they are comparing and list them in the table under the AB column.
   Getting your client to reflect on the "personality traits" or "characteristics" of the other person can be particularly helpful if you are doing some type of marital counseling with your client, working on relationship issues or communication, or trying to build empathy skills with your client.

3. *Use IS Worksheet #5: Communication.* You can use the Venn diagram to build communication strategies or to increase "communication awareness" in your client.
   - In circle A, your client can write down things that are on their mind concerning their partner, coworker, or family member. Some of these thoughts may be positive and some may be negative.
   - In circle B, your client can write down what they think is on the other person's mind, including what they think the other may be thinking about them.
   - In the overlapping circle AB, your client can write down what they would like to say to the other person that they believe would be conducive to strengthening the relationship and improving the overall communication. For example, your client may write in column B that they think their partner is insecure about the relationship. As a result, your client may choose to write in column AB that they will share more words of reassurance with their partner.

4. *Use IS Worksheet #6: Identifying Mutual Goals.* You can use the Venn diagram to identify mutual goals in a relationship.
   - In circle A, your client can identify their goals and list them in the table under column A.
   - In circle B, your client can identify their partner's goals and list those in the table under column B.
   - In the overlapping circle AB, your client can identify mutual goals and list them in the table under column AB.
   - If you are working with a couple, you can have them each fill in their own goals separately and then have them share their goals with each other. They can then work together to identify their mutual goals and write these in column AB.

5. *Use IS Worksheet #7: Open Venn Diagram.* We have provided an "open" Venn diagram if you prefer to have your client write information inside the actual circles instead of writing in a table below the Venn diagram as is the style in IS Worksheets #4, #5, and #6. You can use this open Venn diagram to address any of the themes previously covered (i.e., comparing and contrasting, communication, and identifying mutual goals). On IS Worksheet #7, there is a space to indicate the topic covered and to identify the two themes or people involved (A and B). There is also space at the bottom of the worksheet to write down any notes that are relevant to the discussion.

## USING DIAGRAMS SPONTANEOUSLY: CASE EXAMPLES

Next we present examples of ways we have used visuals spontaneously during therapy sessions. Although details of the actual clinical issues have been modified, we retained the essential clinical theme that was addressed in the session. No identifying information is used so as to protect client confidentiality. The examples are used not to bring attention to any specific clinical problem per se but rather to convey a visually mediated strategy that may be beneficial to use in your own therapy sessions.

These diagrams were drawn during actual therapy sessions to augment, facilitate, or clarify information and concepts that were emerging during the session. For example, some of these diagrams were drawn to help the therapist and client visualize and better understand what the client was saying or what the therapist was saying; assist the client in understanding a concept or to illustrate a coping strategy; bring attention to the "physical act of writing" as a way to illustrate, for example, a client's "mental process;" provide a mechanism to more actively engage a "low verbal" client in the therapy session; or help the client better process the verbal information exchanged in the session (e.g., writing on the white board statements the client was using in the session).

### Case #1: Using the Eraser

Using the eraser on the white board can be very effective in illustrating various processes with your client. The "motoric act" of erasing words, symbols, or images on the white board will illustrate "a change process" and serve as a salient visual reminder to your client of the possibility of "change." Your client's attention will be drawn to this act of "removing" something, which will symbolize that change is possible. Your client will likely remember this event as they later reflect on the session. We have used the eraser to demonstrate the following concepts or change processes addressed in therapy:

1. *Eliminating certain thoughts from one's thought pattern.*

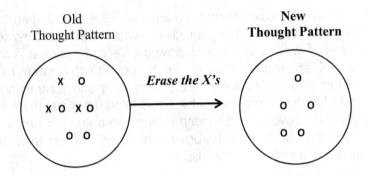

Old
Thought Pattern

New
Thought Pattern

*Erase the X's*

X = Maladaptive Thoughts
O = Adaptive Thoughts

*Erase stressful thoughts symbolized by X's.* This diagram can be effective with clients who are experiencing various stressful thoughts, ruminating, or dwelling on certain events. Erasing the X's can illustrate "the process" of eliminating certain thoughts and learning to focus on more positive or adaptive thoughts. *An alternative method is to draw each diagram one at a time and to show how in the second diagram the X's no longer exist.*

2. *Wiping away negative past memories and moving forward in life.*

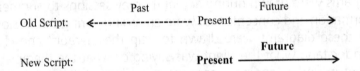

Old Script:  Past --------------- Present --------------- Future

New Script:  **Present** --------------- **Future**

*Erase the line of the past to symbolize moving on.* This diagram can be effective for clients who are stuck in the past and make frequent reference to their past in the therapy session. For example, your client may be dwelling on how their parents treated them in childhood or on certain past negative events that have affected their life. Even though you may already know this information, your client may, out of habit, continue to reflect on this in session. Visually "erasing" the arrow of the past can illustrate moving on and focusing attention on the present and future.

3. *Removing the layers of stress.*

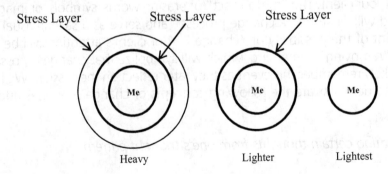

Stress Layer     Stress Layer     Stress Layer

Me     Me     Me

Heavy     Lighter     Lightest

*Erase, one at a time, the outer circles, which represent the different stressors weighing down your client.* This diagram can be effective for clients who are experiencing various stressors or stressful life events. Erasing the circle can "illustrate" the process of managing these events or "eliminating" such stressors so as to feel less burdened. For example, your client may be taking on too many tasks or feeling stressed due to burdensome family responsibilities. As you discuss ways to manage each stressor, you can erase each layer of stress.

**Note**: *It can also be effective during the session to redraw the erased image in any of these different diagrams. This can help "illustrate" how the very problem that you and your client are trying to alleviate can resurface under certain conditions. For instance, in the first example, you could redraw the X's in the circle when you and your client discuss the triggers to experiencing stressful thoughts. In the second example, you can redraw the arrow of the past when discussing things that trigger your client's thoughts of the past. Lastly, in the third example, you can redraw the stress layers around the "me" circle as you and your client discuss the different stressors in their life. Then you can erase the images again as you and your client refocus on coping with and managing these problem areas.*

## Case #2: The Three Worlds

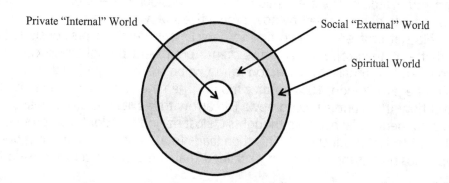

You can use this diagram to explore the "different worlds" of your client and the ways your client navigates these worlds. The diagram can lead to discussions about your client's values, goals, interests, personality features, worries, social interests, and religious beliefs. You can discuss the thoughts, behaviors, and emotions associated with these three different worlds of your client.

The following questions may facilitate discussion and help your client reflect on these three worlds:

1. Tell me about your *private "internal" world*. What is on your mind usually? How do you tend to talk to yourself (critical, neutral, supportive)? Who and what do you tend to think about?

2. What is it like for you in the *social "external" world*? What do you most enjoy about the social world? Least enjoy? What part of you tends to be most visible in the social world? What part of you is least visible?

3. What are your beliefs about the *spiritual world*? Do you do things that serve to connect you to the spiritual world? Who and what is in your spiritual world?

4. In which world are you most content? Least content?

5. How would you like to ideally see yourself in these three worlds? What is one small change you could begin to make to feel more fulfilled and to find more meaning in each of these worlds (e.g., in the *private inner world*, your client may want to engage in more positive self-talk; in the *social external world*, your client may want to share more of themselves in casual social conversations or maybe even join a social group; in the *spiritual world*, your client may want to return to some type of religious practice)? Your client can use three index cards (one for each world) and write down the desired goals for each world.

## Case #3: Old and New Self Profile

The following diagram has been used to help clients adjust to life changes, such as losing a job, going on disability, or needing to adjust to a significant life change. In this example, a client lost her job, which previously served as a strong source of satisfaction and meaning. The client had devoted a considerable amount of time to her job and came to define herself by how productive she was.

The "old self profile" is drawn first to depict how the client previously felt. The arrow that exits the profile leads to the client's prominent thoughts associated with this profile and eventually to her mood rating when she had a job, which was 7 out of 10 (1 = negative mood; 10 = positive mood). Then the "new self profile" is drawn to depict how the client is feeling now. The arrow that exits the profile leads to the client's prominent initial negative thoughts ("I lost my job," "I don't feel productive," and "I need to feel productive"). This then leads to a 3 out of 10 current mood rating. Upon losing her job, the client explained that she experienced depression and felt lost.

We discussed "redefining" herself by identifying other activities she could engage in to find meaning. The activities in the new self profile are identified in the pie graph, with the activity of "work" being notably absent. After exploring other potential interests and values, the client identified new ways that she could spend her time and a new way that she could think about her situation. The diagram then depicted how these new activities and this new way of thinking could bring her mood back up to a 7, which was the mood state she experienced prior to losing her job.

*The diagram can help the client make connections among thoughts, activities, and mood states. It can help the client begin to "envision" the new activities and thoughts that can bring about this new self profile and improved mood.*

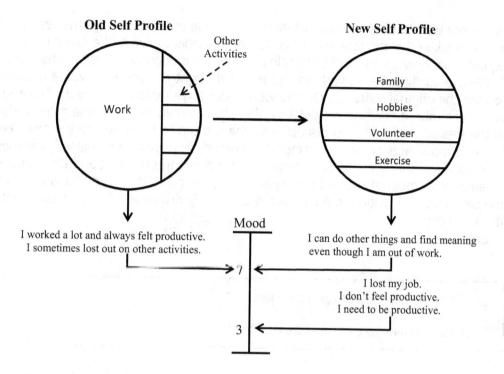

**Old Self Profile**

Other Activities

Work

I worked a lot and always felt productive.
I sometimes lost out on other activities.

**New Self Profile**

Family
Hobbies
Volunteer
Exercise

Mood

I can do other things and find meaning
even though I am out of work.

7

I lost my job.
I don't feel productive.
I need to be productive.

3

## Case #4: Changing the Words

Writing out your client's verbatim thoughts and beliefs can be helpful in allowing your client to more closely examine their thoughts and modify them in such a way that they experience less distress or anxiety. By visualizing their thought process, clients can more directly work with their thoughts and "observe" how they can change their thought process and, in doing so, experience a change in their emotional state. Allowing your client, at times, to do the actual writing in the session can help reinforce how they can directly influence this change process.

Example 1:

> "I caused my grandson's substance abuse problem!"
>
> **care about**
>
> "I ~~caused~~ my grandson's substance abuse problem."

In this example, the client entered therapy due to excessive anxiety secondary to feeling responsible for her grandson's substance abuse problem. She thought she somehow was responsible for this problem by causing her grandson too much stress during his childhood. Entering therapy, she stated that she was obsessively preoccupied with the following thought: "I caused my grandson's substance abuse problem."

We wrote this statement on the white board. As we used some cognitive restructuring to weaken this thought and to evaluate the evidence for it, the client began to consider being less responsible but said she was still preoccupied with the thought.

We eventually came up with an alternative thought and used the white board to reword the original sentence. On the white board, we replaced the word "caused" with "care about." When we did this, the client immediately became more verbal in the session and started to discuss how she wanted to begin to use the new sentence to focus more on ways to support her grandson versus blame herself. She then seemed more optimistic about change. Writing down the thought and then writing an alternative thought seemed to be particularly effective. The act of "crossing out" the old word and writing in a new word concretely illustrated changing the client's thought process.

Example 2:

> "I should have spoken up at the meeting."
>    c
> "I should have spoken up at the meeting."

In this example, the client was using lots of "shoulds" in discussing his behavior. He would frequently make such comments as "I should do this," "I should have done that," "I should always," and "What I should do is this." I mentioned that it is difficult sometimes to notice our thoughts and the specific words we use because our thinking can become habitual. Then I slowly wrote the word "SHOULD" in big capital letters across the white board. Then I crossed out the "SH" and wrote a "C" above it, changing the word "should "to "could." I explained how changing the word can provide the client with more flexibility and minimize feelings of guilt, regret, and shame. We then practiced changing the world "should" to the word "could" in different sentences the client was using. In the previous example, we wrote down the two different versions of the sentence to illustrate how changing a word could be effective. We then used the alternative sentence with the word "could" to help the client feel less pressure in meetings and to give him more flexibility in deciding when and what to say during a meeting. We also talked about the reasons why he sometimes may not say anything at a meeting, and this helped him better appreciate his rationale for sometimes not speaking up.

## Case #5: Getting the Distance Right

This client spontaneously started discussing the change she desired in her daughter. We started talking about what changes she was looking for in her daughter. She was dissatisfied with her daughter's behavior progress so far in improving their relationship. She knew the goals she was aiming for, which included feeling closer to her daughter. She tended to focus on what wasn't working versus what was working in the relationship. The outstretched hands were used to signify that she wanted to be here (the hands were held close together to represent her goal for the relationship; *this is depicted in the following middle image in the diagram chart, under "my expectations for her behavior"*). However, she felt her daughter's behavior was "miles away" from this. The hands were then spread far apart to signify how far she felt her daughter's behavior was compared to what she expected from her (*this is depicted in the first image, under "my perception of my daughter's behavior"*). Then we considered that her daughter may actually be displaying more positive behavior than she realizes because she may be so focused on what is wrong in the relationship that she is missing what is working. The hands were then moved to a moderate distance apart as we discussed this (*this is depicted in the third image, under "my daughter's actual behavior"*). The client did the same with her hands as she started describing what may better represent her daughter's actual behavior. After our discussion, we used the white board to summarize and illustrate these three different perspectives of her daughter's behavior, as illustrated next.

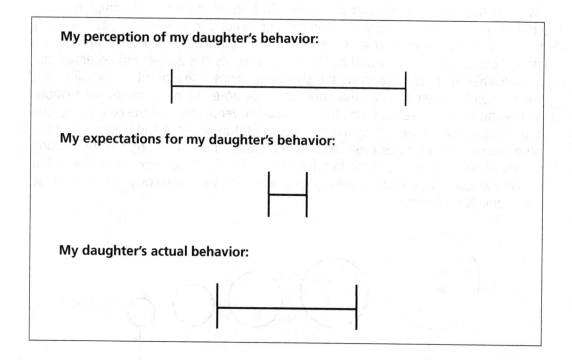

The client continued to discuss the three distance points and what behaviors would fall under these three different areas. As she recognized that a middle position may exist and may be an acceptable position for now, she started to feel less judgmental toward her daughter and more optimistic. Through the aid of the visuals, we discovered that her impatience with the relationship was a driving factor that was preventing her from recognizing the realistic state of her daughter's actual behavior. The client was able to shift the therapy goal from "changing her daughter's behavior" to her identifying her own goal of becoming more patient and less judgmental toward her daughter. It was notable that initially the client felt quite stuck but was able to fairly quickly feel more optimistic about her relationship with her daughter through the aid of the diagram.

## Case #6: Watching the Circles Shrink

This client sought therapy due to panic and social anxiety. I drew a circle during one session to represent the client's life worries. We discussed what some of these life worries were. She mentioned that she felt fairly confident in her ability to typically manage these but that these life worries were still preventing her from reaching all her goals and feeling confident about her future. She then spontaneously picked up the white board, brought it toward her, picked up a marker, and drew a larger circle above the circle of her "life worries." She then said, "This is the fear" and identified this as her "core worry." The core worry was that she would get so anxious someday that she would utterly embarrass herself, lose all respect, and completely lose credibility in the eyes of everyone. She then proceeded to talk about it as the worry that fuels all the other worries. I then progressively drew the top circle smaller and started discussing what it would be like if this worry itself lessened and became more manageable. As I began to draw the shrinking circles, she started to verbalize that she needed to better manage this core worry. Of note, we had met several sessions before this particular session, and the client had never mentioned the core worry. She expressed an interest in making this the focus of future sessions and believed that her other life worries would be even more manageable if her core worry lessened. Using the visual aid enabled the client to reflect more deeply on her anxiety, explore what was at the root of it, and articulate a goal of lessening this core worry to help manage her overall life worries.

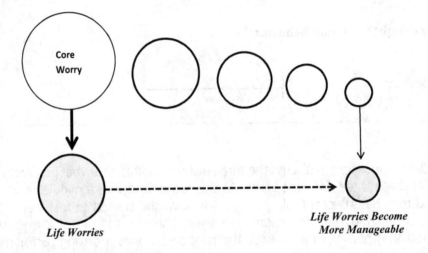

## Case #7: Take Out the Math Sheet

The client, carrying a large cup of coffee, walked into the session and greeted me cheerfully. He slowly sat down in his chair, getting comfortable. He lowered his shoulders, smiled, and inquired about my well-being. What follows is a paraphrasing of the conversation.

| | |
|---|---|
| *Client*: | "How are you?" |
| *Therapist*: | "Good. Thank you. Welcome back. Last time we were discussing some of the things you wanted to work on. What did you want to discuss today?" |
| *Client*: | "Not sure. I haven't done much . . . my dad thinks I should do more . . . I've just been playing video games . . . I always feel tired . . . I'm not sleeping that well." |
| *Therapist*: | "What do you think will help?" |
| *Client*: | "Not sure." |
| *Therapist*: | "How's your mood?" |
| *Client*: | "The same." |

At this time the verbal dialogue is running out. The client looks sleepy and sinks farther into the chair. The client does not offer any other spontaneous verbalizations and has not developed strong conversational skills. I think to myself, *I'm not sure if I can muscle through this verbally. I wonder if I should just keep asking questions and finding ways to get him to discuss his feelings.* I remind myself that he usually says the same things when I ask him how he's feeling.

At this point I start to think of a way I might simply engage my client's thought process. I look at my clipboard on the desk, reach for a math sheet, and attach it to the clipboard. I ask the client if he can fill out a math sheet. He agrees and immediately sits up and looks attentively at me. He accepts the pencil and begins the first problem.

The client then proceeded to read the problems on the sheet, occasionally gazed across the room while doing mental computations, and rehearsed some math strategies out load. He soon began to mention that math was his favorite subject. He talked more about school. He then discussed his interest in returning to school. For the next 5 minutes, he worked carefully and attentively. He finished the worksheet and then attended carefully as we reviewed his work. He noticed that he got most of the questions correct. We then talked the last 15 minutes of the session about his school history and interest in furthering his education. We looked up some information on various education programs and certificates, and he left with some online information about these programs. This was the most productive and engaged that he had ever been during a therapy session.

In follow-up sessions, the client was able to stay engaged in the session by using worksheets to stimulate his thinking and to provide a structure through which he could verbalize his interests and focus on concrete goals (*in Chapter 8 we discuss in more detail some of these paper-and-pencil mind stimulation therapy techniques you* can use with a variety of different clinical populations). We infrequently discussed his symptoms, and rather than relying on spontaneous verbalizations and emotionally laden conversational dialogue, we used the questions and cues on the worksheets to discuss various topics from which we were able to generate practical and realistic therapy goals.

## MISCELLANEOUS DIAGRAMS (APPENDIX D)

There are additional miscellaneous handouts in Appendix D that you may find helpful in teaching a certain coping strategy or discussing a particular topic. These diagrams can be used as needed during your therapy sessions. These miscellaneous diagrams include the following:

*IS Worksheet #8: Genogram*: You can use the genogram diagram to gather relevant information about your client's family history, ethnicity, and religious background and to gather and record information about grandparents, parents, siblings, partners, and children. In the "notes" area, you can record relevant family rituals, behavioral patterns, and personality traits. Ultimately, gathering pertinent background information can assist you in better understanding how your client's family history has shaped their behavior and personality. In the circles you can place the age of the individual or a *D* if the individual is deceased, and for any unused circles, you can simply put an *X* through them. You can also add circles if needed (e.g., if your client has more than four siblings or more than five children).

*CS Handout #1: Cognitive Defusion*: You can use the cognitive defusion diagram to introduce the concept of "fused thoughts." The term *cognitive defusion* was formally introduced in the psychotherapy arena through a form of therapy called acceptance and commitment therapy, which was initiated by Hayes and colleagues (Hayes, & Strosahl, 2004; Hayes, Strosahl, & Wilson 1999). The diagram gives a brief definition of fused thoughts. It may be helpful for your client to identify their own fused thoughts that they seem "attached to" and that seem to have a negative influence on their self-esteem or mood. You can use the diagram at the top of the page as a teaching visual for fused thoughts. The diagram depicts some thoughts being embedded (fused) in the mind of the self and other thoughts floating outside of the self. The diagram depicted on the bottom half of the handout can be used to facilitate the discussion of cognitive defusion coping strategies. The diagram depicts thoughts floating around the self, with no thoughts fused or attached to the self. Explain that the goal is to "defuse" these thoughts through various strategies. Five cognitive defusion strategies are listed on the bottom half of the handout. You can invite your client to practice these strategies to assist them in "getting distance" from stressful thoughts by learning how to "separate" themselves from certain thoughts.

*IS Worksheet #9: Weather Forecast*: You can use this diagram to illustrate the difference between pessimistic and optimistic thinking. This diagram may be helpful for clients whose depression or anger is rooted in a pessimistic belief system. The diagram can assist your client in learning to adopt a more optimistic perspective in their life and to ultimately experience less depression or anger. Under the "Sunny Day Forecast," your client can write down three optimistic statements they can make about themselves or the world. Under the "Cloudy Day Forecast," your client can write three pessimistic statements about themselves or the world. Finally, at the very bottom of the worksheet, using the concept of *weather* as a metaphor for life events and challenges, your client can write out a new weather forecast for their life. This new forecast could include such statements as "Although it may drizzle, it doesn't mean the day is ruined," "Weather can change, but I can stay the same," "The sun never hides forever, clouds always pass, and a day is never ruined due to bad weather," and "I can't control the weather, but I can control my reaction to it."

*DD #5 Monday Morning Quarterbacking*: You can use this diagram to discuss the concept of regret or guilt or if your client thinks that they tend to make bad decisions. The diagram will illustrate how hindsight is 20/20. This is done by depicting the circumstances that existed at the time of the decision (Sunday) and then reviewing your "next day" reflections (Monday) that indicate you should have "known" better, especially now because on Monday you have knowledge of Sunday's outcome. By juxtaposing Sunday's and Monday's "reflection trees," your client will more clearly see how their Monday judgments about their Sunday decisions are unfair, biased, and even at times comical. Call attention to the theme of Monday's reflections, which often suggests that you believe you *should have been able to predict the future*! You can ask your client why on Sunday they weren't following the thinking pattern depicted on Monday. Use *IS Worksheet #10: My Monday Morning Quarterbacking* to review an example from your client's own life when they felt they made a bad decision about something in their life and later regretted it.

*CS Handout #2: S-P-E-A-K*: You can use this diagram to assist your clients in learning how to participate more in social conversations. This can be particularly helpful for clients who may experience, for example, social anxiety or low self-esteem. Sometimes it can be difficult to think of things to discuss with others. For example, if you are feeling nervous or preoccupied with a problem in your life, you may be more focused on thinking about the problem or managing your nervousness and less focused on thinking of topics to discuss with others. One way to help your client to think about possible topics to discuss is to think of the word "SPEAK," which can be used as a mnemonic device to remember conversation topics that your client could talk about as well topics they could ask others about. SPEAK stands for **S**ports, **P**rofession, **E**ducation, **A**ctivities, and **K**in. These are "universal" topics that many people find interesting to talk about. Invite your client to practice participating more in conversations by reviewing the communication tips on the handout.

*IS Worksheet #11: Personal Philosophy Decree*: You can use this handout to invite your clients to engage in a writing exercise to express or formulate their life philosophy. It can be used for clients who see themselves as having lost a certain perspective or purpose in life or for those who are seeking more meaning and may be discouraged about their current life situation. They may see themselves as once having coped better with life and may have expressed that they want to regain the wisdom or philosophy that used to guide their behavior. In other cases, perhaps your client has never had a guiding philosophy, and you can use the handout to assist them in developing a philosophy that can help them derive more meaning in their life. After writing it, your client can provide a title at the top of the decree.

*CS Handout #3: Focus*: This diagram can be helpful for clients with ADHD or organizational difficulties. It can be useful in helping clients to identify specific tasks and to break larger tasks into smaller, more manageable components. The handout can assist your clients in determining what tasks they wish to first address and to actively use the 2Ts strategy to accomplish these tasks. Encourage your clients to break tasks down into manageable steps and to devote a certain amount of time to the task. This will help them sustain attention, stay in the "white zone," and minimize episodes of distractibility. The image at the bottom of the handout can help your client monitor their attention and use redirection strategies when they notice they are "off task" or moving out of the white zone.

*IS Worksheet #12: Traffic Stress*: This diagram can be used with clients who experience traffic stress, road rage, or periodic anger episodes while driving. Using the top half of the worksheet, clients identify their typical driving behaviors and driving stressors. In the bottom half of the worksheet, there is a list of new driving strategies using the mnemonic "TRAFFIC." Review these with your client. Finally, invite your client to use the chart at the bottom of the worksheet to monitor three episodes of traffic stress and to record their success in using new coping strategies.

We conclude the chapter with several tips that can be used during any session. We recommend being flexible and finding ways to use these tips based on the client's particular needs, styles, and goals. You may find that some of the tips may lead to other interventions and strategies that can assist your client in reaching their goals.

## TIPS FOR ENGAGING YOUR CLIENT IN THE THERAPY SESSION

### Use a Dot

To help your client remember to practice a coping strategy or to monitor their thought process, give them a strip of five to six orange sticky dots and have them place these dots in various locations, such as on their cell phone, car dashboard, computer, and bedroom dresser. The dots will remind them of the exercise they need to practice.

## Move the Chairs Around

Use the office computer or an easel to engage a socially anxious client by having them sit next to you. This reduces anxiety triggered by the therapist's facial cues and helps the client attend to more factual and neutral information generated on the easel or computer screen. They can use the computer to write out goals or even search the web for information pertinent to their goals.

## Create a Word Search

Use a word search website in session to have your client create a word search that reflects their interests, favorite activities, favorite music, or even their therapy goals. After creating the word search in session, invite your client to complete it outside of the session. Completing the word search for homework will serve as a reminder of what they are working on in therapy and as a way to further stimulate their interest and engagement in the therapy.

## Take a Picture

After creating or displaying a diagram in the therapy session, invite your client to take a picture of the diagram with their cell phone. This will enable them to easily access and refer to it outside of the therapy session. You may notice that some of your clients will ask to take a picture of the diagram before you even suggest it.

## Take Out the Cell Phone

Use the patient's cell phone to help them share interests, social networks, music, and computer games that may help you learn more about your client. Spend time discussing how they use their phone and how much time they spend on it. Use the information to help them generate practical goals and to use electronic scheduling apps to help them track and monitor their progress in working toward their goals. Invite your client to set their phone alarm to go off two to three times during the day as a reminder to practice a coping strategy discussed in the session or to engage in a brief mindfulness exercise.

## Hand Over the Notepad

Use the act of writing to engage a low verbal or disengaged client. Hand them a blank goals sheet or a notecard, and have them simply begin to write down thoughts and tentative goals without worrying about the viability of the goals. The act of writing will stimulate cognitive processes and help the client better engage in the session's phrases for spontaneously introducing the white board.

## The 30-Second Summary

Start each session with a 30-second summary of the main themes discussed in the therapy and discuss any homework assigned from the last session. Write these themes and the homework assigned on the white board as a visual cue for the client as they enter the room. This will minimize extraneous dialogue, narrow memory retrieval, and help focus the session on the therapy goals and issues.

## The 1-Minute Progress Note

At the end of the session, invite your client to take 1 minute to write down on an index card their progress note for the session. This note can reflect the session's "take-home" message. Invite your client to reflect on the important themes, insights, and strategies that may have been discussed during the therapy and how they will practice these strategies after the session. This is akin to the therapy progress note, but the client gets to write their own.

| Summary of Diagrams | | |
|---|---|---|
| **Miscellaneous Diagrams**<br>*Display Diagrams (DD)*<br>*In-Session (IS) Worksheets*<br>*Coping Strategies (CS) Handouts* | | |
| **Therapy Topic** | **Diagram** | **Appendix D** |
| Busyness<br>Distractibility<br>Worry | The Tree<br>The Tree of My Mind<br>The Tree: Anchoring Strategies | DD #1<br>IS Worksheet #1<br>IS Worksheet #2 |

| Summary of Diagrams | | |
|---|---|---|
| Mood Monitoring | The Barometer<br>My Barometer | DD #2<br>IS Worksheet #3 |
| | | |
| Communication<br>Marital Therapy<br>Relationship Goals | The Venn Diagram<br>Comparing and Contrasting<br>Communication<br>Identifying Mutual Goals<br>Open Venn Diagram | DD #3<br>IS Worksheet #4<br>IS Worksheet #5<br>IS Worksheet #6<br>IS Worksheet #7 |
| | | |
| Family Ethnicity/Religion<br>Family Relationships | Genogram | IS Worksheet #8 |
| | | |
| Managing Thoughts | Cognitive Defusion | CS Handout #1 |
| | | |
| Optimism Versus Pessimism | Weather Forecast | IS Worksheet #9 |
| | | |
| Regret | Monday Morning Quarterbacking<br>My Monday Morning<br>Quarterbacking | DD #5<br>IS Worksheet #10 |
| | | |
| Shyness | S-P-E-A-K | CS Handout #2 |
| | | |
| Developing a Philosophy of<br>Coping | Personal Philosophy Decree | IS Worksheet #11 |
| | | |
| Disorganization | Focus | CS Handout #3 |
| | | |
| Road Rage | Traffic Stress | IS Worksheet #12 |

# 8

## Using Visually Enhanced and Multimodal Interventions with Special Clinical Populations

The focus of this chapter is on using various visually mediated and multimodal strategies to better engage clients who have not responded optimally to traditional verbal therapy. Traditional therapy typically relies heavily on the auditory processing mode and may have limitations for certain clinical populations who present with compromised auditory processing and persistent psychiatric symptoms. These clinical populations may include, for example, clients with persistent psychosis (schizophrenia), behaviorally challenged children and adolescents, and geriatric clients. For certain client populations, we believe that their auditory processing mode may be compromised due to ongoing and persistent preoccupation with and interference from "internal associations" and ruminations. Additionally, these clients may experience some difficulties in maintaining attention, working memory, and other associated cognitive processes that are important for optimal participation in traditional verbal therapy.

Traditional therapy often focuses on discussing emotionally laden personal issues and problems to promote "insight and understanding," with the assumption that the therapeutic discussion will be "internalized and generalized" to effect behavior change outside the therapy session. Clients with persistent psychological and behavioral difficulties may have difficulties processing emotionally laden issues and using the traditional verbal-auditory modality to address and "understand" their persistent behavioral and emotional issues. We take the position that clients with persistent psychiatric and behavioral difficulties who have compromised auditory processing skills can be viable psychotherapy candidates. We believe this can occur by creating a therapy "communication structure" that can assist clients in more easily processing information exchanged during the therapy sessions and thus maximize their participation in and response to therapy (see Figure 8.1).

In our publications, we have provided a rationale for using various visually aided and multimodal strategies to enhance information processing and more effective therapy engagement with certain clinical populations (Ahmed, 1998, 2002, 2016; Ahmed & Boisvert, 2003b, 2006, 2013; Ahmed & Goldman, 1994). As such, using various *visual* and *multimodal techniques* has played a prominent role in our therapy work with these client populations. In this chapter we discuss how to use a variety of visually enhanced and multimodal therapy techniques in both individual and group formats when working with the following clinical populations: behaviorally challenged children and adults, developmentally disabled behaviorally challenged clients, dually diagnosed substance abuse clients, geriatric clients, and clients with persistent psychosis.

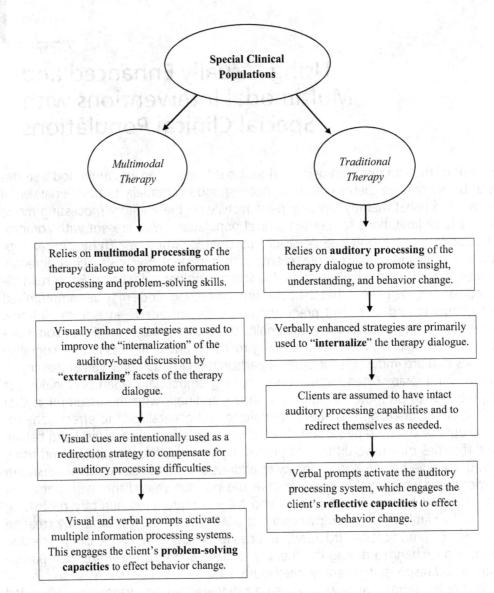

*Figure 8.1* Multimodal Versus Traditional Verbal Therapy

Multimodal strategies are intended to stimulate the client's active engagement in the therapy session by using various visual prompts, cues, strategies, and mind stimulation techniques. Several of the strategies we discuss are derived from our mind stimulation therapy model outlined in our book *Mind Stimulation Therapy: Cognitive Interventions for Persons With Schizophrenia* (Ahmed & Boisvert, 2013). The initial working model (Ahmed & Boisvert, 2003; Ahmed & Goldman, 1994) was developed in the context of working with persons with persistent and chronic psychosis and has expanded to additional populations, which we discuss in this chapter. By incorporating visually cued activities and strategies, clients can better understand, remember, and use the information discussed in therapy to improve their adaptive functioning and thinking capacities. *These strategies are intended to serve as adjunctive therapy interventions that can be incorporated into your clinical work independent of your particular theoretical orientation or approach.*

We next discuss how the different facets of learning theory can provide a framework and rationale for using multimodal therapy strategies in therapy. Learning principles derived from learning theory can inform the development of various interventions and strategies that therapists can use with their clients. These learning principles are presented in the context of conceptualizing therapy as a "psychoeducational encounter" whereby the therapist creates a learning environment to maximize the exchange of information. This environment can be maximized by using various multimodal strategies to assist clients in learning new skills, associating new behaviors with the therapy experience, and using observation, movement, writing, and other activities to reinforce more adaptive behaviors.

## LEARNING THEORY AND MULTIMODAL APPROACHES

Learning theory provides a framework for understanding how behaviors can be acquired, reinforced, maintained, and changed through the therapy process. The core principles of learning theory include the following elements:

a. An *associative learning process* (classical conditioning à la Pavlov) whereby one learns to "emit" certain responses due to associating certain events or stimuli with certain outcomes (e.g., by associating over time the sun with a fun day, one can feel good simply by noticing that it is sunny outside). Learned responses can also generalize and become *habits* (e.g., we may have an unpleasant encounter with a dog and then, through association, fear all dogs).

b. A *reinforcement learning process* (operant conditioning à la Skinner) whereby one becomes aware of the consequences to one's behaviors through reinforcement principles and uses information related to the consequences to change behavior. Behavior that is consistently reinforced may eventually become a *habit* (e.g., a baseball player gets a hit when holding the baseball bat a particular way and learns to hold the bat this way whenever hitting; a child earns a dollar for cleaning her room and as a result continues to clean her room to earn another

171

dollar). Habits can also develop that allow us to avoid negative consequences (e.g., we continually avoid crowded places to prevent anxiety).

c. An *observational learning process* (social learning theory à la Bandura) whereby one uses observation, role-playing, and modeling to change behavior. The same action repeated under similar conditions will eventually become a *habit* (e.g., a child learns how to tie her shoe after watching her mother tie her shoe; we learn the movements of tai chi by observing the instructor).

Psychotherapy, as in any learning environment, involves the implementation, to varying degrees, of these three learning processes to induce new learning and behavior change.

These learning principles shape our behaviors and contribute to the development of certain habits over time. These behavioral habits can predict our reactions to the world around us. For example:

- Our emotional associations to a specific event are often triggered by our internal thinking or by the external social and physical environmental cues that over time have been associated with this event (e.g., we may feel angry, outside of conscious awareness, in the presence of someone simply because over time we have had negative interactions with that person or we get anxious in the grocery store because we previously had a panic attack in the store).

- Our knowledge and experience of the consequences to our behaviors promotes behavior change (e.g., we no longer get anxious when driving because we have practiced driving, and it has led to positive experiences, such as being able to visit friends and increased independence).
- We learn to sense our own body movements and how best to navigate our social and physical world by observing our own and others' behaviors (e.g., we hold the door open for others now because we had noticed that when someone else did this, a smile was exchanged and goodwill was expressed). In similar ways, we learn to engage in certain psychomotor activities, play, and social interactions or we perform various roles that are culturally learned and observed.

Psychotherapy and counseling, as in any learning situation, provide an environment whereby we can better understand our personal learning histories and behavioral habits and use this therapy environment to learn new behaviors and coping strategies to more effectively adapt to and interact with the world and those around us.

## THE MIND STIMULATION THERAPY MODEL

Next we discuss the fundamental elements of the mind stimulation therapy (MST) model, which provides a rationale for using visually aided and multimodal strategies with special clinical populations. The examples of the techniques that we present are primarily drawn from our years of clinical experience using various visual and multimodal techniques to augment traditional therapy with various client populations. MST emphasizes the importance of enhancing "information processing" to promote adaptive thinking, feeling, and behaving. Information processing involves a multisensory process, which assists us in interpreting the information we receive from our physical and social environments so that we can best navigate and adapt to our particular life circumstances and the world around us. In addition to our auditory and verbal processing system, our information processing systems also include the following visual-motor processes:

- Our visual processing of information (e.g., *noticing a stop sign*)
- Our observations of our behaviors, actions, and body movements (e.g., *noticing that our hand is shaking or noticing that we just bumped into a chair*)
- Our observations of the behaviors of others (e.g., *noticing that a woman sitting on a bench is feeding her baby*)
- Our observation of changes in our immediate physical and social environment (e.g., *noticing that it just started to rain*)
- Our engagement in various visual-motor activities, such as walking, exercising, writing, typing, texting, and manipulating objects, to assist us in adapting to our immediate environment (e.g., *noticing that we just received a text message and need to respond to it immediately or participating in our favorite hobby of making puzzles*)

As information processing beings, we are continuously trying to determine how to best respond and adapt to our immediate social and physical environments. The process of adapting to our environment is guided by a variety of cognitive processes, such as attention (e.g., being able to pay attention to details and to sort out relevant and irrelevant aspects of the social world), working memory (e.g., holding information in our mind to mentally solve a problem), immediate or long-term memory (e.g., retrieving information from our immediate or past experiences to make decisions), logical associations (e.g., connecting our thoughts and information in ways that others can understand, agree on, and are logical and goal-directed), and problem-solving (e.g., creating solutions to problems). These cognitive processes, however, may not function optimally when we are experiencing psychological distress or when we are in environments that do not stimulate our multiple information processing systems by providing us with access to a multimodal communication format.

In the growing fields of neuroscience and mental health, various "cognitive stimulation therapies" and memory training programs have been emerging, which show promise in enhancing cognitive functioning and information processing capabilities. The popularity of mind stimulating activities is rapidly growing in the general public through the proliferation of websites and such cognitive skills training programs as Lumosity and CogniFit. Moreover, many apps are now available that are marketed as improving memory, problem-solving, and enhancing cognitive functions.

Research has shown that interventions designed to stimulate cognitive functions can possibly slow the rate of dementia in patients (Matsuda, 2007; Spector & Orrell, 2006; Spector, Orrell, & Woods, 2010; Woods, Thorgrimsen, Spector, Royan, & Orrell, 2006). Cognitive training has also been shown to slow cognitive decline in normal aging (Hertzog, Kramer, Wilson, & Lindenberger, 2008) and to produce sustained improvement in cognitive functions through such programs as the Advanced Cognitive Training for Independent and Vital Elderly (ACTIVE) (Ball et al., 2002). Rebok et al. (2014) conducted a 10-year follow-up for the ACTIVE study and found that the majority of elderly individuals who had improved in their problem-solving skills after cognitive training had sustained these benefits 10 years later. Research has also shown the benefits of memory training programs in improving prefrontal functioning and memory skills in ADHD (Gray et al., 2012; Klingberg, Forssberg, & Westerberg, 2002). Memory and attention training has also been shown to improve learning and memory deficits in children with acquired brain injury (Madsen, Spellerberg, & Kihlgren, 2010).

Research in schizophrenia has focused on cognitive rehabilitation designed to help access clients' intact cognitive functions and ultimately to improve their information processing and problem-solving skills (Kern, Glynn, Horan, & Marder, 2009). The National Institute of Mental Health (NIMH) has recently proposed guidelines for researching and testing interventions in schizophrenia (a program called MATRIS) that targets not only researching newer medications but also cognitive training exercises to help improve the cognitive deficits in schizophrenia (Geyer, 2010; Marder & Fenton, 2004). Cognitive skills training programs, such as Integrated Psychological Therapy (IPT) (Brenner, Roder, Hodel, & Corrigan, 1994; Roder, Müller, Brenner, & Spaulding, 2011), have been found to improve basic cognitive skills in persons with schizophrenia. Additionally, cognitive remediation programs have been used to help clients compensate for deficits in information processing and cognitive functioning (Eack, 2012; Hurford, Kalkstein, & Hurford, 2011; Wykes et al., 2007).

MST strategies are designed, in general, to stimulate information processing, problem-solving, logical thinking, and other cognitive functions. MST provides a multimodal structure to maximize clients' ability to understand and apply the information exchanged in therapy. Ultimately, by processing information more effectively in therapy, clients can better understand the ideas, themes, and concepts discussed and as a result apply this information to improve their adaptive functioning. Next we discuss the core multimodal strategies that we have used with various clinical populations.

## MULTIMODAL TECHNIQUES

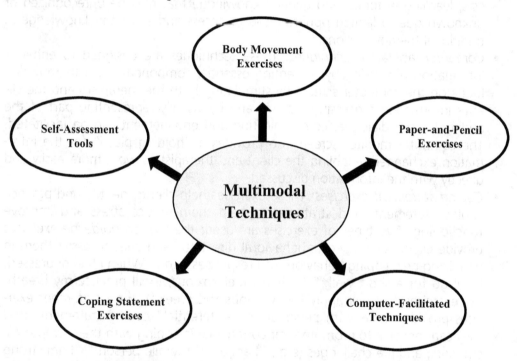

These multimodal techniques, which we describe in detail next, have been used with clients with persistent psychosis or schizophrenia, adolescents with behavior disorders, dual-diagnosed substance abuse clients, high-functioning developmentally disabled adults with challenging behavioral problems, and geriatric clients with compromised physical and psychiatric disabilities. These techniques have been adapted from our MST model and can be used in both individual and group therapy sessions based on the clinical needs and setting. We first discuss the various ways you can use these techniques in your individual sessions and then discuss how to integrate some of these techniques into a group therapy format (*the handouts associated with these multimodal techniques can be found in Appendix E*).

- *Body movement exercises*: These exercises are designed to help your clients focus attention on their own body movement and promote experiential "awareness of being alive." The exercises are also intended to help clients learn how awareness and visualization of movement, anticipation of movement, awareness of one's own and others' bodies, as well as awareness of one's immediate social and physical surroundings, can enhance adaptive thinking and ability to cope with one's present life circumstances.
- *Paper-and-pencil exercises*: These exercises are designed to help develop and stimulate your clients' logical thinking, problem-solving, memory, attention, and abstract thinking skills. These exercises are also intended to access clients' interests, learning histories, and general knowledge that may be unrecognized or unknown due to limited opportunities to access and share this knowledge in traditional therapy sessions.
- *Computer-facilitated techniques*: These techniques are designed to enhance information processing by presenting essential components of a therapy dialogue on the computer screen. By stimulating both the therapist's and the client's information processing systems and by visually representing part of the auditory-based dialogue, communication and engagement can be facilitated. The computer monitor screen also provides a "holding place" for the information exchanged, enabling the client and therapist to work more easily and directly with the information discussed.
- *Coping statement exercises*: These exercises help clients identify and practice coping statements and strategies to help them reduce stress and improve functioning. Two types of exercises are used: the *written guideline* exercises provide clients with specific behavioral directions and cues to assist them in practicing new coping behaviors and responses (e.g., "When I feel depressed, I will go for a short walk;" "When I feel anxious, I will practice my breathing exercises;" "I will apply for two jobs this week"); the *I statement* exercises provide clients with personal "self-referential" coping statements that they can rehearse to promote their confidence in coping with their symptoms, stressors, and life challenges (e.g., "I am a worthwhile person," "I am strong and can manage my depression," "I have always figured out how to cope with difficult situations"). Please note that these coping statements can be "pre-populated" based on the client's style or collaboratively developed. For example, they can be collaboratively developed on a worksheet or by using the computer-facilitated technique to promote more "ownership" in the client in generating the statements.
- *Genogram*: The genogram (see Appendix D) can be used to gather relevant and comprehensive family and historical information in a way that, for some clients, is easier compared to eliciting this information through a more traditional "verbal interview."

- *Self-assessment tools*: These entail brief assessment tools to measure the client's progress in therapy.


## BODY MOVEMENT EXERCISES

Movement signifies to us that we are alive and interacting with our physical surroundings. Research has shown that a part of our brain that controls movement and balance, the cerebellum, is not only important in promoting our coordination but also has "cognitive functions" through its interactions with higher-order parts of the brain associated with reasoning, memory, and learning (Gallese & Lakoff, 2005). Awareness of our body is critical as we navigate our movements in the physical and social world. As we move in our environment, our attention is directed outward as we locate our body in space in our immediate environment. Our brain is attending to the surroundings and assisting us in navigating and adapting to the physical and social world. You can think of movement as a "visually based" attentional activity. Due to the visual and motor attention needed to successfully navigate our surroundings, "internal ruminations" are less noticeable or are "redirected," and abstract reflections on our life are temporarily suspended (e.g., as one moves through a coffee shop locating the menu, standing behind others, reaching for money, and deciding when and what to order, one is likely to be temporality less preoccupied with negative thoughts, such as "I'm depressed and I'll never reach my life goals" or "I wonder if my back pain will ever get better").

The body movement exercises that we discuss have been adapted from the body movement exercises outlined in our MST protocol (Ahmed & Boisvert, 2013). These exercises involve movement activities with visual cues and prompts using principles of observational (visual) learning and modeling that can promote improved attention and well-being. Next we describe variations of these body movement exercises that can be incorporated into individual therapy sessions.


### The Body Movement Exercises

a. In the first version, ask your client to stand up with slightly bended knees, as in a skiing or tai chi position, with the weight on their both feet, having a sense of a firm connection of their body to the ground below (see figure on following page). Then instruct them to practice inhaling through their nose, slowly breathing into the stomach with their mouth closed, and exhaling with their mouth opened (you can also perform the exercise while sitting if it is easier without worrying about maintaining the skiing position if your client has mobility or balance difficulties, such as clients in nursing homes). Direct your client to notice the passage of air through their body as they breathe in and out in a rhythmic fashion (the therapist may demonstrate this first) with the count of 1–10, which can be said out loud as the client and therapist are practicing the exercise.

b. In the second version, your client can move both of their arms while maintaining the bended position and practicing the same rhythmic breathing exercise. The arms need to move up and down, making sure that both arms are always moving (i.e., not stopping at or near the shoulder level) to ensure awareness of constant movement and anticipation of movement before reaching the upper or lower limits. As your client raises their hands and arms, their palms are facing upward. As your client lowers their hands and arms, their palms are facing downward (see figure below).

c. In the third version, your client maintains a similar posture with slightly bended knees and heels anchored to the ground, with their arms and hands outstretched. This time they practice simulating a slow clapping motion, never touching their hands but keeping their hands constantly moving. They withdraw or retract their hands just before they touch, again repeating the exercises in a rhythmic motion coordinated with breathing and counting.

The body movement exercises are designed to promote the following:

- Relaxation
- Awareness of body movements
- Anticipatory movements
- Mental alertness and preparatory response
- Attention and concentration
- Sense of goal attainment
- Practice in positive redirection (when experiencing ruminating negative thoughts and feelings)
- Existential "affirmation" of being alive in the world

The body movement exercises can serve as a "redirection strategy" by directing clients' attention to their movement and by doing so interfering with their negative habits of thinking. Redirection strategies can also help clients access areas in their brain that promote problem-solving, logical thinking, and intact functioning. Engaging in redirection, often achieved through directing our attention to the environment and activating our visual information processing system, is an important process we all need to practice to help us maintain our productive daily routine and to reduce the effect of negative and stressful thoughts. Clients with persistent clinical conditions may characteristically be preoccupied with negative thoughts and feelings, making it difficult to engage in redirection without the aid of visual cues or prompts.

The body movement exercises can also be used to promote an existential perspective of affirming one's existence of being alive. Acknowledging and bringing attention to one's movement and actually "visualizing the movement" of one's body can generate positive feelings about one's continued existence in this world. Discussing existential themes and perspectives allows the therapist to support the client's practice of any spiritual or religious faith that clients may practice. This may be particularly relevant in working with elderly and disabled clients in nursing home settings and helping them cope with disabilities and end-of-life concerns. Many persistent mental health issues for adults may also have deeper roots in a client's "perceived existential crisis." Some clients may have developed unique adaptations to such experiences, expressed through their clinical symptoms, which therapists may need to integrate and attempt to understand in their psychotherapy work with the client (e.g., a client may report hearing voices and getting reassurance from the voices or using the experience of hearing voices as an affirmation that they are alive, have company, and are interacting with the world).

The body movement exercises can also promote awareness of how one is interacting with and responding to one's immediate environment. Clients can learn to be more aware of others and the elements in their immediate surroundings. Some clients may lose touch with this awareness of their body in relation to their surroundings due in part to limited social experiences and long-term adherence to a regimented daily routine that reinforces habitual actions and movements. Some clients have learned through association to perform some of their actions and movements outside of conscious awareness. Additionally, some may be preoccupied with their psychological problems, which may make them less aware of their body movements within the immediate environment (e.g., some clients may chronically bump into objects or people, not readily acknowledge or recognize others in their immediate personal surroundings, or forget to hold the door open for someone behind them).

Additionally, the body movement exercises can also be used to promote awareness of boundaries between oneself and others and to address the behavioral issues of "aggression" or boundary violations that involve some form of aggressive-like behavior. The body movement exercises can be incorporated into discussions of how, for example, free play and sports can promote such awareness. This awareness of our body movements and actions in relation to those around us, who also share our immediate environment, can be helpful in more carefully monitoring our behaviors in the presence of others and practicing more self-control. It may also help one from being a potential victim of another's unwanted physical closeness (which can sometimes border on physical or sexual assault) by making one more aware of the importance of ensuring that others understand and respect the limits and boundaries of one's physical space.

## Suggestions

- Post the instructions describing the body movement exercises as a reminder to practice the exercises.
- The time and schedule for individual practice of the exercises can be determined based on the client's style and motivation. Ideally, the exercise should be practiced at least once a day. Routine daily practice will allow the formation of a "habit," which your client can later "activate" when feeling distracted or distressed.
- Chart daily practice using body movement exercise recording chart. The chart can be used to evaluate compliance and progress and to record the benefits of the exercises.
- Encourage your client to develop a list of potential movement exercises that they can incorporate into their daily or weekly routine. For example, these exercises could include moving around the home periodically; vacuuming; cleaning one's bedroom; doing the dishes; painting; coloring; practicing tai chi, yoga, or stretching exercises; fixing something that is broken; working on a craft or light project; lifting light weights; gardening; or going for a walk in the neighborhood, at the mall, or at a local park.

## PAPER-AND-PENCIL EXERCISES

Paper-and-pencil exercises can be used to facilitate your client's engagement in the therapy sessions. "Neutral" paper-and-pencil exercises that are not specifically related to your client's psychiatric symptoms or behavioral problems can stimulate your client's attention and information processing. We promote the idea that discussing personal problems and developing therapy goals with less verbal clients or with clients who are not typical verbal therapy candidates can be facilitated by engaging in paper-and-pencil exercises for brief periods of time. This can occur prior to or after discussing the client's problem areas. If introduced early in the session, the paper-and-pencil exercises can stimulate the client's clarity of thinking, attention, logical reasoning, and memory processes and thus make them more "cognitively amenable" to discussing relevant mental health issues and topics. If the exercises are introduced later in the session, the exercises can stimulate the client's problem-solving and thinking skills and lead to a discussion of how to develop and practice effective coping skills to better manage their symptoms and problem areas.

> Paper-and-pencil exercises can enhance your client's degree of participation in the therapeutic dialogue. Using these exercises can be conceptualized as "tuning up the engine of the mind" (analogous to a car engine) so that the mind can function optimally in the therapeutic dialogue. As part of our daily routine, many of us engage in various forms of mind-stimulation activities involving the "visual information processing mode." These include such activities as reading newspapers, articles, or books; watching TV or news programs; browsing the Internet or social media sites; or engaging in other activities and hobbies, such as crossword puzzles, word searches, knitting, or crocheting. These activities involve our visual processing systems and serve to keep our mind alert, stimulate our cognitive functioning, and engage our inherent problem-solving capacities.

The paper-and-pencil exercises are intended to stimulate cognitive functions, such as logical thinking, reasoning, attention, abstract thinking, general knowledge, and memory functioning. Using these exercises in the therapy session can stimulate various cognitive functions and problem-solving skills that are intact but may be "dormant" or underused by your clients due to limited opportunities to practice these skills. The various paper-and-pencil exercises include analogies, similarities, grouping, classifying, categorizing, synonyms, antonyms, math, general knowledge, visual matching, and word searches.

## Guides for Using the Paper-and-Pencil Exercises

- Instructions: *"Let us do a couple of exercises to help you practice your thinking, problem-solving, and memory skills so that '**your mind can get tuned up like a car engine**' (you can use or omit this phrase depending on your client's age, personality, and functional level) and you can think better for yourself. This will help you get the most out of our therapy session and help you to better manage your current behavior by using your thinking and problem-solving skills to figure out what you need to do."*

- Select any of the sample exercises or any others that are relevant to the therapy topics and the client's particular style and interests.
- Use the exercises for brief periods of time or for any amount of time that is justified based on the client's performance of and tolerance for the exercises.
- Consider developing individual binders or "mini workbooks" that your clients can use for homework (additional exercises can be drawn or adapted from various educational resource workbooks or websites). For example, you can use various websites, such as word search websites (e.g., www.armoredpenguin.com/wordsearch/) to develop a word search on your client's favorite topic.
- Residential, school, or ward staff can use these exercises as a redirection strategy to interrupt certain behaviors by prompting clients who may be behaviorally disruptive to engage in a paper-and-pencil exercise. This allows staff to use positive redirection rather than processing or confronting long-entrenched behavioral habits that clients may have difficulty explaining or "reasoning away" through verbal interventions. For example, asking the client why they are acting a certain way or reminding them of the rules in the hope that the reminder will serve as a future deterrent to such behavior may serve to increase the client's agitation.

## COMPUTER-FACILITATED TECHNIQUES

Our published work going back to the 1990s has extensively highlighted ways to effectively use computer-facilitated therapy techniques in the therapy session. This entails using the computer monitor screen to visually represent the essential components of the therapy dialogue (see Figure 8.2). This technique has been used with clients with schizophrenia (Ahmed, 1998, 2002; Ahmed, Bayog, & Boisvert, 1997; Ahmed & Boisvert, 2006) and with adolescents (Ahmed, 2016; Ahmed & Boisvert, 2006). Figure 8.2 provides a diagrammatic presentation of the computer-facilitated therapy technique that we have used in our clinical practice with these client populations.

The computer word processing technique that we describe has been used with inpatient clients with persistent psychosis experiencing hallucinations and delusions who were regarded as being incapable of engaging in "reality-based conversations" and thus not considered "appropriate" for traditional conversational therapy and with residential and community support clients receiving services from community mental health centers (Ahmed, 1998, 2002, 2016; Ahmed, Bayog, & Boisvert, 1997). The computer-facilitated techniques were used to collaboratively engage the client in the following ways:

- Discussing and identifying current functioning and goals
- Developing cognitive behavioral coping strategies
- Developing reminder lists of "behavioral guides," such as how to adhere to a productive daily routine and how to manage specific symptoms, including anxiety, depression, or anger

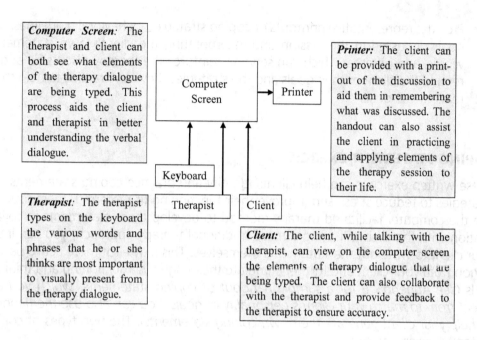

**Computer Screen:** The therapist and client can both see what elements of the therapy dialogue are being typed. This process aids the client and therapist in better understanding the verbal dialogue.

**Printer:** The client can be provided with a print-out of the discussion to aid them in remembering what was discussed. The handout can also assist the client in practicing and applying elements of the therapy session to their life.

**Therapist:** The therapist types on the keyboard the various words and phrases that he or she thinks are most important to visually present from the therapy dialogue.

**Client:** The client, while talking with the therapist, can view on the computer screen the elements of therapy dialogue that are being typed. The client can also collaborate with the therapist and provide feedback to the therapist to ensure accuracy.

*Figure 8.2* Computer-Facilitated Therapy Work Station

- Identifying personal goals, current functioning, history of past and current interventions, obstacles to goals, and steps to reach goals with behaviorally disordered adolescents (Ahmed & Boisvert, 2006) (see *IG Worksheet #13: Goal-Setting Chart* in Appendix A, which can be reproduced on the computer if using it as a computer-facilitated therapy technique)

## Features of the Computer-Facilitated Method

- Visually represents important elements or themes spoken or discussed in the collaborative therapeutic dialogue session to maximize communication and understanding and to assist the client in focusing more logically and coherently on a given topic or therapy theme
- Promotes effective communication for both the client and the therapist by allowing them to "visually evaluate" what is being discussed
- Promotes a more reality-based conversation between the therapist and client, ensuring that both understand more fully what the other is saying
- Promotes a more interactive and collaborative dialogue for clarifying personal goals, current functioning, identifying clinical problems and issues, and identifying the steps that clients need to take to reach their goals. The collaborative framework allows clients to take more ownership in addressing their therapy goals and in developing strategies to reach their goals

- Provides representative printouts of coping strategies, behavioral guidelines, and goals discussed in the session and incorporating the client's own statements, words, and phrases, which can serve to reinforce the therapy discussion and to remind the client of their goals and the strategies they can practice to help them reach these goals

## COPING STATEMENT EXERCISES

These written exercises can help clients identify and practice coping statements and strategies to reduce stress and improve their functioning (if preferred, therapists can use the computer-facilitated therapy method to develop these statements in collaboration with the client). If using a more traditional therapy approach, you can invite your client to write out the statements themselves. This may elicit more active participation from your client and further stimulate their cognitive functioning and thinking skills (*see Appendix E for a sample handout of coping statements, which you can select from to match your client's personality or goals. You can also use the handout to help your client generate their own coping statements*). The two types of coping statement exercises are:

a. *Behavioral statements*: These exercises provide clients with specific behavioral directions and cues to assist them in practicing new coping behaviors and responses (e.g., "When I feel depressed, *I will* go for a short walk;" "When I feel anxious, *I will* practice my breathing exercises;" "*I will* apply for two jobs this week"). You will notice that these are written as *action statements*.

b. *I statements*: These exercises provide clients with personal "self-referential" coping statements they can rehearse to promote their confidence in coping with their symptoms, stressors, and life challenges (e.g., "*I am a worthwhile person;*" "*I am strong* and can manage my depression;" "*I am smart* and have always figured out how to cope with difficult situations"). You will notice that these are written as *personality statements*.

## GENOGRAMS

The genogram is a popular technique that is presented here to emphasize the importance of using visually mediated strategies to elicit more comprehensive historical information from such populations as children and adolescents with learning disabilities, adults with auditory memory difficulties, and elderly psychiatric patients. These clients may have difficulty sharing affect-laden associations of family relationships and may provide only limited information during a more traditional "verbal interview." The genogram can serve as a "holding place" for the information, where the therapist and client can gather information though the visual structure of the genogram.

This allows the client to proceed at their own pace and gives them the freedom and control to discuss and provide whatever information they deem relevant.

The genogram can also cue the client's memory without requiring that they discuss or address any particular issue. We believe that by eliciting the information in this format, some clients may feel more comfortable exploring issues and themes at their own pace given that there are no specific "discussion" requirements. This may make them feel more comfortable sharing their feelings and deciding what they want to discuss. We believe that ultimately clients can more productively engage in discussing meaningful family history issues and their own emotional and behavioral issues when visual methods are used to prompt their responses (*see Appendix D for IS Worksheet #8: Genogram*).

## SELF-ASSESSMENT TOOLS

Today's business, medical, educational, and related service cultures routinely use questionnaires to solicit information from consumers and service recipients to assess their perceived satisfaction with the services and products they receive. In the mental health field, Seligman (1995) made a strong case for using such techniques as a legitimate evaluation tool in mental health practice. We have developed and used various self-evaluation tools and questionnaires to assess our clients' perceptions of their progress in reaching their goals. For some of our individual therapy clients, we have constructed self-rating scales for specific symptoms that they can rate in between sessions to monitor their status and to review with their therapist in future sessions. For some clients, such as developmentally disabled adolescents and adults or adults with persistent psychosis, we have assisted staff in constructing assessment scales that address targeted behaviors and goals. Both staff and clients can rate or review these scales and incorporate the information in follow-up sessions.

### Benefits of Using Self-Assessment Tools

- There is less time pressure in formulating responses and more opportunity to revisit and revise responses when one completes a questionnaire versus when one responds orally to questions.
- One can more objectively review one's progress over time by reviewing and reflecting on the recorded data versus relying on auditory memory.
- It allows therapists more time to review and reflect on a client's recorded responses.
- It is easy for therapists to present the data in a graphic chart form to assess progress or to use the data to communicate the client's status with other members of the clinical team.
- Thinking can become more focused and organized when one is provided with visual cues. Reading questionnaire items and providing written responses can

help reduce interference from internal preoccupations that may be more likely to occur when answering questions orally.

- Clients using visually presented targeted questions can become more reflective and objective in their assessments compared to when reporting their responses orally. They can review their responses and then more easily explain or clarify why they may have provided a certain response.

## THE MST GROUP FORMAT

Next we discuss ways to use various multimodal strategies in a group format for therapists who may be facilitating groups. We provide a framework developed from our MST model (Ahmed & Boisvert, 2013).

The group format we present, using a "simulated classroom structure," helps to promote a positive learning-teaching environment. We believe that such learning environments are integral to maximizing the therapy experience and to fostering positive and collaborative client-therapist interactions. This "classroom-like structure" minimizes emotional arousal or associations that can be triggered when discussing mental health issues in a more traditional therapy framework. The structure can also stimulate school learning behaviors and create a "mind-set" that activates the "learner" in clients and as such better prepares them to participate in the group activities. The group format is composed of the following activities:

1. *Body movement exercises*: The group will begin with a 2 to 3-minute body movement exercise to promote relaxation and to develop a "mental set" to prepare clients for the group.
2. *Group discussion*: The next phase of the group entails discussing various topics. The group discussions follow these two formats:
   a. *Reporting of the past week's events*: Group members take turns sharing an event or activity from their past week as well as an activity they have planned for the upcoming week. This helps clients stay focused on their present life events, interests, and activities.
   b. *Discussion of various topics using a classroom educational format:* Therapists may use any of the group members' "utterances" of any idea or thought and turn it into a discussion topic for the group. This may entail paraphrasing a statement from the client or, if needed, using a "browsing technique" that entails "clicking" on to a word, phrase, or topic that the client shared and using it to further explore a topic (e.g., similar to how one searches the web and clicks on to various links to open up new documents of information).
3. *Paper-and-pencil exercises:* These exercises are introduced after the group discussion phase. The exercises are designed to stimulate memory, abstract thinking, general knowledge, and problem-solving skills. In our group experiences, clients who may be somewhat distracted or unfocused during other group activities tended to become more focused during the paper-and-pencil exercises. The

visual cuing and novelty of the exercises promote more noticeable concentration, interest, and focused task involvement for many clients. The paper-and-pencil exercises should be selected so as to enable all clients independent of their educational background to achieve some level of success.

The exercises can be introduced in the following way: *"Some of you may find the exercises very easy to do and some may find them more challenging; this might reflect your different learning and educational backgrounds. It is not important to be able to finish all the items on a given exercise or to compare your performance to others. What is important is that you try your best and that you are doing some 'mind tuning' by exercising attention, concentration, thinking, reasoning, and stimulating your memory. All these are important skills to practice to help you figure out how best to solve or cope with your personal difficulties and goals."* It is not always necessary to give "corrective feedback" to clients during these exercises. It will depend on the degree of "cognitive rigidity" or "emotional arousal" that may be provoked by such feedback. Feedback can sometimes be more effective when it comes from other group members. During the process of feedback, however, the therapist may be able to introduce the importance of following social and conversational rules and the need for us to validate our thinking with others to help us best adjust to the current situation and to promote our recovery.

4. *Body movement exercises:* Ending the group with body movement exercises allows clients to achieve closure to the group with a sense of relaxation and positive feelings.

## GENERAL SUGGESTIONS

- *Be flexible with the group sequence.* Therapists can use their judgment in following the suggested group sequence. For example, therapists may sometimes choose to use the paper-and-pencil exercises following the body movement exercises if group members need assistance in settling in to the group process. Alternatively, if the discussion appears to be an engaging topic for all group members, you may choose to omit the paper-and-pencil exercise for the session.
- *Use co-facilitators if available.* Very often in group sessions, we have had the opportunity to have co-facilitators, such as graduate student interns or externs in various mental health fields, including doctoral-level clinical or counseling psychology students, master's-level psychologists, mental health counselors, and social worker clinicians or students. We have also used mental health clinicians working in inpatient or community residence programs who were able to provide individual attention or coaching to group members during the various group activities. Involving mental health workers in residential programs also allowed us to suggest using certain exercises as part of the resident's weekly or daily routine and to encourage the mental health workers to reinforce the resident's practice of the coping strategies outside of the group setting.

- *Discuss personal issues within a framework of universal themes.* Therapists can also use the group format to discuss any personal "trauma-related issue" that a client may choose to discuss. We recommend paraphrasing the discussion in a way to promote a general discussion about how people cope with "traumas" or other challenging experiences. The therapist can determine the overall sensitivity and privacy of a particular issue and may suggest further follow-up of the issue in individual therapy or with other mental health staff who may be working with the client.

- *Use an easel, white board, or blackboard.* Although in previous chapters we have discussed using the white board as a visual technique in outpatient therapy, we also recommend using it or an equivalent method (e.g., easel or blackboard) as a communication strategy for group counseling with the clinical populations we have mentioned. In group therapy you can use the blackboard, white board, or easel to enhance information processing and communication in a way that is analogous to a traditional classroom setting.

- *Be flexible with client participation.* Sometimes there are clients who choose to participate in only one or two aspects of the MST model and who may be reluctant to participate in other group activities. Instead of requiring that these clients participate in these activities, you can encourage them to continue to sit through the group, even allowing them to self-talk or to move around if needed. Therapists may also prompt them to do some other activities of their choice, such as paper-and-pencil drawings or doodling or even leaving the session for a brief period of time, as long as their behavior is not disruptive to the group.

## GUIDELINES FOR SPECIAL CLINICAL POPULATIONS

Next we suggest guidelines for using multimodal strategies as an adjunct to your typical sessions with your clients. At times the strategies can be used as "stand-alone" interventions whereby you choose to conduct an entire session focused on incorporating a specific intervention or strategy. You may also choose to design a series of brief sessions focused on incorporating a few of the interventions. In other cases, you may find it helpful to briefly incorporate one of the interventions into your typical sessions with some clients (e.g., you may decide to begin a session with a client using a brief body movement exercise or a paper-and-pencil exercise and then conduct the rest of the session using your typical approach). Given the wide variability of functioning between and within age groups and clinical populations, you may need to use your judgment on a session-by-session basis as to what elements of the MST multimodal strategies are appropriate for your clients or for a specific session with a client.

## CHILD CASES

Therapists can choose any of the following strategies in working with children with emotional and behavioral challenges who are seen in outpatient settings or who are receiving special education services in school settings:

1. *Body Movement Exercises*
   a. The exercises should be introduced with a clear explanation as to how practicing the exercises will promote one's functioning in educational, social, and family situations. Clinicians can emphasize that the body movement exercises can help us practice important skills, such as setting goals, controlling body movements, focusing attention, and learning ways to relax.
   b. Some of these exercises can be incorporated into traditional group play therapy for young children whereby a group member who may need individualized attention can be provided with a 10-minute individual session facilitated by a co-therapist while the other members continue to participate in the group session.
   c. For behaviorally challenged children attending a special education classroom, you may take a student out of the classroom for individualized attention for a 10- to 15-minute session.
   d. In individual therapy in private practice, you can begin and end a session with a body movement exercise to promote task involvement and direct engagement in the session.
2. *Paper-and-Pencil Exercises*
   a. Use as needed to engage the client and to build rapport and explore interests. You can adapt the exercises to the reading and interest levels of your client.

## ADOLESCENT CASES

Therapists may choose any of the following strategies in either individual or group psychotherapy with adolescents with behavioral challenges who may be receiving services in any of the following settings: special education programs, psychiatric inpatient units, community residences, home-based services, or outpatient settings. The strategies can be used as needed based on the client's interests and goals. You may find that during some sessions, some exercises work better than others and that your client is more responsive to certain exercises during a particular session. Some of the exercises can be used briefly to engage the client, and others may be used for longer periods based on the session's goals.

## Suggested Strategies

1. Body movement exercises (can use a recording form to monitor practice outside of the session)
2. Genogram exercise
3. Paper-and-pencil exercises (can be used for homework geared to the client's cognitive functioning)
4. Self-assessment exercises
5. Use a white board or easel to discuss and explore general knowledge, personal memory, and mental health issues
6. Computer-facilitated technique (can be used specifically in developing personal goals, identifying current functioning, evaluating current response to various treatment interventions, understanding the dynamics of one's mental health issues, and collaborating with clinician in identifying steps to reach one's goals [Ahmed, 2016] and also to develop specific cognitive behavioral statements or coping statements)
7. *Case example*: An adolescent client with ADHD was able to settle down more easily in talking about psychological and behavioral issues when the body movement and paper-and-pencil exercises were introduced at the beginning of a session or during "conversational therapy" when the client tended to demonstrate "hyperactive" and "off-task" behaviors. Often during the session, the therapist observed or noted difficulties without making comments and continued to engage the client in the exercises. Once a positive rapport was established by engaging the client in neutral paper-and-pencil exercises, the therapist was able to follow-up on the observed behaviors with staff and the family to further investigate the client's learning, school, and relationship difficulties.

## DEVELOPMENTALLY DISABLED ADOLESCENTS AND ADULTS WITH PERSISTENT BEHAVIORAL ISSUES

In working with these populations, it is important to consider the following:

- Psychotherapy and behavioral intervention plans should be actively supplemented with consultation with the client's program staff and family as deemed appropriate.
- Therapeutic strategies and prompts that are found to be effective in sessions with clients should be integrated using active prompts, reminders, and supports in the client's milieu and home environment so as to promote generalization of the interventions.
- It is important for the clinician providing psychotherapy to actively involve program staff, including working closely with the behavior analyst of the program in identifying the target mood status and behaviors for the intervention. Developing a behavior recording process can be helpful (e.g., one can use time-sampled measures that

staff can incorporate in their daily work routine) in evaluating behavior change and functioning, including the client's psychiatric medication response.

• The following suggested strategies can be incorporated during individual sessions and implemented in the client's milieu or home environment with staff and family assistance. It is often helpful to coordinate a "homework plan" for clients and discuss with staff and family members the value and rationale for using certain strategies and activities. Staff and family members can help monitor the client's progress and reinforce the importance of practicing the various strategies and activities that follow.

## Suggested Strategies

1. Body movement exercises (can use a recording form to monitor practice outside of the session)
2. Genogram exercise (can be completed with family members)
3. Paper-and-pencil exercises (can be used in session and for homework)
4. Self-assessment exercises (family and staff can share their impressions as well)
5. Coping statements

## CLIENTS WITH PERSISTENT PSYCHOSIS AND DUALLY DIAGNOSED CLIENTS WITH SUBSTANCE ABUSE AND MENTAL ILLNESS

In working with these populations, it is important to be flexible and to use the suggested strategies based on your clients' skills, needs, and interests. It can also be helpful to work with staff and family as needed to reinforce the client's practice of the exercises. Based on the client's treatment setting and program, you can adapt these strategies to individual and group formats and decide which elements of the exercises will be most effective. The exercises can be used in various ways to explore your client's interests, engage them in discussing various topics, help them to improve attention and concentration, and provide them with activities to assist them in thinking more clearly and working toward their individual goals.

## Suggested Strategies

1. Body movement exercises (can use a recording form to monitor practice outside of the session)
2. Paper-and-pencil exercises (can be used for homework geared to the client's cognitive functioning)
3. Self-assessment exercises
4. Coping statements
5. Use a white board or easel to discuss and explore general knowledge, personal memory, mental health issues

6. Computer-facilitated therapy (can follow the steps previously outlined in the adolescent section)

7. *Case examples*: These case examples illustrate how we have used some of these multimodal strategies with these clinical populations in a group format.

*Case #1*: A dual-diagnosed (schizophrenia and substance abuse) client in a community residential setting often kept quiet in the group sessions but was observed readily engaging in paper-and-pencil exercises. However, the client showed considerable difficulty in completing basic math and reasoning exercises. The client accepted feedback from the group when responses were shared in the group but continued to show limited involvement in the discussion phase, where he appeared to get easily confused. The client was also seen in individual sessions where he acknowledged having school learning difficulties and always struggled with learning basic math operations and reading comprehension. He was not diagnosed as a "special needs child" but appeared to have good practical knowledge and intact visual learning skills. Given this information, it was possible to do individual and group counseling with this client in a more effective manner by providing him with exercises and activities that he could accomplish and tolerate.

*Case #2*: An inpatient forensic psychiatric client (who was judged not guilty for a first-degree murder on account of mental illness) would not share any personal information in any previous therapy encounters other than nodding yes or no to basic routine questions. The client started attending the MST group and complied readily with the body movement exercises and the paper-and-pencil cognitive exercises. However, the client sat quietly during the group discussion phase, often refusing to say anything beyond one or two words, and never shared any personal information. Despite this, the client was able to do very well with the body movement exercises and the paper-and-pencil exercises. He chose to selectively respond only to immediate personal events but not to any remote personal or childhood memories or to any mental health questions.

## PHYSICALLY AND PSYCHIATRICALLY COMPROMISED GERIATRIC AND NURSING HOME CLIENTS

In working with these populations, it is important to consider the following:

- Consider the nature of the various forms of cognitive and physical disabilities that clients may exhibit.
- In most nursing homes, individual sessions often must be conducted in the client's bedroom or on the general ward with limited privacy.
- Record reviews and note-taking by staff often take place in the central open nursing stations.

- Formal or informal consultation and information exchange often occurs in the open ward or in the nurses' station.
- Sessions are most effective if they are brief (15–20 minutes) due to many nursing home clients having various physical and psychiatric disabilities that are compounded by their advancing age, which can influence their ability to sustain attention and endure certain activities.
- Consultation and suggestions must be very brief and clearly articulated with very little ambiguity, whether given orally or in writing. One needs to be brief in highlighting any history, personal dynamics, or therapy process. The focus should be on highlighting the most important elements that one needs to convey to staff, which can be unlike other clinical situations where clinicians may have more time to process, prepare, and communicate their reports to staff.
- In consulting with staff, one may consider the following guiding questions to help target realistic goals, specific client needs, and staff expectations for client change.

  - What is the client doing?
  - When is the behavior observed?
  - What are the realistic options that can be implemented by the staff and client to address the issue?
  - What is the expectation of change to observe in the client?

## Suggested Strategies

1. Use the body movement exercises (with wheelchair or bedridden patients, one can instruct clients to gently practice squeezing the wheelchair handles or bed bars and putting and releasing pressure to create a movement exercise). Please note that the body movement exercises are not designed to substitute for physical therapy exercises that may be recommended for some client's recovery from an injury. Rather, the body movement exercises rely on the client's intact "body movement functioning." One needs to be flexible and creative in designing appropriate exercises for clients, considering both their physical capabilities and their limitations. We have also provided consultation to physical therapy and occupational therapy personnel in nursing home settings to incorporate some of the body movement strategies primarily to prime client's receptivity to their other therapy and rehabilitation services. We have also encouraged other clinicians, including medication prescribers and mental health clinicians, to use elements of the body movement exercises as they deem appropriate to promote clients' engagement in and receptivity to services.
2. Use the genogram to promote discussion of family relationships and personal memory-related topics. Specifically, it can help some clients disengage from persistently reporting their long history of entrenched psychiatric symptoms, such as hallucinations and delusions.

3. Use neutral paper-and-pencil cognitive exercises, specifically simple math, word search, logical association, or general knowledge exercises, without necessarily giving any corrective feedback. Use the content to explore cognitive functioning and to identify areas of strength and "intact functioning" that can be productively used in the counseling process.

4. Use handouts related to the client's specific daily routine or coping statements that clients can be prompted to practice by the staff.

5. *Case example*: A nursing home client with reasonable high-functioning social skills and a history of mental illness (e.g., schizo-affective disorder) exhibited overt tremors and anxiety symptoms associated with a stroke. During counseling to address mood stabilization and anxiety issues, the client revealed problems with math exercises but otherwise displayed intact reasoning skills. Upon probing, the client admitted having a difficult childhood, having been placed in an orphanage for a "parental abandonment-related issue," and having an arithmetic learning issue for which he did not receive any special services. He managed to hold a job as a janitor but developed an alcohol addiction and a mood disorder. He had never shared these chronically bothersome negative school and childhood experiences with anyone. He was able to discuss these issues after completing various neutral mind stimulating exercises designed to stimulate his thinking, memory, and attention.

# 9

# Conclusion

We have tried to highlight and provide a strong rationale for the value of using various visually aided methods to augment traditional verbal therapy. We believe that the techniques we have described can serve as effective communication strategies to more actively engage clients' thinking, problem-solving, and communication skills during therapy sessions. By providing visual, auditory, behavioral, and movement interventions, we believe that therapists can facilitate clients' ability to access information, skills, knowledge, and responses that may not be as evident or accessible during ordinary therapy sessions. We believe that by using a multimodal communication format, both you and your clients will be able to collaboratively engage in creating a more focused and goal-directed therapeutic dialogue. Augmenting your therapy approach with these various techniques and methods can also provide you and your clients with a new "therapy structure." This visually mediated structure, incorporating the various diagrams, worksheets, and handouts presented throughout the book, can provide you with unique ways to design and augment therapy sessions with a wide range of outpatient clients. Additionally, the visually mediated and multimodal strategies that we described in Chapter 8 provide diverse strategies and interventions for a wide range of challenging clinical populations who display more persistent difficulties and behaviors that have not responded optimally to more traditional approaches.

To facilitate more optimal communication and engagement between the therapist and the client, we encourage you to be flexible in implementing a variety of multimodal strategies in your therapy sessions (see Figure 9.1 for the full VET model). We believe that by actively incorporating various VET techniques and elements of the mind stimulation therapy model, you will stimulate more active participation from your clients. You may already use some of these techniques we have described by, for example, providing written materials, handouts, assessment questionnaires, or homework assignments. However, we hope that our book offers new strategies and interventions to augment the interventions you may typically use and enables you to develop more confidence in using these visually aided therapeutic strategies creatively with your clients.

In using the various strategies we have discussed, it is important to be flexible and to adjust to the interests, skills, styles, and intentions of your client. Some clients will respond better to certain techniques, interventions, and approaches. It is also important to consistently display the core relationship-building skills with all clients (Norcross, 2011) and to regularly seek feedback (Prescott, Maeschalck, & Miller, 2017) to ensure that your approach is meeting your clients' needs and helping your clients

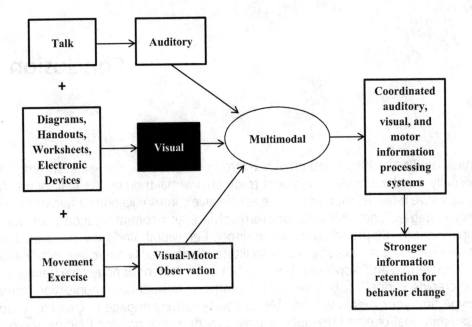

*Figure 9.1* Visually Enhanced Therapy Model

reach their goals. The amount of time you spend on any visually enhanced therapy method will depend on how your client responds to these methods and the observed and articulated benefits your client seems to be deriving from such methods. Some clients may be most comfortable in using a particular therapy session primarily for relationship support, which relies on using the more traditional conversational therapy mode. At times some clients may be overtly or covertly hesitant to use techniques that may require more focused attention on issues or problems. We encourage you to use your judgment as to the timing and readiness for certain clients to engage in some of the multimodal interventions.

We encourage you to try different visually mediated strategies as the need arises and as you and your clients work toward therapy goals. You may use visually mediated strategies more with some clients and less with others. For example, some clients will be eager to write during the session and may even reach for writing materials once they understand that this can be part of the therapy session. Other clients may be more comfortable at times with less structure and more traditional verbal exploration. Despite your clients' individual preferences and styles, most, if not all, will likely derive some benefit from using visually mediated strategies. Using written and visual materials can evoke a client's school learning experiences and naturally facilitate information processing through the multimodal methods available to them. Most of your clients will likely appreciate the novelty of the various visually mediated methods and may find themselves engaged in the session in ways that differ from how they have engaged in more traditional verbal therapy sessions.

## SOME FINAL SUGGESTIONS

- Equip your office and therapy station with visual materials and prompts. This will cue you and your client to use these materials in both planned and spontaneous ways in therapy sessions.
- Balance leading and following. Be mindful of when clients may be engaging in "reusable utterances" and reinforcing negative thinking habits by focusing too long on already established problem areas, but make sure you get the full story. Actively use redirection strategies when needed to keep clients focused on their therapy goals.
- Be creative, flexible, and practical in how you facilitate the session and in what you address.
- Allow your client to lead when needed and to use written materials as needed.
- Become familiar with the main teaching points that accompany the clinical topics and themes. This will enrich the therapy discussion and the relevance of the diagrams that accompany the clinical topics.
- Always maintain rapport and discover what your client responds to best in the session.
- Be creative and flexible with homework and follow-up on any tasks assigned.
- Assume the role of both teacher and student in working with your clients. This will enable you and your client to share and learn information during the therapy process and to establish an effective working alliance that acknowledges your client's needs, skills, and knowledge.
- Lastly, this book, with its diverse interventions, can be used by a variety of mental health disciplines, including mental health counselors, marriage and family therapists, social workers, school counselors, psychologists, and rehabilitation counselors. The psychoeducational nature of the book may also appeal to a broader range of clinicians, such as psychiatric nurses, psychiatrists, occupational therapists, physical therapists, recreational therapists, speech therapists, and nurse educators, all of whom function in the role of health-care providers. These roles often entail providing clients with information, teaching them skills, and facilitating the therapeutic learning process. The psychoeducational nature of the book provides a format that may appeal to this learning process. Facets of the book may also appeal to consumers and the lay public, as many of the concepts, handouts, and diagrams can be used selectively for self-help or self-growth.

# References

Ahmed, M. (1998). Computer-facilitated therapy: Reality-based dialogue with people with schizophrenia. *Journal of Contemporary Psychotherapy, 28*, 397–403.

Ahmed, M. (2002). Computer-facilitated dialogue with patients who have schizophrenia. *Psychiatric Services, 53*, 99–100.

Ahmed, M. (2016). Computer-facilitated therapeutic dialogue with adolescents with behavior disorders. *Adolescent Psychiatry, 6*, 140–147.

Ahmed, M., Bayog, F., & Boisvert, C. M. (1997). Computer-facilitated therapy for inpatients with schizophrenia. *Psychiatric Services, 48*, 1334–1335.

Ahmed, M., & Boisvert, C. M. (2003a). Multimodal integrative cognitive stimulating group therapy: Moving beyond the reduction of psychopathology in schizophrenia. *Professional Psychology: Research and Practice, 34*, 644–651.

Ahmed, M., & Boisvert, C. M. (2003b). Enhancing communication through visual aids in clinical practice. *American Psychologist, 58*, 816–817.

Ahmed, M., & Boisvert, C. M. (2006). Using computers as visual aids to enhance communication in therapy. *Computers in Human Behavior, 22*, 847–855.

Ahmed, M., & Boisvert, C. M. (2013). *Mind stimulation therapy: Cognitive interventions for persons with schizophrenia*. New York, NY: Routledge.

Ahmed, M., & Goldman, J. A. (1994). Cognitive rehabilitation of adults with severe and persistent mental illness: A group model. *Community Mental Health Journal, 30*, 385–394.

American Psychiatric Association. (2013). *The diagnostic and statistical manual of mental disorders* (5th ed.). Washington, DC: Author.

Anderson, T., Lunnen, K. M., & Ogles, B. M. (2010). Putting models and techniques in context. In B. L. Duncan, S. D. Miller, B. E. Wampold, & M. A. Hubble (Eds.), *The heart and soul of change* (2nd ed., pp. 143–166). Washington, DC: American Psychological Association.

Anderson, T., Ogles, B. M., Patterson, C. L., Lambert, M. J., & Vermeersch, D. A. (2009). Therapist effects: Facilitative interpersonal skills as a predictor of therapist success. *Journal of Clinical Psychology, 65*, 755–768.

Artino, A. R. (2008). Cognitive load theory and the role of learner experience: An abbreviated review for educational practitioners. *AACE Journal, 16*, 425–439.

Ayres, P., & Paas, F. (2012). Cognitive load theory: New directions and challenges. *Applied Cognitive Psychology, 26*, 827–832.

Baddeley, A. (1992). Working memory. *Science, 255*, 556–559.

Baddeley, A. (1998). *Human memory*. Boston, MA: Allyn & Bacon.

Baer, R. A. (2003). Mindfulness training as a clinical intervention: A conceptual and empirical review. *Clinical Psychology: Science and Practice, 10*, 125–143.

Ball, K., Berch, D. B., Helmers, K. F., Jobe, J. D., Leveck, M. D., Marsiske, M., . . . Willis, S. L. (2002). Effects of cognitive training interventions with older adults: A randomized controlled trial. *Journal of the American Medical Association, 288*, 2271–2281.

Barlow, D. H. (2014). *Clinical handbook of psychological disorders: A step-by-step treatment manual* (5th ed.). New York, NY: Guilford Press.

Beck, J. S. (2011). *Cognitive behavior therapy: Basic and beyond* (2nd ed.). New York, NY: Guilford Press.

Berends, L. (2011). Embracing the visual: Using timelines with in-depth interviews on substance use and treatment. *The Qualitative Report, 16*, 1–9.

Bourne, E. J. (2015). *The anxiety and phobia workbook* (6th ed.). Oakland, CA: New Harbinger.

Brenner, H. D., Roder, V., Hodel, B., & Corrigan, P. (1994). *Integrated psychological therapy for schizophrenic clients*. Seattle, WA: Hogrefe & Huber.

Brna, P. (2001). Learning to think and communicate with diagrams: 14 questions to consider. *Artificial Intelligence Review, 15*, 115–134.

Brown, K. W., & Ryan, R. M. (2003). The benefits of being present: Mindfulness and its role in psychological well-being. *Journal of Personality and Social Psychology, 84*, 822–848.

Burmack, L. (2002). *Visual literacy: Learn to see, see to learn*. Alexandria, VA: Association for Supervision and Curriculum Development.

Caudill, M. A. (2016). *Managing pain before it manages you* (4th ed.). New York, NY: Guilford Press.

Cavicchio, F., Melcher, D., & Poesion, M. (2014). The effects of linguistic and visual salience in visual world studies. *Frontiers in Psychology, 5*, 176. doi:10.3389/fpsyg.2014.00176

Chmielewski, T., & Dansereau, D. F. (1998). Enhancing the recall of text: Knowledge mapping training promotes implicit transfer. *Journal of Educational Psychology, 90*, 407–413.

Coffey, K. A., & Hartman, M. (2008). Mechanisms of action in the inverse relationship between mindfulness and psychological distress. *Complementary Health Practice Review, 13*, 79–91.

Conway, M. A., & Bekerian, D. A. (1987). Organization in autobiographical memory. *Memory & Cognition, 15*, 119–132.

Cowan, N. (2010). The magical mystery four: How is working memory capacity limited, and why? *Current Directions in Psychological Science, 19*, 51–57.

Czuchry, M., Newbern-McFarland, D., & Dansereau, D. F. (2009). Visual representation tools for improving addiction treatment outcomes. *Journal of Psychoactive Drugs, 41*, 181–187.

Dansereau, D. F. (2005). Node-link mapping principles for visualizing knowledge and information. In S. O. Tergan & T. Keller (Eds.), *Knowledge and information visualization* (pp. 61–81). Heidelberg, Germany: Springer-Verlag.

Dansereau, D. F., Dees, S. M., & Simpson, D. D. (1994). Cognitive modularity: Implications for counseling and the representation of personal issues. *Journal of Counseling Psychology, 41*, 513–523.

Dansereau, D. F., Joe, G. W., & Simpson, D. D. (1993). Node-link mapping: A visual representation strategy for enhancing drug abuse counseling. *Journal of Counseling Psychology, 40*, 385–395.

Dansereau, D. F., & Simpson, D. D. (2009). A picture is worth a thousand words: The case of graphic representations. *Professional Psychology: Research and Practice, 40*, 104–110.

Didonna, F. (Ed.). (2009). *Clinical handbook of mindfulness*. New York, NY: Springer.

Duncan, B. L., Miller, S. D., Wampold, B. E., & Hubble, M. A. (Eds.). (2010). *The heart and soul of change* (2nd ed.). Washington, DC: American Psychological Association.

Dunn, A. L., Trivedi, M. H., Kampert, J. B., Clark, C. G., & Chambliss, H. O. (2005). Exercise treatment for depression: Efficacy and dose-response. *American Journal of Preventive Medicine, 28* (1), 1–8.

Eack, S. M. (2012). Cognitive remediation: A new generation of psychosocial interventions for people with schizophrenia. *Social Work, 57*, 235–246.

Faust, D., & Ahern, D. C. (2011). Visuals in cases involving mental health evidence: Examples and illustrations. In D. Faust (Ed.), *Coping with psychiatric and psychological testimony* (6th ed., pp. 1025–1093). New York, NY: Oxford University Press.

Fletcher, J. D., & Tobias, S. (2005). The multimedia principle. In R. E. Mayer (Ed.), *The Cambridge handbook of multimedia learning* (pp. 117–133). New York: Cambridge University Press.

Freud, S. (2010). *The interpretation of dreams* (J. Strachery, Trans.). New York, NY: Basic Books.

Gallese, V., & Lakoff, G. (2005). The brain concepts: The role of sensory-motor systems in conceptual knowledge. *Cognitive Neuropsychology, 22*, 455–479.

Garrett, B. L. (2014). *Brain & behavior: An introduction to biological psychology* (4th ed.). Thousand Oaks, CA: Sage.

Gass, J. R. (2011). Trying cases visually: Understanding the effective use of visual communications in your legal practice. In D. Faust (Ed.), *Coping with psychiatric and psychological testimony* (6th ed., pp. 1005–1024). New York, NY: Oxford University Press.

Geyer, M. A. (2010). New opportunities in the treatment of cognitive impairments associated with schizophrenia. *Current Directions in Psychological Sciences, 19*, 264–269.

Gray, S. A., Chaban, P., Martinussen, R., Goldberg, R., Gotleib, H., Kronitz, R., . . . Tannock, R. (2012). Effects of a computerized working memory training program on working memory, attention, and academics in adolescents with severe LD and comorbid ADHD: A randomized controlled trial. *Journal of Child Psychology and Psychiatry, 53*, 1277–1284.

Hayes, S. C., & Strosahl, K. (2004). *A practical guide to acceptance and commitment therapy.* New York, NY: Springer.

Hayes, S. C., Strosahl, K., & Wilson, K. G. (1999). *Acceptance and commitment therapy: An experiential approach to behavior change.* New York, NY: Guildford Press.

Hertzog, C., Kramer, A. F., Wilson, R. S., & Lindenberger, U. (2008). Enrichment effects on adult cognitive development: Can the functional capacity of older adults be preserved and enhanced? *Psychological Science, 9*, 1–65.

Hill, L. H. (2006). Using visual concept mapping to communicate medication information to patients with low health literacy: A preliminary study. In A. J. Canas & J. D. Novak (Eds.), *Concept maps: Theory, methodology, technology. Proceedings of the Second International Conference on Concept Mapping* (pp. 621–628). San Jose, Costa Rica: Universidad de Costa Rica.

Hoffman, M. H. G. (2011). Cognitive conditions of diagrammatic reasoning. *Semiotica, 186*, 189–212.

Huettig, F., Mishra, R. K., & Olivers, C. N. (2012). Mechanisms and representations of language-mediated visual attention. *Frontiers in Psychology, 2*, 394. doi:10.3389/fpsyg.2011.00394

Hurford, I. M., Kalkstein, S., & Hurford, M. O. (2011). Cognitive rehabilitation in schizophrenia: Strategies to improve cognition. *Psychiatric Times, 28*, 43–47.

Jensen, E. P. (2008). *Brain-based learning: The new paradigm of teaching* (2nd ed.). Thousand Oaks, CA: Corwin.

Kabat-Zinn, J. (1990). *Full catastrophe living: Using the wisdom of your body and mind to face stress, pain, and illness.* New York, NY: Delacorte.

Kabat-Zinn, J. (1994). *Wherever you go, there you are: Mindfulness meditation in everyday life.* New York, NY: Hyperion.

Kabat-Zinn, J. (2015). Mindfulness. *Mindfulness, 6*, 1481–1483.

Kern, R. S., Glynn, S. M., Horan, W. P., & Marder, S. R. (2009). Psychosocial treatments to promote functional recovery in schizophrenia. *Schizophrenia Bulletin, 35*, 347–361.

Klingberg, T., Forssberg, H., & Westerberg, H. (2002). Training of working memory in children with ADHD. *Journal of Clinical and Experimental Neuropsychology, 24*, 781–791.

Kumar, S. (2010). *The mindful path through worry and rumination: Letting go of anxious and depressive thoughts*. Oakland, CA: New Harbinger.

Lambert, M. J., & Ogles, B. M. (2004). The efficacy and effectiveness of psychotherapy. In M. J. Lambert (Ed.), *Bergin and Garfield's handbook of psychotherapy and behavior change* (5th ed., pp. 139–193). New York, NY: Wiley.

Larkin, J. H., & Simon, H. A. (1987). Why a diagram is (sometimes) worth ten thousand words. *Cognitive Sciences, 11*, 65–99.

Leahy, R. L. (2006). *The worry cure: Seven steps to stop worry from stopping you*. New York, NY: Three Rivers Press.

Leahy, R. L. (2018). *Cognitive therapy techniques: A practitioner's guide* (2nd ed.). New York, NY: Guilford Press.

Leahy, R. L., Holland, S. J. F., & McGinn, L. K. (2011). *Treatment plans and interventions for depression and anxiety disorders* (2nd ed.). New York, NY: Guilford Press.

Ma, W. J., Husain, M., & Bays, P. M. (2014). Changing concepts in working memory. *Nature Neuroscience, 17*, 347–356.

Mace, C. (2008). *Mindfulness and mental health: Therapy, theory and science*. New York, NY: Routledge.

Madsen, S. N., Spellerberg, S., & Kihlgren, M. (2010). Training of attention and memory deficits in children with acquired brain injury. *Acta Paediatrica, 99*, 230–236.

Marder, S. R., & Fenton, W. (2004). Measurement and treatment research to improve cognition in schizophrenia: NIMH MATRICS initiative to support the development of agents for improving cognition in schizophrenia. *Schizophrenia Research, 72*, 5–9.

Martell, C. R., Dimidjian, S., & Herman-Dunn, R. (2010). *Behavioral activation for depression: A clinician's guide*. New York, NY: Guilford Press.

Matsuda, O. (2007). Cognitive stimulation therapy for Alzheimer's disease: The effect of cognitive stimulation therapy on the progression of mild Alzheimer's disease in patients treated with donepezil. *International Psychogeriatrics, 19*, 241–252.

Mayer, R. E. (2005). *The Cambridge handbook of multimedia learning*. New York, NY: Cambridge University Press.

Mckay, M., Davis, M., & Fanning, P. (2011). *Thoughts & feelings* (4th ed.). Oakland, CA: New Harbinger.

Miller, G. A. (1956). The magical number seven, plus or minus two: Some limits on our capacity for processing information. *Psychological Review, 63*, 81–97.

Miller, J. B., deWinstanley, P., & Carey, P. (1996). Memory for conversations. *Memory, 4*, 615–631.

Mousavi, S. Y., Low, R., & Sweller, J. (1995). Reducing cognitive load by mixing auditory and visual presentation modes. *Journal of Educational Psychology, 87*, 319–334.

Nathan, P. E., & Gorman, J. M. (Eds.). (2015). *A guide to treatments that work* (4th ed.). New York, NY: Oxford University Press.

Nesbit, J. C., & Adescope, O. O. (2006). Learning with concept and knowledge maps: A meta-analysis. *Review of Educational Research, 76*, 413–448.

Norcross, J. C. (Ed.). (2011). *Psychotherapy relationships that work: Evidence-based responsiveness* (2nd ed.). New York, NY: Oxford University Press.

Novak, J. D. (1990). Concept mapping: A useful tool for science education. *Journal of Research in Science Teaching, 27*, 939–949.

Prescott, D. S., Maeschalck, C. L., & Miller, S. D. (2017). *Feedback-informed treatment in clinical practice: Reaching for excellence*. Washington, DC: American Psychological Association.

Rebok, G. W., Ball, K., Guey, L. T., Jones, R. N., Kim, H. Y., King, S. L., . . . Willis, S. L. (2014). Ten-year effects of the advanced cognitive training for independent and vital elderly cognitive training trial on cognition and everyday functioning in older adults. *Journal of the American Geriatric Society, 62*, 16–24.

Roder, V., Müller, D. R., Brenner, H. D., & Spaulding, W. D. (2011). *Integrated psychological therapy (IPT) for the treatment of neurocognition, social cognition, and social competency in schizophrenia patients*. Cambridge, MA: Hogreffe.

Rogers, C. (1951). *Client-centered therapy: Its current practice, implications and theory*. London, England: Constable.

Roodenrys, K., Agostinho, S., Roodenrys, S., & Chandler, P. (2012). Managing one's own cognitive load when evidence of split attention is present. *Applied Cognitive Psychology, 26*, 878–886.

Ross, M., & Sicoly, F. (1979). Egocentric biases in availability and attribution. *Journal of Personality and Social Psychology, 37*, 322–336.

Roth, A., & Fonagy, P. (2004). *What works for whom? A critical review of psychotherapy research* (2nd ed.). New York, NY: Guilford Press.

Sapolsky, R. (2004). *Why zebras don't get ulcers: An updated guide to stress, stress-related diseases, and coping* (3rd ed.). New York, NY: W. H. Freeman.

Seligman, M. E. P. (1995). The effectiveness of psychotherapy: The Consumer Reports study. *American Psychologist, 50*, 965–974.

Spector, A., & Orrell, M. (2006). A review of the use of cognitive stimulation therapy in dementia management. *British Journal of Neuroscience Nursing, 2*, 381–385.

Spector, A., Orrell, M., & Woods, B. (2010). Cognitive Stimulation Therapy (CST): Effects on different areas of cognitive function for people with dementia. *International Journal of Geriatric Psychiatry, 25*, 1253–1258.

Stafford, L., & Daly, J. A. (1984). Conversational memory: The effects of recall mode and memory expectancies on remembrances of natural conversations. *Human Communication Research, 10*, 379–402.

Standing, L. (1973). Learning 10,000 pictures. *Quarterly Journal of Experimental Psychology, 25*, 207–222.

Stenning, K., & Oberlander, J. (1995). A cognitive theory of graphical and linguistic reasoning: Logic and implementation. *Cognitive Sciences, 19*, 97–140.

Stiller, K. D., Freitag, A., Zinnbauer, P., & Freitag, C. (2009). How pacing of multimedia instructions can influence modality effects: A case of superiority of visual texts. *Australasian Journal of Educational Technology, 25*, 184–203.

Stokes, S. (2001). Visual literacy in teaching and learning: A literature perspective. *Electronic Journal for the Integration of Technology in Education, 1* (1), 10–19.

Susskind, J. E. (2005). PowerPoint's power in the classroom: Enhancing students' self-efficacy and attitudes. *Computers & Education, 45*, 203–215.

Sweller, J. (1988). Cognitive load during problem solving: Effects on learning. *Cognitive Science, 12*, 257–285.

Sweller, J. (1993). Some cognitive processes and their consequences for the organisation and presentation of information. *Australian Journal of Psychology, 45*, 1–8.

Sweller, J. (2003). Evolution of human cognitive architecture. In B. Ross (Ed.), *The psychology of learning and motivation* (pp. 215–266). San Diego, CA: Academic Press.

Sweller, J. (2005). Implications of cognitive load theory for multimedia learning. In R. E. Mayer (Ed.), *The Cambridge handbook of multimedia learning*. New York, NY: Cambridge University Press.

Sweller, J., Ayres, P., & Kalyuga, S. (2011). *Cognitive load theory*. New York, NY: Springer.

Sweller, J., Van Merrienboer, J., & Paas, F. (1998). Cognitive architecture and instructional design. *Educational Psychology Review*, *10*, 251–296.

Tanenhaus, M. K., Spivey-Knowlton, M. J., Eberland, K. M., & Sedivy, J. C. (1995). Integration of visual and linguistic information in spoken language comprehension. *Science*, *268*, 1632–1634.

Titsworth, B. S. (2001). The effects of teacher immediacy, use of organizational lecture cues, and students' notetaking on cognitive learning. *Communication Education*, *50*, 282–297.

Todman, J. (2002). Pragmatic aspects of communication. *Proceedings seventh ISAAC research symposium* (pp. 68–75). Odense, Denmark, ISAAC: Toronto.

Tufte, E. (2006). *Beautiful evidence*. Cheshire, CT: Graphics Press.

Venn, J. (1880). On the diagrammatic and mechanical representations of propositions and reasoning. *London, Edinburgh, and Dublin Philosophical Magazine and Journal of Science*, *9*, 1–18.

Wade, N. J., & Swanston, M. T. (2013). *Visual perception: An introduction* (3rd ed.). New York, NY: Psychology Press.

Wampold, B. E. (2001). *The great psychotherapy debate: Model, methods, and findings*. Mahwah, NJ: Erlbaum.

Ware, C. (2008). *Visual thinking for design*. New York, NY: Morgan Kaufman.

Watkins, E. R. (2016). *Rumination-focused cognitive-behavioral therapy for depression*. New York, NY: Guilford Press.

Witt, P. L., Wheeless, L. R., & Allen, M. (2004). A meta-analytical review of the relationship between teacher immediacy and student learning. *Communication Monographs*, *71*, 184–207.

Woods, B., Thorgrimsen, L., Spector, A., Royan, A., & Orrell, M. (2006). Improved quality of life and cognitive stimulation therapy in dementia. *Aging & Mental Health*, *10*, 219–226.

Wykes, T., Reeder, C., Landau, S., Everitt, B., Knapp, M., Patel, A., & Romeo, R. (2007). Cognitive remediation therapy in schizophrenia. *British Journal of Psychiatry*, *190*, 421–427.

Zhang, J. (1991). The interaction of internal and external representations in a problem solving task. *Proceedings of the thirteenth annual conference of cognitive science society* (pp. 954–958). Hillsdale, NJ: Erlbaum.

Zhang, J. (1997). The nature of external representations in problem solving. *Cognitive Science*, *21*, 179–217.

Zhang, J. (2000). External representations in complex information processing tasks. In A. Kent (Ed.), *Encyclopedia of library and information science* (Vol. 68, pp. 164–180). New York, NY: Marcel Dekker.

# Appendices

# Appendix A

## Information-Gathering Tools

| Information-Gathering Tools | | |
| --- | --- | --- |
| *Information-Gathering (IG) Worksheets* *Coping Strategy (CS) Handouts* | | |
| **Method** | **Diagram** | |
| Timelines | Biographical Timeline—Adolescent Biographical Timeline—Adult Stressful Events Timeline Positive Events Timeline Clinical Condition Timeline Life Memories Timeline | IG Worksheet #1 IG Worksheet #2 IG Worksheet #3 IG Worksheet #4 IG Worksheet #5 IG Worksheet #6 |
| | | |
| Pie Graphs | Current Values Pie Graph Values Pie Graph Current Health Choices Pie Graph Health Choices Pie Graph Current Weekly Activities Pie Graph Weekly Activities Pie Graph Weekly Schedule Current Self Pie Graph The Self Pie Graph | IG Worksheet #7 CS Handout #1 IG Worksheet #8 CS Handout #2 IG Worksheet #9 CS Handout #3 CS Handout #4 IG Worksheet #10 CS Handout #5 |
| | | |
| Personal Interests Worksheet | Personal Interests Worksheet | IG Worksheet #11 |
| | | |
| Goal-Setting Worksheets | Therapy Problem Areas Goal Planning Goal-Setting Chart Brainstorming Life Goals Life Goals Plan (Health/Relationships) Life Goals Plan (Career/Financial) Life Goals Plan (Spiritual/Social) | IG Worksheet #12 CS Handout #6 IG Worksheet #13 IG Worksheet #14 CS Handout #7 CS Handout #8 CS Handout #9 |
| | | |
| Mind Maps | Mapping the Mind Remapping the Mind | IG Worksheet #15 CS Handout #10 |

# Timelines

# Biographical Timeline
# Adolescent

**Title:** _____

**Age**

| Childhood | Adolescence | Adulthood |
|:---:|:---:|:---:|

**Event**

## Reflections

Childhood:

Adolescence:

Adulthood:

# Biographical Timeline
## Adult

**Title:** _____

**Age**

| Childhood | Adolescence | Adulthood |
|---|---|---|

**Event**

**Reflections**

| |
|---|
| Childhood: |
| Adolescence: |
| Adulthood: |

# Stressful Events
# Timeline

**Events**

| Year | | | | | | | | |
|------|---|---|---|---|---|---|---|---|
|      |   |   |   |   |   |   |   |   |

**Reaction**

# Reflections

Themes

Coping Behaviors

Coping Philosophy _____

# Positive Events
# Timeline

**Events**

| Year | | | | | | | | |
|------|--|--|--|--|--|--|--|--|
| | | | | | | | | |

**Age**

## Reflections

Effect of Events

Interests and Skills

# Clinical Condition
# Timeline

**Condition:** _____

**Age**

| Childhood | Adolescence | Adulthood |
|---|---|---|

**Event**

## History

Triggers to Symptoms

|  |
|---|

Treatment

| **Medications:** _____ |
|---|
| **Therapy:** _____ |
| **Self-Help:** _____ |
| **Support Groups (AA/Church/Others):** _____ |

Most Effective Coping Strategies

|  |
|---|

# Life Memories
# Timeline

| Health (medical conditions, illness) | Family (parents, siblings) | Social (peers, dating, marriage) | Education (schooling, jobs, hobbies) |
|---|---|---|---|

**Positive Memories:**

**Negative Memories:**

**Positive Memories:**

**Negative Memories:**

**Positive Memories:**

**Negative Memories:**

**Positive Memories:**

**Negative Memories:**

Most Positive Memories: _____
_____
_____

Most Negative Memories: _____
_____
_____

Significant Medical and Mental Health Services: _____
_____
_____

Things You Are Most Satisfied With in Your Life: _____
_____
_____

# Pie Graphs

## Current Values—Pie Graph #1

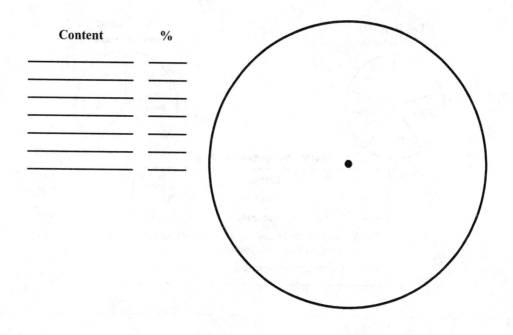

Content      %

_____   _____

_____   _____

_____   _____

_____   _____

_____   _____

_____   _____

## Desired Values—Pie Graph #2

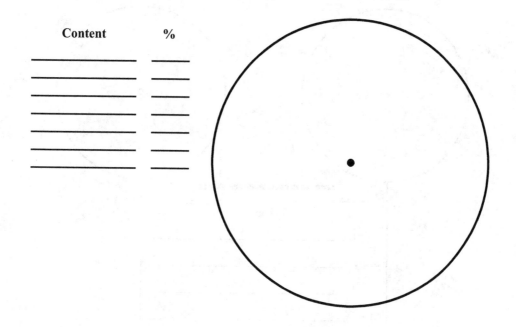

Content      %

_____   _____

_____   _____

_____   _____

_____   _____

_____   _____

_____   _____

# Values Pie Graph

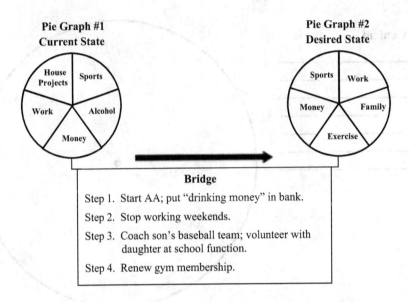

**Pie Graph #1**
**Current State**

**Pie Graph #2**
**Desired State**

**Bridge**

Step 1. Start AA; put "drinking money" in bank.

Step 2. Stop working weekends.

Step 3. Coach son's baseball team; volunteer with daughter at school function.

Step 4. Renew gym membership.

# Values

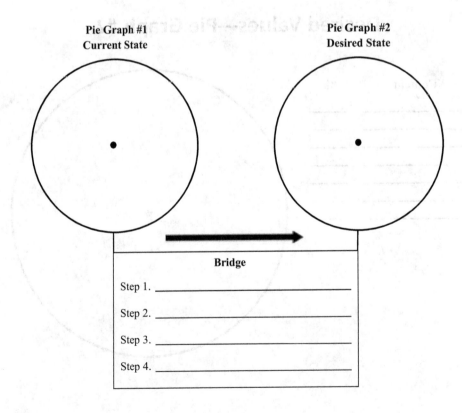

**Pie Graph #1**
**Current State**

**Pie Graph #2**
**Desired State**

**Bridge**

Step 1. _____

Step 2. _____

Step 3. _____

Step 4. _____

# Current Health Choices—Pie Graph #1

Content      %

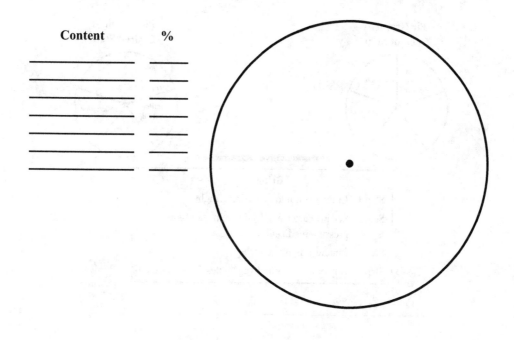

# Desired Health Choices—Pie Graph #2

Content      %

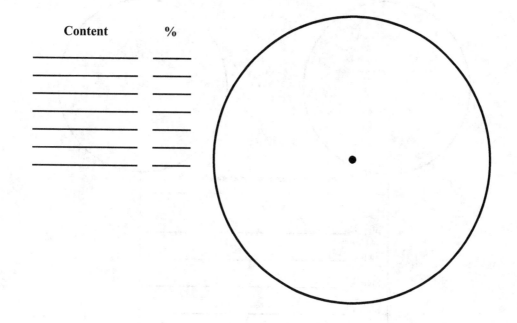

# Health Choices Pie Graph

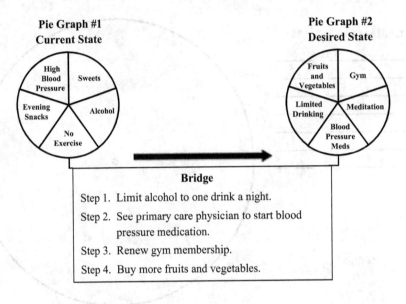

**Pie Graph #1**
**Current State**

High Blood Pressure | Sweets | Alcohol | No Exercise | Evening Snacks

**Pie Graph #2**
**Desired State**

Fruits and Vegetables | Gym | Meditation | Blood Pressure Meds | Limited Drinking

**Bridge**

Step 1. Limit alcohol to one drink a night.

Step 2. See primary care physician to start blood pressure medication.

Step 3. Renew gym membership.

Step 4. Buy more fruits and vegetables.

# Health Choices

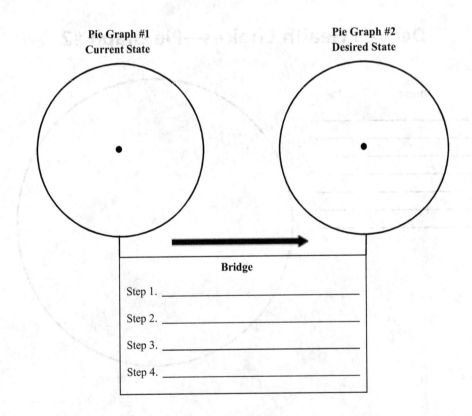

**Pie Graph #1**
**Current State**

**Pie Graph #2**
**Desired State**

**Bridge**

Step 1. _____

Step 2. _____

Step 3. _____

Step 4. _____

# Current Weekly Activities—Pie Graph #1

Content      %

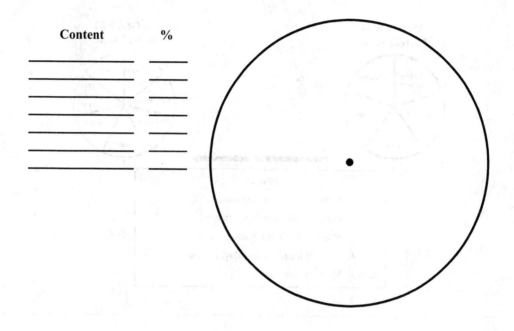

# Desired Weekly Activities—Pie Graph #2

Content      %

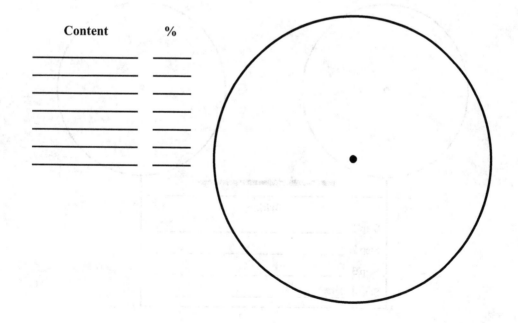

# Weekly Activities Pie Graph

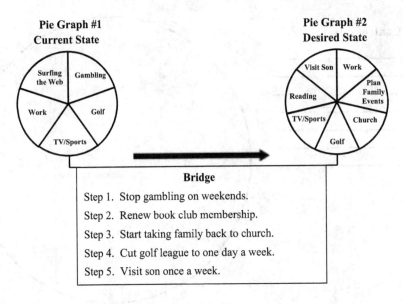

### Bridge

Step 1. Stop gambling on weekends.
Step 2. Renew book club membership.
Step 3. Start taking family back to church.
Step 4. Cut golf league to one day a week.
Step 5. Visit son once a week.

# Weekly Activities

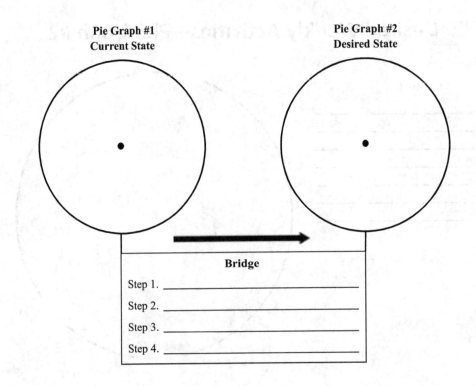

### Bridge

Step 1. _____
Step 2. _____
Step 3. _____
Step 4. _____

# Weekly Schedule

| Day | Mon. | Tues. | Wed. | Thurs. | Fri. | Sat. | Sun. |
|---|---|---|---|---|---|---|---|
| **Date:** | | | | | | | |
| 8–9 a.m. | | | | | | | |
| 9–10 a.m. | | | | | | | |
| 10–11 a.m. | | | | | | | |
| 11–12 p.m. | | | | | | | |
| 12–1 p.m. | | | | | | | |
| 1–2 p.m. | | | | | | | |
| 2–3 p.m. | | | | | | | |
| 3–4 p.m. | | | | | | | |
| 4–5 p.m. | | | | | | | |
| 5–6 p.m. | | | | | | | |
| 6–7 p.m. | | | | | | | |
| 7–8 p.m. | | | | | | | |

# Current Self—Pie Graph #1

Content        %

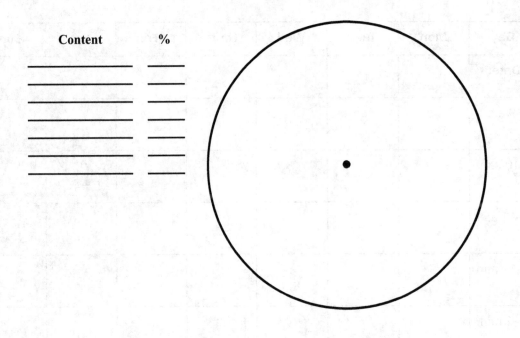

# Desired Self—Pie Graph #2

Content        %

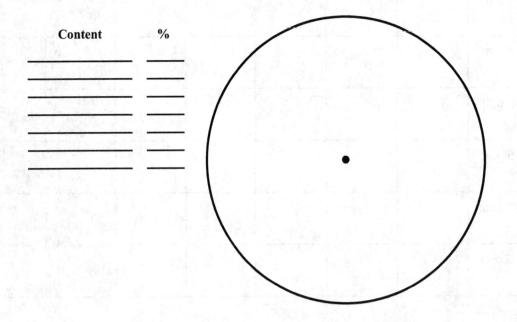

# The Self Pie Graph

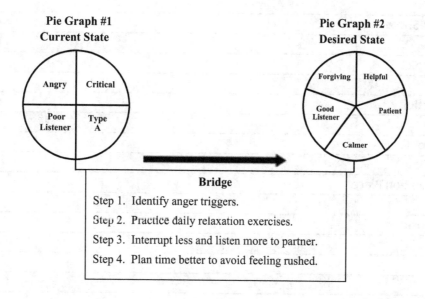

**Pie Graph #1**
**Current State**

Angry | Critical
Poor Listener | Type A

**Pie Graph #2**
**Desired State**

Forgiving | Helpful
Good Listener | Patient
Calmer

**Bridge**

Step 1. Identify anger triggers.

Step 2. Practice daily relaxation exercises.

Step 3. Interrupt less and listen more to partner.

Step 4. Plan time better to avoid feeling rushed.

# The Self

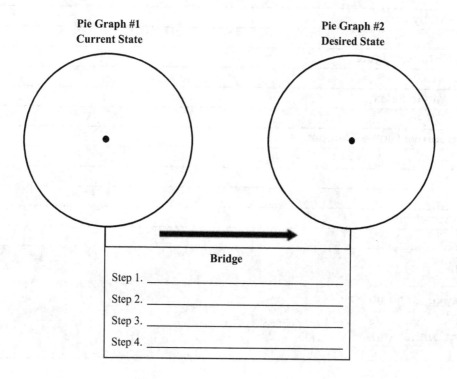

**Pie Graph #1**
**Current State**

**Pie Graph #2**
**Desired State**

**Bridge**

Step 1. _____

Step 2. _____

Step 3. _____

Step 4. _____

# Personal Interests Worksheet

| | |
|---|---|
| **Favorite TV Show** | |
| **Favorite Book** | |
| **Favorite Activity** | |
| **Favorite Movie** | |
| **Favorite Vacation Place** | |
| **Favorite Music** | |
| **Religion** | |
| **Favorite Discussion Topic** | |
| **Favorite Weekend Activity** | |
| **Favorite Hobby** | |
| **Favorite Historical Figure** | |
| **Favorite Way to Relax** | |
| **Most Supportive Family Member** | |
| **Best Friend** | |
| **Favorite Social Event** | |
| **Ideal day:** | |
| **Ideal way to spend time alone:** | |
| **Ideal time with friends:** | |

# Therapy Problem Areas

**Problem Areas (*circle all that apply*):** alcohol use, anger management, anxiety, avoidance, chronic pain, communication, depression, disorganization, distractibility, gambling, health problems, low motivation, low self-esteem, panic, parenting, phobias, procrastination, relationships, sleep problems, substance use, time management, work stress, other: _____

## Prioritize and Rate the Problems

|  | Severity 1–10 (1 = mild; 10 = severe) | Duration of Problem | Confidence in Resolving Problem (1 = low; 10 = high) |
|---|---|---|---|
| 1. _____ | _____ | _____ | _____ |
| 2. _____ | _____ | _____ | _____ |
| 3. _____ | _____ | _____ | _____ |
| 4. _____ | _____ | _____ | _____ |

## Therapy Goals

1. _____

_____

_____

2. _____

_____

_____

3. _____

_____

_____

# Goal Planning

**Goal #1:** _____

    **Step 1:** _____

    **Step 2:** _____

    **Step 3:** _____

    **Step 4:** _____

    **Estimated completion time (*circle one*):** next 1–2 weeks; next 1–2 months; next 3–6 months; next 6–12 months; next 1+ years

---

**Goal #2:** _____

    **Step 1:** _____

    **Step 2:** _____

    **Step 3:** _____

    **Step 4:** _____

    **Estimated completion time (*circle one*):** next 1–2 weeks; next 1–2 months; next 3–6 months; next 6–12 months; next 1+ years

---

**Goal #3:** _____

    **Step 1:** _____

    **Step 2:** _____

    **Step 3:** _____

    **Step 4:** _____

    **Estimated completion time (*circle one*):** next 1–2 weeks; next 1–2 months; next 3–6 months; next 6–12 months; next 1+ years

# Goal-Setting Chart

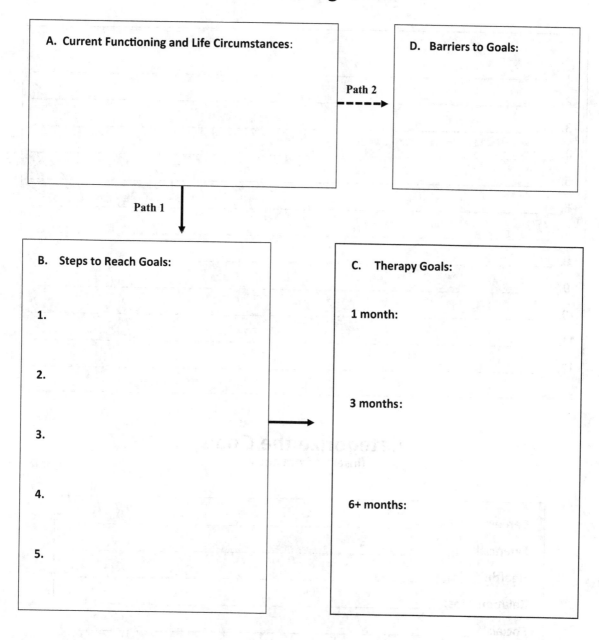

**A.  Current Functioning and Life Circumstances:**

**D.  Barriers to Goals:**

Path 2

Path 1

**B.  Steps to Reach Goals:**

1.

2.

3.

4.

5.

**C.  Therapy Goals:**

1 month:

3 months:

6+ months:

The goal-setting chart can be used to identify current functioning, therapy goals, and the steps needed to reach these goals. The chart is also used to identify barriers to reaching therapy goals. The aim is to follow path 1 versus path 2 to achieve success in reaching one's goals. *Notice that there is no arrow leading from the barriers to the goals. The only arrow that leads to the goals is the arrow coming from the steps.*

# Brainstorming Life Goals

1. _____
2. _____
3. _____
4. _____
5. _____
6. _____
7. _____
8. _____
9. _____
10. _____
11. _____
12. _____

# Categorize the Goals
### (insert # from above)

Career: _____

Financial: _____

Health: _____

Relationships: _____

Social: _____

Spiritual: _____

Other: _____

# Life Goals Plan

| Category | | 1–4 Weeks | 1–3 Months | 3–6 Months | 1 Year |
|---|---|---|---|---|---|
| **Career** | **Goals** | | | | |

**Steps**

1. _____

2. _____

3. _____

4. _____

5. _____

| | | 1–4 Weeks | 1–3 Months | 3–6 Months | 1 Year |
|---|---|---|---|---|---|
| **Financial** | **Goals** | | | | |

**Steps**

1. _____

2. _____

3. _____

4. _____

5. _____

# Life Goals Plan

| Category | | 1–4 Weeks | 1–3 Months | 3–6 Months | 1 Year |
|---|---|---|---|---|---|
| **Health** | **Goals** | | | | |
| | **Steps** | | | | |
| | 1. _____ | | | | |
| | 2. _____ | | | | |
| | 3. _____ | | | | |
| | 4. _____ | | | | |
| | 5. _____ | | | | |

| Category | | 1–4 Weeks | 1–3 Months | 3–6 Months | 1 Year |
|---|---|---|---|---|---|
| **Relationships** | **Goals** | | | | |
| | **Steps** | | | | |
| | 1. _____ | | | | |
| | 2. _____ | | | | |
| | 3. _____ | | | | |
| | 4. _____ | | | | |
| | 5. _____ | | | | |

# Life Goals Plan

| Category | | 1–4 Weeks | 1–3 Months | 3–6 Months | 1 Year |
|---|---|---|---|---|---|
| **Social** | **Goals** | | | | |
| | **Steps** | | | | |

1. _____

2. _____

3. _____

4. _____

5. _____

| Category | | 1–4 Weeks | 1–3 Months | 3–6 Months | 1 Year |
|---|---|---|---|---|---|
| **Spiritual** | **Goals** | | | | |
| | **Steps** | | | | |

1. _____

2. _____

3. _____

4. _____

5. _____

# Mapping the Mind

| Topics | Rarely (1) | Sometimes (2) | Often (3) |
|---|---|---|---|
| Past Events or Mistakes | | | |
| Future Events | | | |
| Family Members Certain People | | | |
| Work | | | |
| Health | | | |
| Exercise | | | |
| Spiritual Themes | | | |
| Household Tasks | | | |
| Politics Current Events | | | |
| Sports | | | |
| Success | | | |
| Finances | | | |
| Hobbies | | | |
| Other | | | |

For each topic place a check in the column (1, 2, or 3) that best reflects how often you think of the topic.

The way you would describe your mind (*circle all that apply*): noisy, calm, positive, negative, critical, supportive, reflective, detail-oriented, task-oriented, practical, rigid, flexible, confused

**Mind State Rating:** [    ]    1-------------10
                                    Calm        Noisy

# Remapping the Mind

**Current Mind**

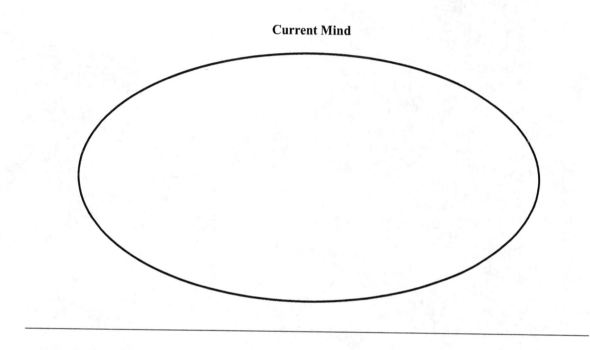

**New Mind**

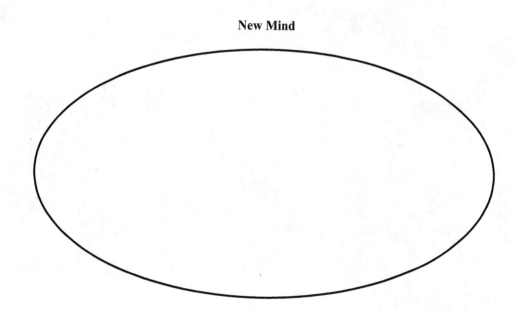

# Remapping the Mind

# Universal Therapy Topics: Diagrams, Worksheets, and Handouts

| Universal Therapy Topics | | |
|---|---|---|
| *Display Diagrams (DD)*<br>*In-Session (IS) Worksheets*<br>*Coping Strategies (CS) Handouts* | | |
| **Therapy Topic** | **Diagram** | |
| Mindfulness | The Time Circles<br>Visiting the Time Circles<br>Coping With the Time Circles<br>Staying in the Present | DD #1<br>IS Worksheet #1<br>CS Handout #1<br>CS Handout #2 |
| | | |
| Ambivalence | Ambivalence<br>Decision Making: The T-Path<br>Resolving Ambivalence: The 2As<br>Decision-Making: Pros and Cons | DD #2<br>IS Worksheet #2<br>CS Handout #3<br>CS Handout #4 |
| | | |
| Uncertainty | Uncertainty<br>Shining the Light of Certainty<br>Adjusting the Light of Certainty | DD #3<br>IS Worksheet #3<br>CS Handout #5 |
| | | |
| Stress | Stress Monitoring<br>Stress Meter<br>Stress Monitoring Form<br>Stress Management Strategies | DD #4<br>IS Worksheet #4<br>CS Handout #6<br>CS Handout #7 |
| | | |
| Communication | The Song of Communication<br>Tuning the 2Ts of Communication<br>Playing a New Station: The 3Ls<br>Communication Ambiguity | DD #5<br>IS Worksheet #5<br>CS Handout #8<br>CS Handout #9 |

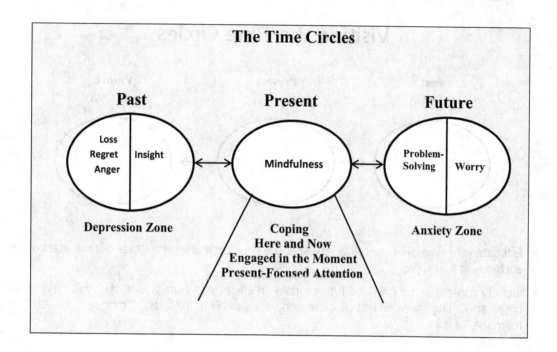

**The Time Circles**

Past        Present        Future

Loss
Regret
Anger | Insight

Mindfulness

Problem-
Solving | Worry

Depression Zone

Coping
Here and Now
Engaged in the Moment
Present-Focused Attention

Anxiety Zone

# Visiting the Time Circles

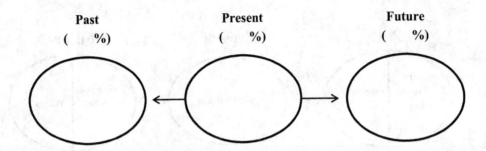

**Past**
(    %)

**Present**
(    %)

**Future**
(    %)

- Estimate your time circle *percentages* (list above each circle the percentage of time that you spend each day in that circle)
- Identify *content* in the past and future circles (in each circle write down what you tend to reflect on when visiting these time circles; use general words like "parents," "money," "health," "past marriage," etc.)

Purpose of visiting the circles (write down what your intended purpose is in visiting these circles; try to answer the question "Why do I visit these circles?")

Past: _____

_____

_____

Future: _____

_____

_____

# Coping With the Time Circles

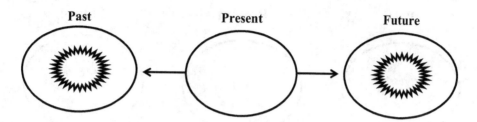

**⚙ Triggers:** Notice what triggers you to move into the past or future. Triggers can include other people, situations, conversations, memories, news events, activities, or times of day, such as nighttime. Write these triggers below.

**Past Triggers**

_____

_____

_____

**Future Triggers**

_____

_____

_____

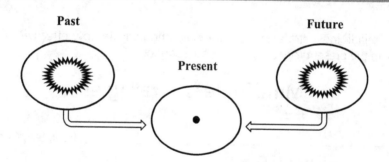

**● Redirection:** When you notice that you find yourself in a past or future zone, practice a redirection strategy to bring yourself back to the present. For example, you can practice a deep-breathing exercise, reengage in a task, or focus on an object in the room. Below, write the redirection strategies you practiced and how effective the strategy was (*circle one:* poor, fair, or good).

## Redirection Strategies

1. _____ Poor, Fair, Good

2. _____ Poor, Fair, Good

3. _____ Poor, Fair, Good

# Staying in the Present

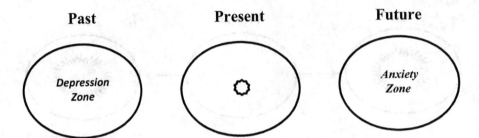

Signs that you might be starting to drift away from the present may include losing concentration, daydreaming, getting restless, or experiencing stress. Catching these early-waring signs is helpful in preventing yourself from entering the circle of the past or the circle of the future.

⬡ **Mindfulness:** You can practice various mindfulness strategies to keep yourself in the present. Some of these strategies may include practicing a breathing exercise, staying focused on the task at hand by devoting a specific amount of time to it before taking a break, reciting a favorite saying or prayer, writing out a to-do list, fixing something, talking to a friend, reading, going for a walk, or exercising.

Below, write the mindfulness strategies you practiced and indicate how effective the strategy was in helping you stay in the present (*circle one:* poor, fair, or good).

# Mindfulness Strategies

1. _____ Poor, Fair, Good

2. _____ Poor, Fair, Good

3. _____ Poor, Fair, Good

4. _____ Poor, Fair, Good

5. _____ Poor, Fair, Good

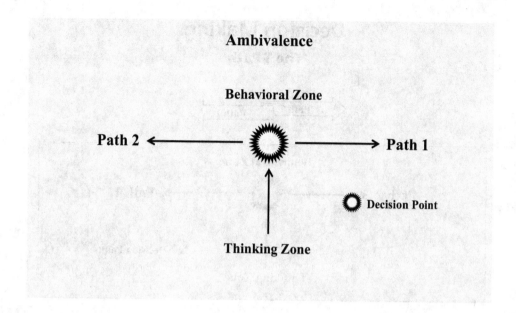

**Ambivalence**

**Behavioral Zone**

Path 2 ←                    → Path 1

○ Decision Point

**Thinking Zone**

# Decision Making
## The T-Path

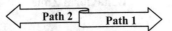

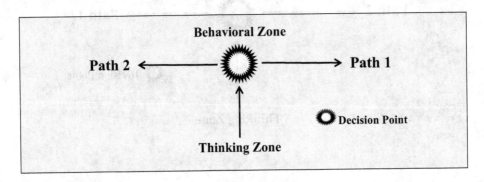

**Thinking Zone:** Write down ways you have made decisions in the past. What do you tend to reflect on in your thinking zone, such as the effect your decisions will have on others, your confidence in yourself, your ability to deal with the outcome of your decisions, or support or agreement you will get from others?

_____

_____

_____

_____

**Type of Decisions:** Below, list the types of decisions you need to make, such as financial, relationship, health, work, or family. Then describe the specific decision you need to make. Choose the appropriate CS handout to develop a plan (see the following example).

| Type of Decision | Specific Decision I Need to Make |
|---|---|
| **Example:** Relationship | Should I ask my partner to drink less? (CS Handout #3) |
| **Example:** Work | Should I work weekends or evenings? (CS Handout #4) |
| _____ | _____ |
| _____ | _____ |
| _____ | _____ |

# Resolving Ambivalence
## The 2As

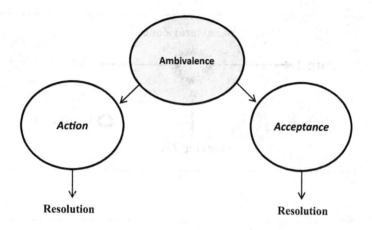

**Decision to Make:** _____

**My Decision** (*circle one*):                    **Action**                              **Acceptance**

---

**Action Plan** (I want to do something different by taking action. Below is my action plan)

1.

2.

3.

4.

**Acceptance Plan** (I don't really need to change anything. I can learn to just accept this and focus on other things. Below is how I will accept this situation).

1.

2.

3.

4.

---

# Decision Making
## Pros and Cons

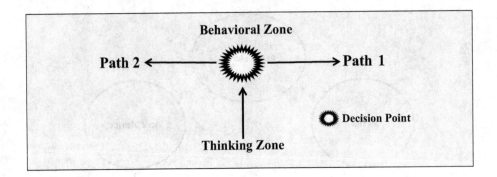

**Decision to Make:** _____

Behavioral Zone: Pros (+) Cons (–)

| Path 1 | Path 2 |
|---|---|
| **(+)** | **(+)** |
| 1. _____ <br> 2. _____ <br> 3. _____ | 1. _____ <br> 2. _____ <br> 3. _____ |

| **(–)** | **(–)** |
|---|---|
| 1. _____ <br> 2. _____ <br> 3. _____ | 1. _____ <br> 2. _____ <br> 3. _____ |

| Decision (*circle one*): | Path 1 | Path 2 |
|---|---|---|

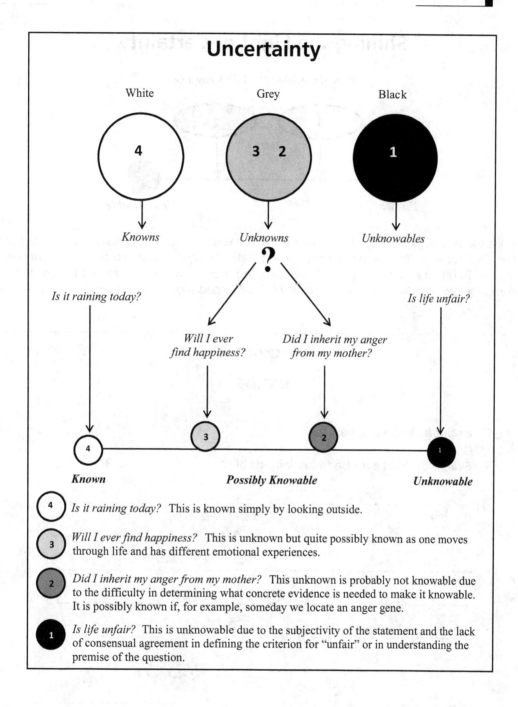

# Uncertainty

White        Grey        Black

**4**      **3  2**      **1**

*Knowns*     *Unknowns*     *Unknowables*

**?**

*Is it raining today?*         *Is life unfair?*

*Will I ever find happiness?*     *Did I inherit my anger from my mother?*

4    3    2    1

**Known**      **Possibly Knowable**      **Unknowable**

**4** *Is it raining today?* This is known simply by looking outside.

**3** *Will I ever find happiness?* This is unknown but quite possibly known as one moves through life and has different emotional experiences.

**2** *Did I inherit my anger from my mother?* This unknown is probably not knowable due to the difficulty in determining what concrete evidence is needed to make it knowable. It is possibly known if, for example, someday we locate an anger gene.

**1** *Is life unfair?* This is unknowable due to the subjectivity of the statement and the lack of consensual agreement in defining the criterion for "unfair" or in understanding the premise of the question.

# Shining the Light of Certainty

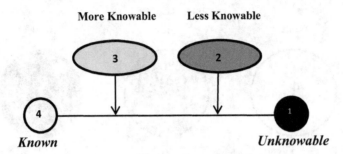

More Knowable    Less Knowable

3    2

4    1

*Known*    *Unknowable*

Below, list the events, behaviors, or questions for which you tend to seek certainty. Items listed should be posed as a question. Two examples are provided. Rate each question based on the *light of certainty scale* above. To rate the item, ask yourself the following: *How easy will it be to find the answer to the question? How will I know if I found the answer? What evidence do I need to answer the question?*

**UNKNOWNS**

**RATING**

*Example*: Will I live past age 75?    **1**

*Example*: Will I ever be financially stable?    **3**

_____    _____

_____    _____

_____    _____

_____    _____

_____    _____

_____    _____

_____    _____

_____    _____

# Adjusting the Light of Certainty

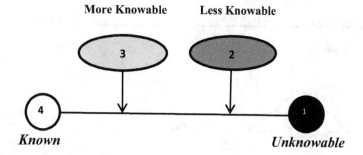

Below, list from IS Worksheet #3 the unknowns you identified. For unknowns you rated 2, put them in the "Less Knowable Column." For unknowns you rated 3, put them in the "More Knowable Column." Add any additional unknowns you struggle with to either column. In the bottom columns, write how you could either *answer* or *settle* these unknowns.

| More Knowable (3) | Less Knowable (2) |
|---|---|
| 1. *Example*: Are my GI symptoms cancer? | 1. *Example*: Did my deceased mom ever really love me? |
| 2. | 2. |
| 3. | 3. |
| 4. | 4. |
| 5. | 5. |
| **Ways to *answer* these unknowns** | **Ways to *settle* these unknowns** |
| 1. *Example*: Schedule an appointment with a GI doctor | 1. *Example*: She must have tried her best to love me but had trouble showing it at times. |
| 2. | 2. |
| 3. | 3. |
| 4. | 4. |
| 5. | 5. |

# Stress Monitoring

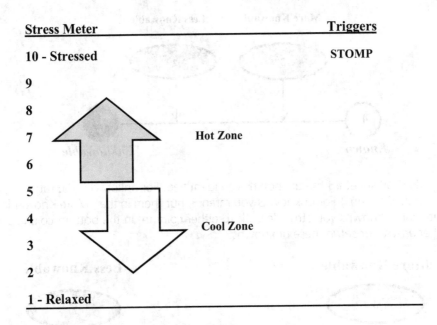

| Stress Meter | Triggers |
|---|---|
| 10 - Stressed | STOMP |
| 9 | |
| 8 | |
| 7 | Hot Zone |
| 6 | |
| 5 | |
| 4 | Cool Zone |
| 3 | |
| 2 | |
| 1 - Relaxed | |

## STOMP Triggers

**S**ituations: "I hate traffic." "Long lines at the grocery store bother me."

**T**houghts: "I never have anything interesting to say."

**O**verall Stress Level: "My chronic health problems always seem to stress me out."

**M**emories: "Why did my father always tell me what to say when I was a kid?"

**P**eople: "My aunt is talking about politics again. She always thinks she's right."

Notice small movement (e.g., 4 to 5) up the scale caused by STOMP triggers (You are getting upset, *stomping* your foot, and moving up the scale!).

# Stress Meter

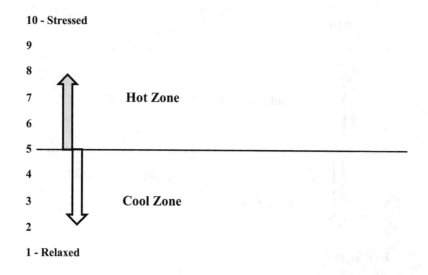

10 - Stressed

9

8

7       **Hot Zone**

6

5

4

3       **Cool Zone**

2

1 - Relaxed

---

### STOMP Triggers

**S**ituations: _____

**T**houghts: _____

**O**verall Stress Level: _____

**M**emories: _____

**P**eople: _____

---

Coping Strategies:

**1.** _____

**2.** _____

**3.** _____

# Stress Monitoring Form

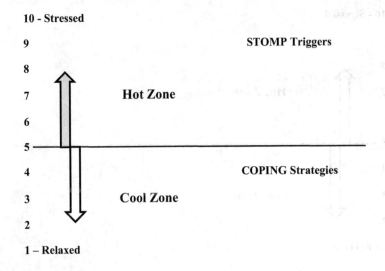

10 - Stressed

9                                          STOMP Triggers

8

7                    Hot Zone

6

5

4                                          COPING Strategies

3                    Cool Zone

2

1 – Relaxed

| Triggers: | **S**ituations | **T**houghts | **O**verall **S**tress | **M**emories | **P**eople |
|-----------|----------------|--------------|------------------------|--------------|------------|
| **Coping:** | **C**ount | **O**rder | **P**ause | **I**magine | **N**otice | **G**uess |

| STOMP Trigger | Rating | Coping Strategies | New Rating |
|---------------|--------|-------------------|------------|
|               |        |                   |            |
|               |        |                   |            |
|               |        |                   |            |
|               |        |                   |            |
|               |        |                   |            |

Use abbreviations for the STOMP triggers. Notice small movement (e.g., 4 to 5) up the scale caused by these triggers (e.g., you are getting upset, *stomping* your feet, and moving up the scale!).

©2019, *Using Diagrams in Psychotherapy*, Charles M. Boisvert and Mohiuddin Ahmed, Routledge

# Stress Management Strategies

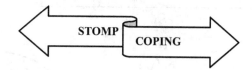

## STOMP Triggers

**S**ituations: "I hate going to this place; it's always so loud."

**T**houghts: "I never have anything interesting to say."

**O**verall Stress: "My chronic health problems always seem to stress me out."

**M**emories: "Why did my father always tell me what to say when I was a kid?"

**P**eople: "My aunt talks about politics all the time. She always thinks she's right."

## COPING Strategies

**C**ount:     Count to 10 slowly to center yourself.

**O**rder:     Order your priorities by deciding what is most important to do at this very moment to calm yourself. What would you order or put at the top of the list?

**P**ause:     Pause and slow down. Move more slowly. This will reduce stress in your body and slow down your thoughts.

**I**magine:   Imagine your future. How will it be influenced by what is happening right now? Is this event or situation critical, important, significant, or just a passing nuisance?

**N**otice:    Notice what you are thinking. Try to think of the situation in a different way.

**G**uess:     Guess or estimate your level of stress. Try to move the number down one notch.

# The Song of Communication

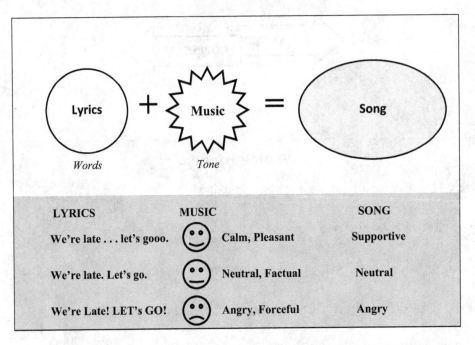

| LYRICS | MUSIC | SONG |
|---|---|---|
| We're late . . . let's gooo. | Calm, Pleasant | Supportive |
| We're late. Let's go. | Neutral, Factual | Neutral |
| We're Late! LET's GO! | Angry, Forceful | Angry |

*The same lyrics, combined with different music, can produce a different song.*

**The 2Ts of Communication**

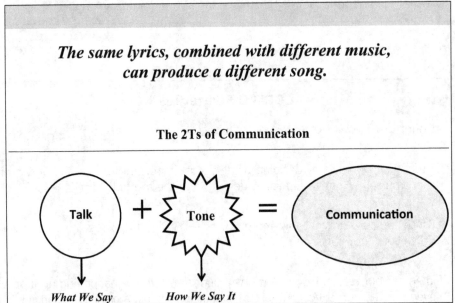

# ☀ **Tuning the 2Ts of Communication** ☀

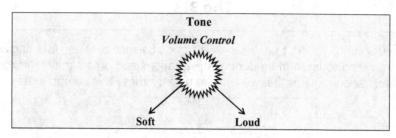

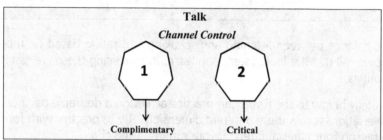

**In general, I would classify my communication style as (*circle all that apply*):**

a. **Tone** (*volume*): soft, loud, moderate, fast, slow, forceful, rushed, hesitant, emphatic

b. **Talk** (*channel*): complimentary, critical, complaining, supportive, detailed, inquisitive

### List below how you would like to change the *tone* and *talk* of your communication

| **Volume Control** | **Channel Control** |
|---|---|
| (*Change Tone*) | (*Change Talk*) |

_____     _____

_____     _____

_____     _____

CS Handout #8

# Playing a New Station
## The 3Ls

Effective communication requires that we achieve a good balance between listening and speaking. Some people may tend to listen more during conversations and others may tend to speak more. Effective communication requires that we learn to balance these two components.

To achieve a good balance between listening and speaking (a 3 rating based on the scale above), we can practice what we call the 3Ls: look, listen, and learn. By practicing these we can improve our communication with others.

Follow the 3Ls strategy below to see if you can practice achieving a desirable balance. Use the chart to monitor your conversations across these different dimensions. Try to practice with four different people or with the same person four times and record your ratings in the chart.

**Look** 👀 **Good eye contact, relaxed face**

**Listen** 👂 **Focused attention, head nods, encouragers ("Yeah," "Uh-huh," "Right")**

**Learn** 📝 **Check for understanding (reflect back story, feelings, meaning, and words)**

| Monitoring My Communication | | | | | |
| --- | --- | --- | --- | --- | --- |
| Person | L–S Rating | Look | Listen | Learn | Outcome |
| | | | | | |
| | | | | | |
| | | | | | |
| | | | | | |

**Rate yourself using the following scales: L–S:** (Listening 1–5 Speaking); **Looking:** (Poor 1–5 Excellent); **Listening:** (Poor 1–5 Excellent); **Learning:** (Poor 1–5 Excellent); **Outcome:** (Negative 1–5 Positive)

©2019, *Using Diagrams in Psychotherapy*, Charles M. Boisvert and Mohiuddin Ahmed, Routledge

# Communication Ambiguity

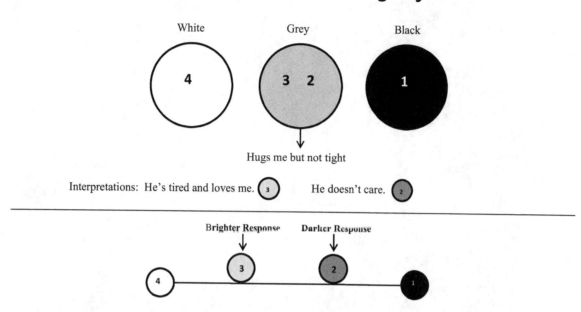

White      Grey      Black

4     3 2     1

Hugs me but not tight

Interpretations: He's tired and loves me. 3     He doesn't care. 2

Brighter Response     Darker Response

4     3     2     1

### Ambiguous Communication in My Relationship:

1. _____     2. _____

Possible Interpretations        Possible Interpretations

_____     _____

_____     _____

_____     _____

Brightest Interpretation        Brightest Interpretation

_____     _____

*Communication in relationships can often be in the grey or "difficult to interpret" areas and can cause us to pause and wonder why another is behaving or communicating in a certain way. A genuine intention from another may be misinterpreted as a self-serving or manipulative "maneuver." Our interpretation is likely to be based on such factors as our current state of mind and the history of the relationship. As you reflect on ambiguous communication in your relationships, notice the various interpretations you tend to make. Certain interpretations are "darker" while others are "brighter." It will often be difficult to know the "correct interpretation." Your interpretation won't necessarily confirm the "truth value" of the communication but will likely determine your ultimate mood and behavior. Work toward brighter interpretations.*

Communication Ambiguity

# Appendix C

## Common Clinical Problems: Diagrams, Worksheets, and Handouts

| Common Clinical Problems | | |
|---|---|---|
| *Display Diagrams (DD)* *In-Session (IS) Worksheets* *Coping Strategies (CS) Handouts* | | |
| **Therapy Topic** | **Diagram** | |
| Worry | The Worry Zones My Worry Zones Coping With the Worry Zones Managing Worry: The 2Rs | DD #1 IS Worksheet #1 CS Handout #1 CS Handout #2 |
| | | |
| Pain | The Pain Circuits My Pain Circuits Rewiring My Pain Circuits | DD #2 IS Worksheet #2 CS Handout #3 |
| | | |
| Rumination | Rumination The Hamster Wheel Managing Rumination: The 3Ds | DD #3 IS Worksheet #3 CS Handout #4 |
| | | |
| Mood Regulation | The Mood Wave Watching the Wave Depression Ditches and Joy Jolts Launching the Anger Arrows Resetting the Anger Arrows | DD #4 IS Worksheet #4 CS Handout #5 CS Handout #6 CS Handout #7 |
| | | |
| Motivation | Motivation Movement Goal Sheet Weekly Chart Immediate Goals: Plan | DD #5 IS Worksheet #5 IS Worksheet #6 CS Handout #8 |
| | | |
| Self-Esteem | Self-Esteem Shifting the Balance Self-Talk | DD #6 IS Worksheet #7 CS Handout #9 |

| Common Clinical Problems | | |
|---|---|---|
| Panic | The Wave of Panic<br>Mapping Panic: The Body Mines<br>Managing Panic: The Body Minds<br>The Changing Wave of Panic | DD #7<br>IS Worksheet #8<br>CS Handout #10<br>CS Handout #11 |
|  |  |  |
| Urges | The Hunger Urge<br>Detecting Urge Triggers<br>Surfing the Urge | DD #8<br>IS Worksheet #9<br>CS Handout #12 |

# The Worry Zones

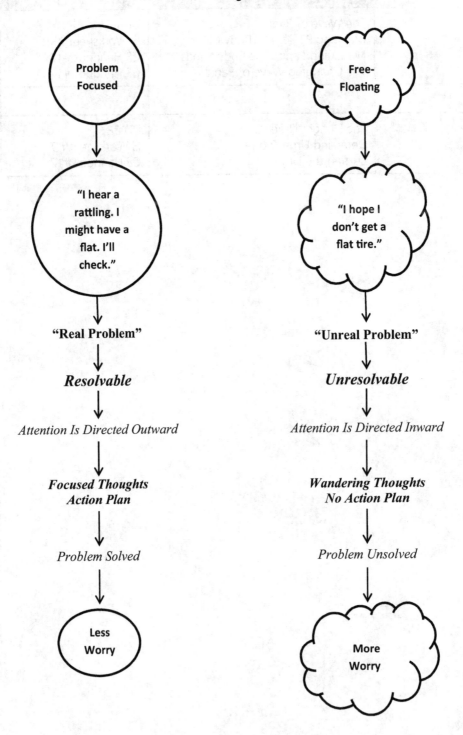

# My Worry Zones

**Problem-Focused Worries**

*Free-Floating Worries*

### My Problem-Focused Worries

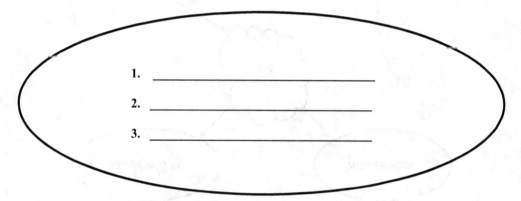

1. _____
2. _____
3. _____

### *My Free-Floating Worries*

1. _____
2. _____
3. _____

# Coping With the Worry Zones

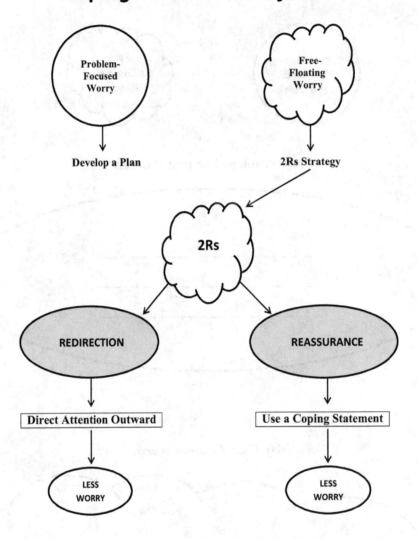

# Managing Worry:
# The 2Rs

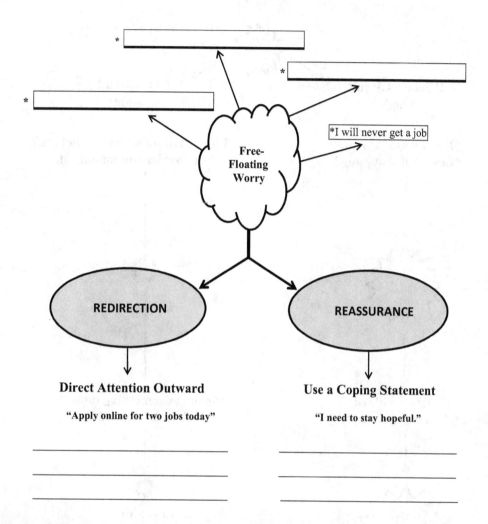

*I will never get a job

REDIRECTION

REASSURANCE

**Direct Attention Outward**

"Apply online for two jobs today"

_____

_____

_____

**Use a Coping Statement**

"I need to stay hopeful."

_____

_____

_____

* Write three of your free-floating worries at the top of the diagram. Then choose one and practice applying redirection and reassurance strategies to help you manage this worry. Under the categories of "Reassurance" and "Redirection," write the strategies you could use to cope with your worry. An example of each coping strategy is provided.

# The Pain Circuits

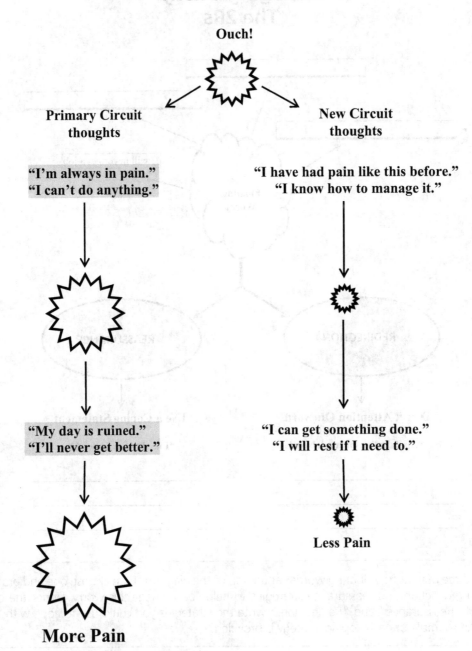

Ouch!

**Primary Circuit thoughts**

"I'm always in pain."
"I can't do anything."

"My day is ruined."
"I'll never get better."

**More Pain**

**New Circuit thoughts**

"I have had pain like this before."
"I know how to manage it."

"I can get something done."
"I will rest if I need to."

Less Pain

# My Pain Circuit

**Thought:** [                                        ]

**Thought:** [                                        ]

**Emotional Reactions:** [                                ]

**Behavioral Reactions:** [                                ]

[                                ]

[                                ]

## My Relationship to My Pain

**Example:** "I hate my pain." "I swear at my pain." "I'm always looking over my shoulder to see when my pain will show up." "My pain has disrupted my entire life and frequently causes me to cancel plans." "I wish it would just go away, but I feel it has taken over my life and I can't control it."

_____

_____

_____

_____

# Rewiring My Pain Circuits

**Ouch!**

↓

**New Circuit**

New Thought: ⬜

New Thought: ⬜

↓

New Emotional Reactions: ⬜

New Behavioral Reactions: ⬜

## My New Relationship to My Pain

_____

_____

_____

## Ways to Manage My Pain Triggers

**Example:** "Move more slowly." "Rearrange draws and shelves so that I stoop less." "Reduce stress by practicing breathing exercises three times a day." "Get up from my desk every hour to stretch."

_____

_____

_____

# Rumination

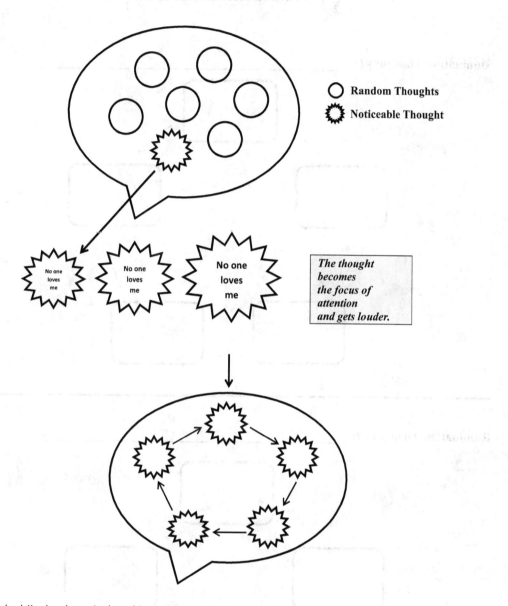

The thought hijacks the mind and is continuously repeated.

#  The Hamster Wheel

**Rumination Thought #1:** _____

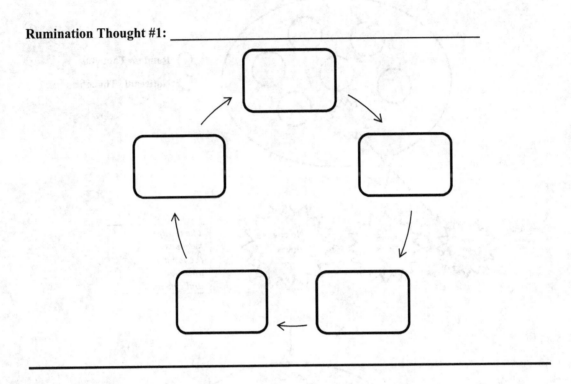

**Rumination Thought #2:** _____

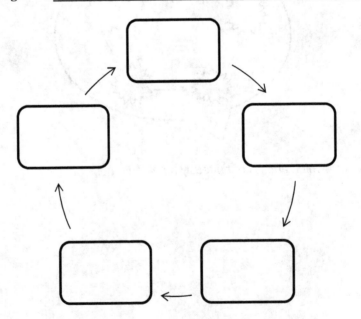

# Managing Rumination
## The 3Ds

*Detect* ⟶ *Decide* ⟶ *Dismiss*

| | |
|---|---|
| **Detect** the thought: | *Notice that you are ruminating again.* |
| **Decide** to stop: | *Make a decision to stop ruminating.* |
| **Dismiss** the thought: | *Dismiss the thought by redirecting attention.* |

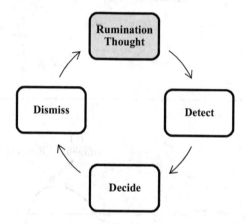

**Rumination Thought**: _____

| | Detect | Decide | Dismiss |
|---|---|---|---|
| | *What I noticed* | *What I said* | *What I did* |
| ***Example:*** **Home alone on Friday night** | I started thinking "nobody loves me." | I said to myself, "Stop thinking that. It only worsens my mood." | I decided to watch my favorite movie and then read a short book. |
| **Episode 1:** | | | |
| **Episode 2:** | | | |
| **Episode 3:** | | | |

Use the chart to practice managing the rumination thought you listed above. Record your responses for three different episodes.

# The Mood Wave

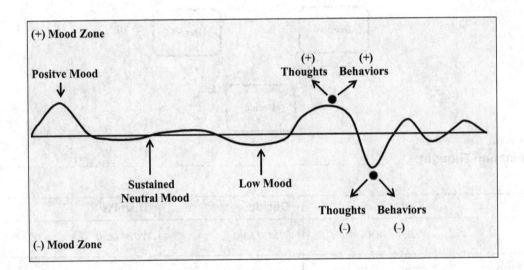

# Watching the Wave

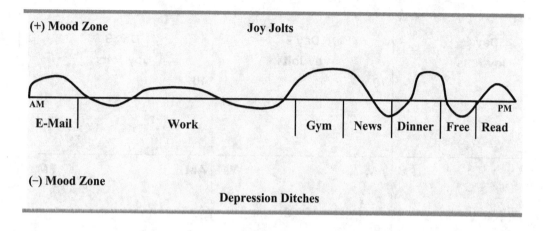

(+) Mood Zone

_____

AM                                                                    PM

(–) Mood Zone

| Vulnerable Periods (Depression Ditches) | Stable Periods (Joy Jolts) | Triggers (+) (–) |
|---|---|---|
| _____ | _____ | _____ |
| _____ | _____ | _____ |
| _____ | _____ | _____ |
| _____ | _____ | _____ |

# Depression Ditches and Joy Jolts

| Day 1 Joy Jolts | Day 2 Joy Jolts | Day 3 Joy Jolts |
|---|---|---|
| 10 | 10 | 10 |
| 5_____ | 5 | 5 |
| AM          PM | AM          PM | AM          PM |
| 1 | 1 | 1 |
| Depression Ditches | Depression Ditches | Depression Ditches |

| | Joy Jolts | | | | Depression Ditches | | |
|---|---|---|---|---|---|---|---|
| | *Example* | Episode 1 | Episode 2 | | *Example* | Episode 1 | Episode 2 |
| **Direction of Change** | 5→7 | | | | 5→2 | | |
| **Duration of Change** | 3 hours | | | | 30 minutes | | |
| **Internal Triggers (thoughts, memories)** | Kept thinking it was a nice day; was grateful for my family | | | | Told myself while sitting at my desk that I always make mistakes | | |
| **External Triggers (people, time of day, activity)** | Praised by boss; son called me; nice weather | | | | Woke up late; rushed to work; forgot my lunch | | |

**Mood-Elevating Strategies:** _____

_____

# Launching the Anger Arrows

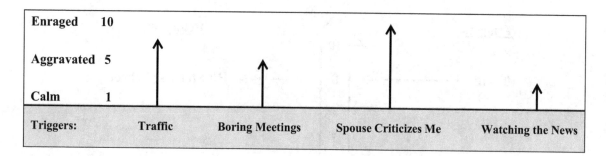

## My Anger Arrows

| Enraged | 10 |
| Aggravated | 5 |
| Calm | 1 |
| Triggers: | |

## Launching My Anger Arrows

| Triggers | Rating | Thoughts | Behaviors |
|---|---|---|---|
| What started it | 1–10 | What I thought | What I did |
| **Example**: Traffic jam | 8 | "I'm late again." | Hit steering wheel |
| | | | |
| | | | |
| | | | |
| | | | |

# Resetting the Anger Arrows

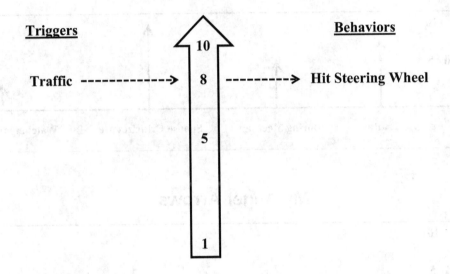

**Triggers**                                   **Behaviors**

Traffic - - - - - - - - → 8 - - - - - - - → Hit Steering Wheel

10

5

1

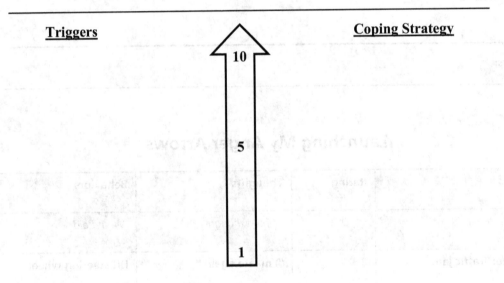

**Triggers**                                   **Coping Strategy**

10

5

1

# Motivation Movement

**A** = Mood     **B** = Activity

*Feeling Your Way Into a New Mood*

---

**Current Approach:** "When my mood improves, then I will exercise."

A ——————————————→ B

**A = Mood Improves**
**B = Exercise**

---

*Moving Your Way Into a New Mood*

---

**New Approach:** "When I start to exercise, then my mood will improve."

B ——————————————→ A

**B = Exercise**
**A = Mood Improves**

---

**Start "B" Activities to Improve Your Mood**

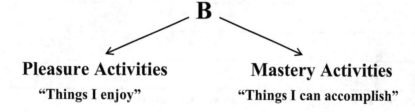

**Pleasure Activities**
"Things I enjoy"

**Mastery Activities**
"Things I can accomplish"

# Goal Sheet

## Immediate Goals

_____          _____

_____          _____

_____          _____

_____          _____

## Prioritizing Immediate Goals

|  | Complete Goals by This Day | Estimated Time to Complete |
|---|---|---|
| 1. _____ | _____ | _____ |
| 2. _____ | _____ | _____ |
| 3. _____ | _____ | _____ |
| 4. _____ | _____ | _____ |
| 5. _____ | _____ | _____ |
| 6. _____ | _____ | _____ |
| 7. _____ | _____ | _____ |
| 8. _____ | _____ | _____ |

*Note*. Use IS Worksheet #7 to insert projected completion dates into the weekly chart.

# Weekly Chart

| Day | Mon. | Tues. | Wed. | Thurs. | Fri. | Sat. | Sun. |
|---|---|---|---|---|---|---|---|
| **Date:** | | | | | | | |
| 12–7 a.m. | | | | | | | |
| 7–8 a.m. | | | | | | | |
| 8–9 a.m. | | | | | | | |
| 9–10 a.m. | | | | | | | |
| 10–11 a.m. | | | | | | | |
| 11–12 p.m. | | | | | | | |
| 12–1 p.m. | | | | | | | |
| 1–2 p.m. | | | | | | | |
| 2–3 p.m. | | | | | | | |
| 3–4 p.m. | | | | | | | |
| 4–5 p.m. | | | | | | | |
| 5–6 p.m. | | | | | | | |
| 6–7 p.m. | | | | | | | |
| 7–8 p.m. | | | | | | | |
| 8–9 p.m. | | | | | | | |
| 9–10 p.m. | | | | | | | |
| 10–11 p.m. | | | | | | | |
| 11–12 a.m. | | | | | | | |

# Immediate Goals

## Plan

| Goal | Steps | Completion Date |
|------|-------|-----------------|
| **1.** | _____ <br> _____ | |
| **2.** | _____ <br> _____ | |
| **3.** | _____ <br> _____ | |
| **4.** | _____ <br> _____ | |
| **5.** | _____ <br> _____ | |
| **6.** | _____ <br> _____ | |
| **7.** | _____ <br> _____ | |
| **8.** | _____ <br> _____ | |

# Self-Esteem

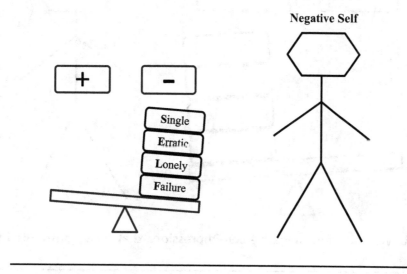

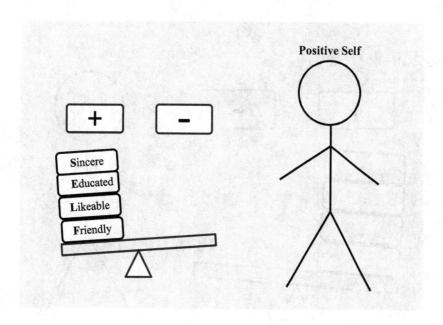

# Shifting the Balance

**Old Self**

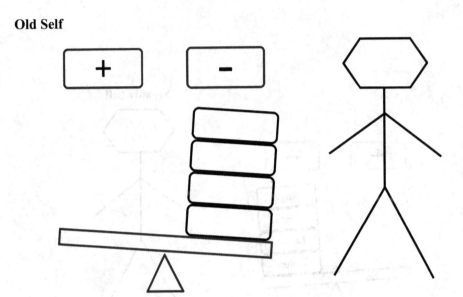

**In the boxes above, write four negative self-impressions that have contributed to low self-esteem.**

**New Self**

**In the boxes above, write four positive self-impressions that can contribute to improved self-esteem.**

# Self-Talk

## Positive Self-Statements

1. _____

2. _____

3. _____

4. _____

5. _____

6. _____

7. _____

8. _____

**My Go-To Positive Self Statement:** _____

_____

# The Wave of Panic

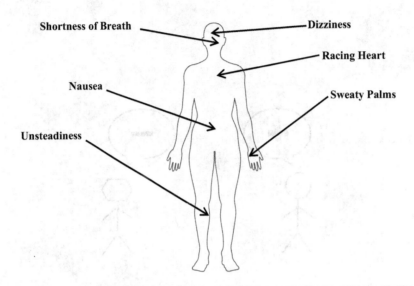

Shortness of Breath · Dizziness · Racing Heart · Nausea · Sweaty Palms · Unsteadiness

Panic is characterized by a variety of physical symptoms that can be experienced in different parts of the body. A wave of panic often circulates around the body.

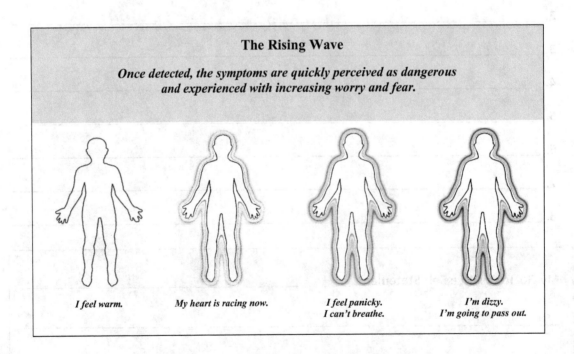

**The Rising Wave**

*Once detected, the symptoms are quickly perceived as dangerous and experienced with increasing worry and fear.*

*I feel warm.* · *My heart is racing now.* · *I feel panicky. I can't breathe.* · *I'm dizzy. I'm going to pass out.*

# Mapping Panic:
# The Body Mines

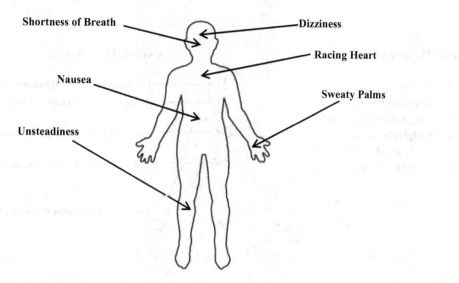

Shortness of Breath — Dizziness

Nausea — Racing Heart

Unsteadiness — Sweaty Palms

Panic is characterized by a variety of physical symptoms that can be experienced in different parts of the body. You can think of these parts of the body as "mines" that erupt during panic. This eruption produces a wave of panic that circulates around the body.

**Circle your panic symptoms:** racing heart, rapid breathing, heart palpitations, dizziness, shortness of breath, tingling in hands, nausea, sweaty palms, unsteadiness, muscle tension, dry mouth, blurred vision, shaking, chills, heat sensations, chest pain, choking sensations

**Using the diagram above as a guide, locate on the figure your most active mines.**

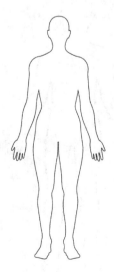

# Managing Panic
## The Body Minds

*Panic Thoughts*

1. *I will faint*
2. *I will stop breathing.*
3. *I might have a heart attack.*
4. *I might throw up.*
5. *My hands shouldn't s weat.*
6. *I will fall down.*

Coping Thoughts

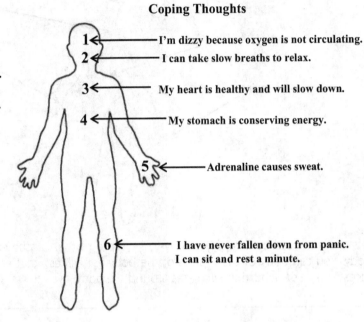

1← I'm dizzy because oxygen is not circulating.
2← I can take slow breaths to relax.
3← My heart is healthy and will slow down.
4← My stomach is conserving energy.
5← Adrenaline causes sweat.
6← I have never fallen down from panic.
I can sit and rest a minute.

---

## *"Minding the Mines"*

*My Panic Thoughts*                    Coping Thoughts

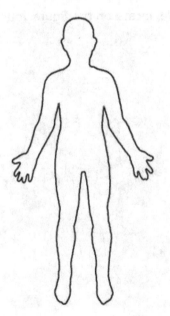

# The Changing Wave of Panic

**The Rising Wave**

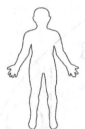 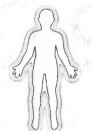 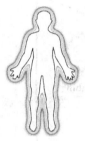 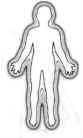

*I feel warm.*  *My heart's racing now.*  *I feel panicky.*  *I'm dizzy.*
*I can't breathe.*  *I'm going to passout.*

**The Fading Wave**

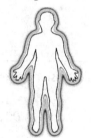 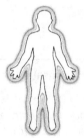 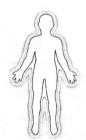 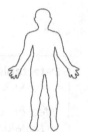

*I have felt these symptoms before.*  *There's nothing dangerous.*  *These symptoms will pass.*  *I'm okay now.*

| The Fight-or-Flight Response | |
|---|---|
| **Bodily Symptom** | **Biological Change and Adaptive Purpose** |
| Heart Rate Increases Blood Pressure Increases | Blood and $O_2$ are delivered more quickly throughout the body Promotes strength and optimizes functioning of organs |
| Nauseous | Blood supply is reduced to stomach and GI track Conserves resources, prevents hunger, and decreases digestion |
| Breathing Rate Increases | $O_2$ is distributed more quickly to the heart and muscles and throughout the body Strengthens heart and muscles for action |
| Pupils Dilate | Allows more light to enter the eye Enhances vision, improves detection of danger, and improves night vision |
| Extremities Become Cold | Blood supply is directed to vital internal organs Conserves resources and minimizes blood loss to vulnerable body parts |
| Pain Tolerance Increases | Increased circulation of endorphins Enables one to endure pain, sustain threats and defend oneself |

# The Hunger Urge

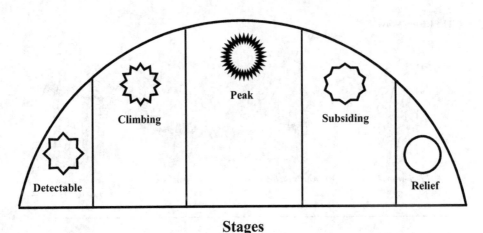

**Stages**

| | |
|---|---|
|  | **Detectable:** Thoughts, images, and sensations of mild tension are experienced as the urge is triggered.<br><br>*"I feel hungry. I just noticed a twinge in my stomach. It's only 11:00 a.m. I think McDonald's serves lunch starting at 11:00 a.m."* |
|  | **Climbing:** Distracted, increased tension and stomach pains, thoughts and behaviors aimed at ways to satisfy the urge; food images, mild irritability, and focused attention on the urge.<br><br>*"I'll leave in 15 minutes. I can finish this work after lunch. I'll check my wallet to see if I have money. I'd love a large fry and two cheeseburgers."* |
|  | **Peak:** The urge is at its greatest. Behaviors aimed to satisfy the urge are initiated (e.g., eating). Attention is hyperfocused on satisfying the urge.<br><br>*"I'm starving. Why is this drive through so busy? I should have left earlier. It's so slow. I'm starving. I'll have a large fry and two cheeseburgers, please. Wow, these fries taste great. Those cheeseburgers—they're next!"* |
|  | **Subsiding:** Tension is reduced. Hunger pains lessen. A sensation of satisfaction is initiated. Attention broadens to focus on other stimuli and behaviors, such as post-lunch activities.<br><br>*"That last cheeseburger was good. Almost time to get back to the office. I think I'll come here again tomorrow for lunch. I'm starting to feel full."* |
| ○ | **Relief:** Relief and satisfaction are experienced. The urge is satisfied. Attention is redirected to other activities.<br><br>*"I'm full and ready for a nap. That tasted good. I'll go back to the office now to finish that report."* |

# Detecting Urge Triggers

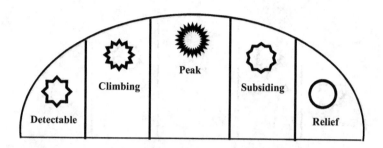

Detectable    Climbing    Peak    Subsiding    Relief

**My Urges** (e.g., drinking alcohol, cursing, cleaning, ordering, picking skin, pulling hair, gambling, social media, yelling, injuring self, injuring others, watching pornography, expressing critical comments, spending money, sending disagreeable e-mails, throwing objects, overeating, purging, using substances)

_____          _____

_____          _____

**My Urge Triggers** (e.g., people, places, situations, stress, boredom, certain days or times of day)

_____          _____

_____          _____

| High-Risk Situations | Urge |
|---|---|
| 1. _____ | _____ |
| _____ | |
| 2. _____ | _____ |
| _____ | |
| 3. _____ | _____ |
| _____ | |
| 4. _____ | _____ |
| _____ | |

# Surfing the Urge

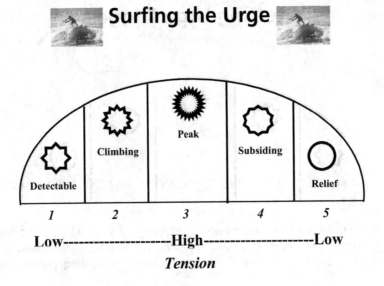

Peak

Climbing

Detectable

Subsiding

Relief

*1*    *2*    *3*    *4*    *5*

Low--------------------High--------------------Low
*Tension*

---

### Interventions

**Stage 1: Distract the urge.** Focus on something else. Don't engage the urge.

**Stage 2: Delay the urge.** Notice the urge but tell yourself that you will respond to the urge in a few minutes. Continue to engage in an activity. Delay responding to the urge for as long as you can. The urge will eventually weaken if you delay it long enough.

**Stage 3: Surf the urge.** If the urge gets to its peak, ride the urge by just noticing it. Rehearse in your mind what you are noticing. Move around. Remind yourself of the importance of not giving in to the urge. Tell yourself that the urge will eventually weaken and subside. If needed, engage in activity that requires focused attention. Reward yourself if you resisted the urge.

*Note.* Implementing interventions during stage 1 (*detectable*) is important. It becomes increasingly difficult to manage urges as they approach stage 3 (*peak* stage).

---

| Urge | Situation | Strategy | Outcome |
|------|-----------|----------|---------|
|      |           |          |         |
|      |           |          |         |
|      |           |          |         |

**Use the chart to monitor your urges and to practice the intervention strategies.**

# Appendix D

## Miscellaneous Diagrams

| Miscellaneous Diagrams | | |
|---|---|---|
| *Display Diagrams (DD)*<br>*In-Session (IS) Worksheets*<br>*Coping Strategies (CS) Handouts* | | |
| **Therapy Topic** | **Diagram** | |
| Busyness<br>Distractibility<br>Worry | The Tree<br>The Tree of My Mind<br>The Tree: Anchoring Strategies | DD #1<br>IS Worksheet #1<br>IS Worksheet #2 |
| | | |
| Mood Monitoring | The Barometer<br>My Barometer | DD #2<br>IS Worksheet #3 |
| | | |
| Communication<br>Marital Therapy<br>Relationship Goals | The Venn Diagram<br>Comparing and Contrasting<br>Communication<br>Identifying Mutual Goals<br>Open Venn Diagram | DD #3<br>IS Worksheet #4<br>IS Worksheet #5<br>IS Worksheet #6<br>IS Worksheet #7 |
| | | |
| Family Ethnicity/Religion<br>Family Relationships | Genogram | IS Worksheet #8 |
| | | |
| Managing Thoughts | Cognitive Defusion | CS Handout #1 |
| | | |
| Optimism Versus Pessimism | Weather Forecast | IS Worksheet #9 |
| | | |
| Regret | Monday Morning Quarterbacking<br>My Monday Morning<br>Quarterbacking | DD #5<br>IS Worksheet #10 |
| | | |
| Shyness | S-P-E-A-K | CS Handout #2 |

| Miscellaneous Diagrams | | |
|---|---|---|
| Developing a Philosophy of Coping | Personal Philosophy Decree | IS Worksheet #11 |
| | | |
| Disorganization | Focus | CS Handout #3 |
| | | |
| Road Rage | Traffic Stress | IS Worksheet #12 |

# The Tree

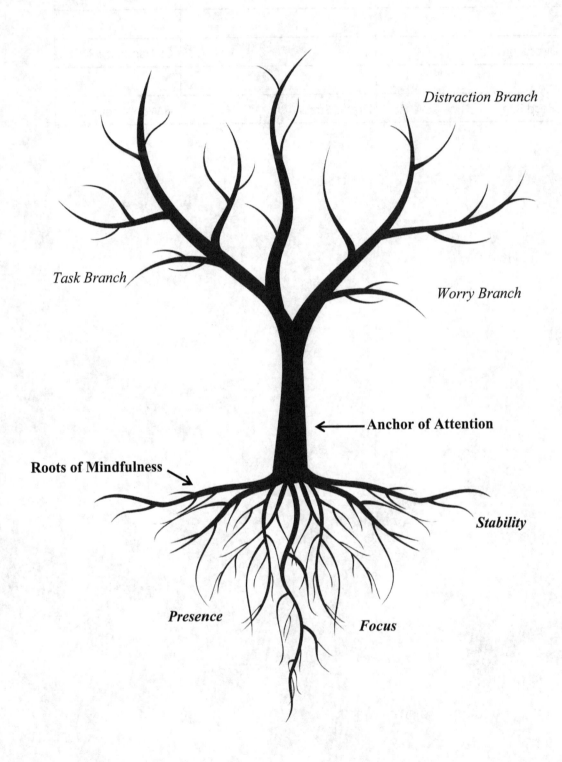

# The Tree of My Mind

*Busyness Tree*        *Worry Tree*        *Distractibility Tree*

**Type of Tree:** _____

**My Tree Branches**

_____
_____
_____
_____

**Triggers to Branching**

_____
_____
_____
_____

# The Tree

**Anchoring Strategies**

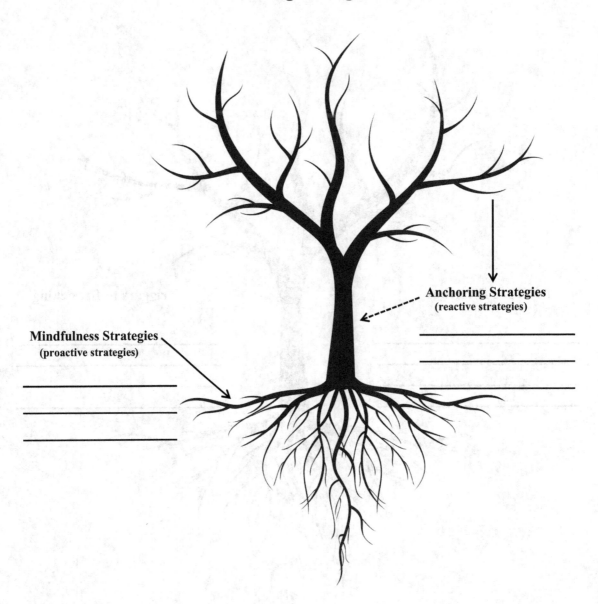

**Anchoring Strategies**
(reactive strategies)

_____

_____

**Mindfulness Strategies**
(proactive strategies)

_____

_____

# The Barometer

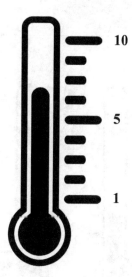

# The Changing Barometer

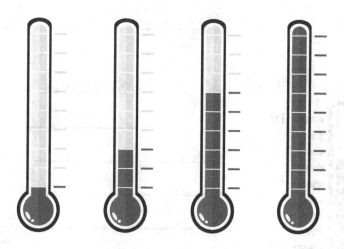

# My Barometer

_____

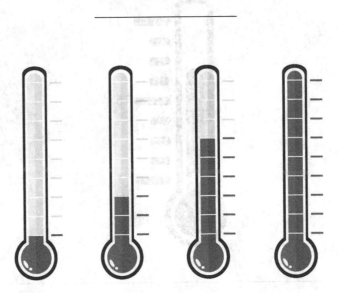

# Triggers

_____     _____     _____

## Strategies

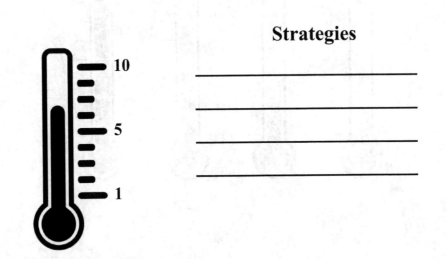

_____

_____

_____

_____

# The Venn Diagram

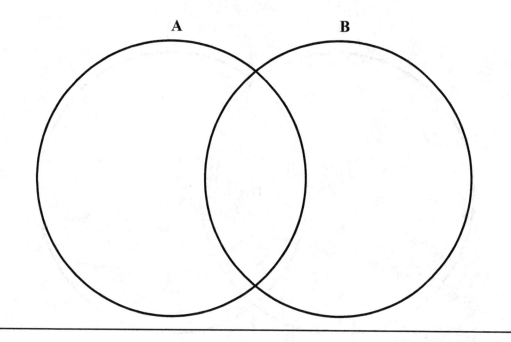

A          B

Comparing and Contrasting

Communication

Identifying Mutual Goals

# Comparing and Contrasting

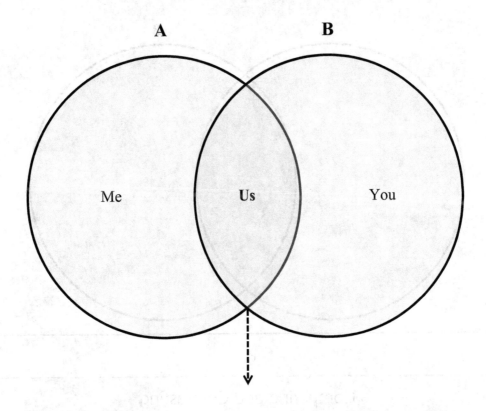

| A | AB | B |
|---|---|---|
|  | 1. |  |
|  | 2. |  |
|  | 3. |  |
|  | 4. |  |
|  | 5. |  |

# Communication

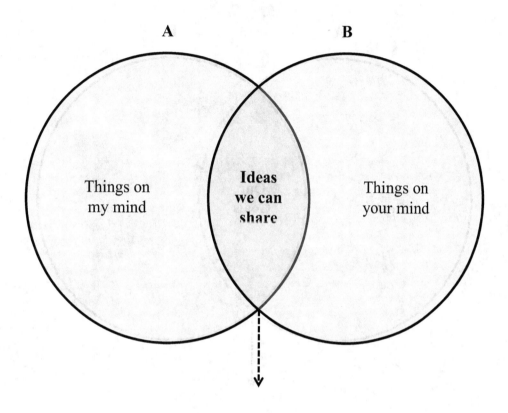

| A | AB | B |
|---|---|---|
|  | 1. |  |
|  | 2. |  |
|  | 3. |  |
|  | 4. |  |
|  | 5. |  |

# Identifying Mutual Goals

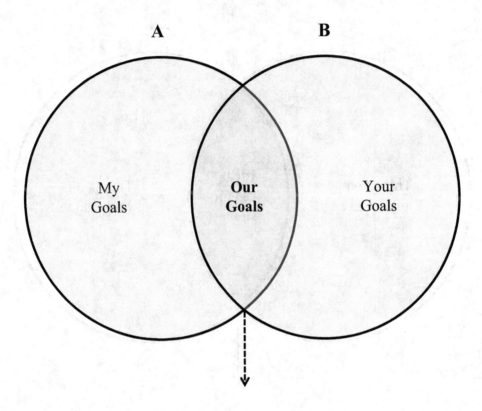

A

B

My
Goals

Our
Goals

Your
Goals

| A | | AB | B | |
|---|---|---|---|---|
| | | 1. | | |
| | | 2. | | |
| | | 3. | | |
| | | 4. | | |
| | | 5. | | |

# Open Venn Diagram

**Topic:** _____

**A** _____    **B** _____

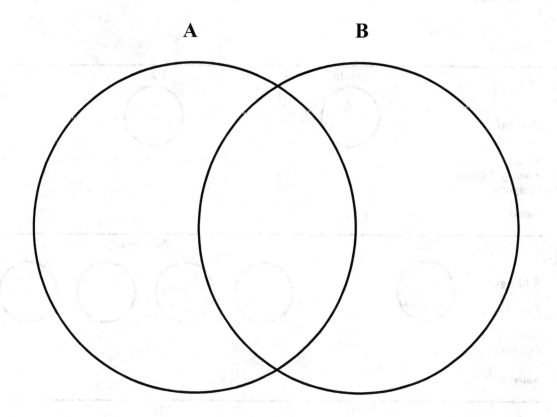

**Notes:**

_____

_____

_____

_____

# Genogram

**GM**   **GF**                          **GM**   **GF**

**Grandparents**

*Names:*
*Ethnicity/Religion:*
*Occupation:*

**Notes:**

**Mom**                          **Dad**

**Parents**

*Names;*
*Ethnicity/Religion:*
*Occupation:*

**Notes:**

**Me**                          **Siblings**

**Siblings**

*Names:*
*Occupation:*

**Notes:**

**Partner**                          **Me**

**Spouse or**
**Significant Other**

*Ethnicity:*
*Religion:*
*Occupation:*
**Notes:**

**Children**

**Notes:**

# Cognitive Defusion

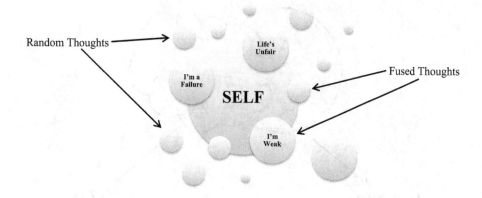

*Fused thoughts are negative thoughts that seem "attached to you." They can frequently "feel like facts" and have often come to define your self-worth, emotional well-being, and future.*

---

**Cognitive Defusion Strategies:** Below are five strategies or ways of thinking about your thoughts that can help release fused thoughts from your mind. These cognitive defusion strategies can also help minimize negative feelings that are generated from your fused thoughts.

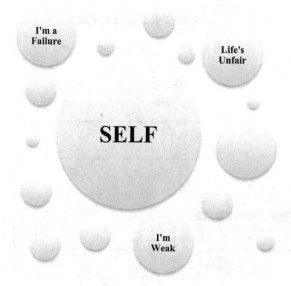

- Get distance from your thoughts by becoming an observer and not a victim of your thoughts.

- Remember that thoughts are just thoughts.

- Notice but don't evaluate or engage your thoughts. Simply say to yourself, "Oh, that's interesting, I'm having the thought that . . ."

- Actively tell yourself that your thoughts are not you and that your thoughts do not by themselves define reality.

- Don't try to suppress or control your thoughts but rather accept your thoughts as momentary experiences that will drift away.

# Weather Forecast

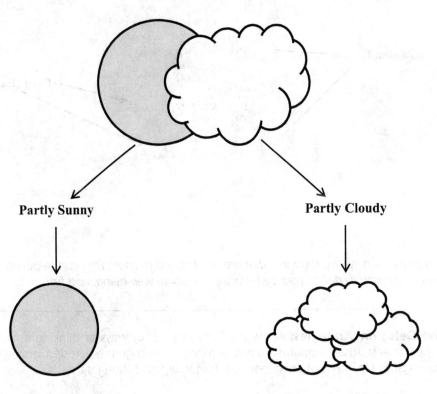

**Partly Sunny**

**Partly Cloudy**

**A Sunny Day Forecast**

Ex: Pack my bathing suit, go to the beach

_____

_____

_____

**A Cloudy Day Forecast**

Ex: Pack my umbrella, cancel plans

_____

_____

_____

## My New Weather Forecast:

_____

_____

_____

# Monday Morning Quarterbacking

**Sunday**

*What you thought Sunday morning*

**Monday**

*\*What you think you **should have been thinking** on that Sunday morning!*

It looks like it won't rain. The sun's out and there are only a few clouds. It will stay sunny.

↓

I'll leave my umbrella at home.

↓

It's still not raining. It's just partly cloudy. The sun will probably come out.

↓

Oh no! It's raining now. *\*I should have decided to take my umbrella!*

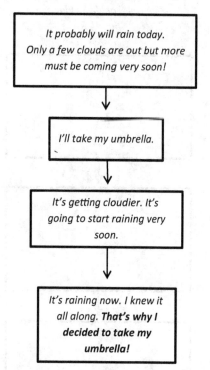

*It probably will rain today. Only a few clouds are out but more must be coming very soon!*

↓

*I'll take my umbrella.*

↓

*It's getting cloudier. It's going to start raining very soon.*

↓

*It's raining now. I knew it all along. **That's why I decided to take my umbrella!***

---

**Warning Statements That You May Be Monday Morning Quarterbacking**

I should have known better!

It was obvious!

I knew it all along!

It was so stupid to do that!

I told you so!
*(Monday morning quarterback someone else)*

---

# My Monday Morning Quarterbacking

**Regret or Theme:** _____

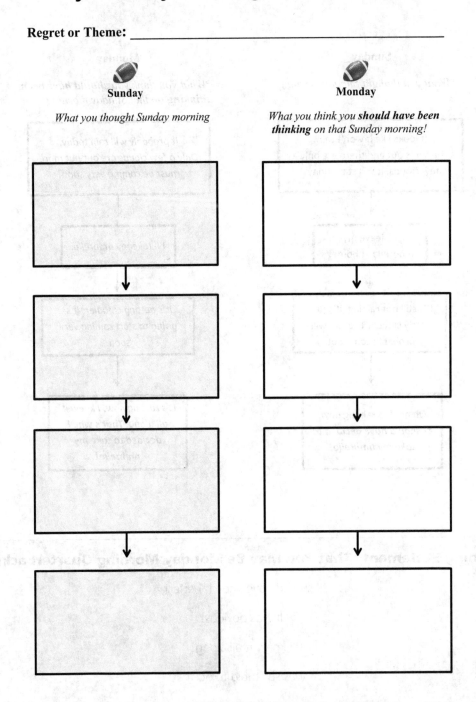

**Sunday**

*What you thought Sunday morning*

**Monday**

*What you think you **should have been** thinking on that Sunday morning!*

*Note.* The regret or theme can be in the form of a statement, such as "I should have done such and such or I should have known better when . . ." This can be the event that is reviewed in the flowchart. Invite your client to give as much detail as possible under the "Sunday" flowchart for what they were specifically thinking at the time when they made their original decision on "Sunday." Then under the "Monday" flowchart, record in detail what your client started to specifically think later on "Monday" once they knew the outcome of the situation.

# S-P-E-A-K

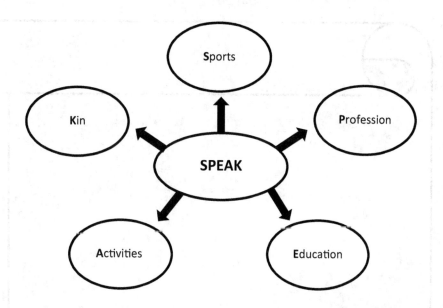

One way to think about possible topics to discuss is to think of the word "**SPEAK**." The word SPEAK stands for the following universal topics: **S**ports, **P**rofession, **E**ducation, **A**ctivities, and **K**in.

**S**ports—Many people enjoy discussing *sports* and their favorite sports teams.

**P**rofession—Many people like to discuss their *profession* and what it entails.

**E**ducation—Think of *education* as learning and personal knowledge you can share with others.

**A**ctivities—This can include any *activities*, events, hobbies, or clubs that you participate in.

**K**in—Think of **kin** as family. People like to discuss what is going on with their family, such as family events, pets, vacations, accomplishments, or activities with their children.

## Communication Tips

- Introduce a topic or contribute to a conversation at any time and in any way.
- Wait for a natural pause when others stop talking and then say something.
- Ask a question or make a comment about the topic.
- Make good eye contact and listen carefully to what others are saying.
- Share a similar experience or similar thought about the topic.
- Share your knowledge about the topic.
- Ask for information on a topic.

# Personal Philosophy Decree

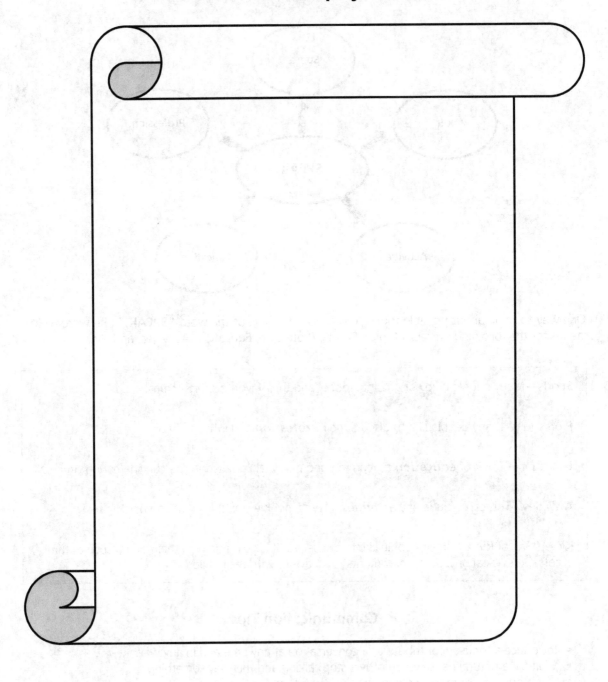

# FOCUS

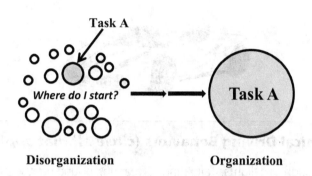

Task A

**Where do I start?**

Task A

**Disorganization**          **Organization**

---

## Organizational Strategies

1. Identify a starting point.
2. Use the 2Ts strategy (*task* and *time*):
   *Task*: Break larger tasks down into smaller tasks (e.g., clean one section of a room).
   *Time*: Devote a certain amount of time to a task that is realistic and practical (e.g., spend 20 minutes cleaning a room and then take a break).
3. Distractibility can occur because of internal stimuli, such as thoughts and memories, or external stimuli, such as people or situations. This can make it difficult to sustain your attention on a task.
4. Managing triggers to distractibility is important. Triggers can include such things as computers, cell phones, boredom, noises, hunger, pain, and temperature.
5. Manage distractibility by adhering to the 2Ts strategy and by knowing what zone you are in (see the following diagram). Notice the times you tend to be in the ● zone and actively redirect yourself to back to your task.

---

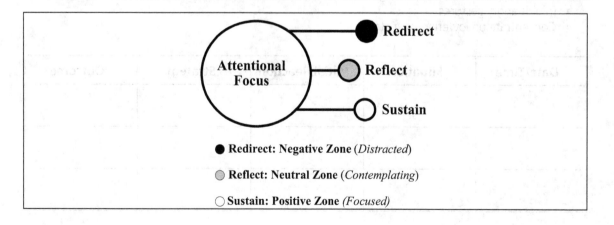

Attentional Focus

● **Redirect**

◉ **Reflect**

○ **Sustain**

● **Redirect: Negative Zone** (*Distracted*)

◉ **Reflect: Neutral Zone** (*Contemplating*)

○ **Sustain: Positive Zone** (*Focused*)

---

# Traffic Stress

---

### Typical Driving Behaviors (*circle all that apply*):

speeding, going through red lights, tailgating, swearing, pounding the steering wheel, hand gestures, using the horn, others: _____

### Typical Driving Stressors (*circle all that apply*):

speeders, tailgating, no blinkers, cell phone use, heavy traffic, slow drivers, construction sites, pedestrians, parking lots, highways, single-lane roads, animals, panhandlers, bridges, one-way streets, parking, shopping centers, snow, rain, night driving, school buses, motorcycles, bicyclists, police officers, ambulances, fire trucks, tractor trailers, broken-down cars, speed bumps, school zones, others: _____

---

## New Driving Strategies

- **T**ake your time.
- **R**elax with deep breaths.
- **A**void commentary on other drivers.
- **F**ocus attention straight ahead.
- **F**ind your place and limit passing.
- **I**nhibit angry gestures.
- **C**oncentrate on lowering your stress.

| Date/Time | Situation | Initial Reaction | Strategy | Outcome |
|---|---|---|---|---|
| | | | | |
| | | | | |
| | | | | |

Use the chart to monitor three episodes of traffic stress.

# Appendix E

## Mind Stimulation Exercises and Handouts

- **Body Movement Exercise**

- **Paper-and-Pencil Exercises**

- **Coping Statements**

- **Self-Assessment Tools**

# Body Movement Exercise

While standing up, slightly bend your knees to feel the weight of your body grounded to the floor. Your stance should be similar to a skiing position. If you have trouble standing, the exercise may be completed while sitting in a chair.

Move both of your hands with your palms up as you breathe in through your nose and move both of your hands with your palms down as you breathe out through your mouth. The movement of your hands should be continuous—that is, your hands should keep moving during the exercise. It is important to focus on your hands and to notice your hand movements. The hands moving up and then moving down count for one complete repetition.

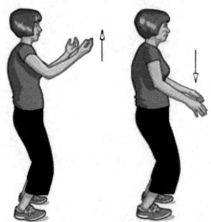

Perform the breathing exercise 10 times by counting to 10. Count each complete repetition until you reach 10. Remember, as you breathe in with your mouth closed, raise your hands. As you breathe out with your mouth slightly opened, lower your hands. After you have reached a count of 10, sit quietly for 1 minute and notice your surroundings.

Directing your attention to your hand movements will help you concentrate and focus on your behavior in the immediate moment. By doing this you will be less distracted by negative thoughts.
Note. Adapted from Ahmed and Boisvert (2013), pp. 36–39.

## Body Movement Exercises
## Recording Chart

| Day | Time | Rating 1 Calm Before | 10 Tense After | Comments |
|-----|------|----------------------|----------------|----------|
| Monday | | | | |
| | | | | |
| Tuesday | | | | |
| | | | | |
| Wednesday | | | | |
| | | | | |
| Thursday | | | | |
| | | | | |
| Friday | | | | |
| | | | | |
| Saturday | | | | |
| | | | | |
| Saturday | | | | |
| | | | | |

# Paper-and-Pencil Exercises

# Analogies

Circle the correct answer from the choices given and write the answer on the line.

1. Dark is to light as tall is to: _____

   a. High          b. Right          c. Short          d. Straight

2. Old is to ancient as glad is to: _____

   a. Sad          b. Scared          c. Happy          d. New

3. Plummer is to wrench as surgeon is to: _____

   a. Scalpel          b. Patient          c. Hospital          d. Medicine

4. Foot is to shoe as hand is to: _____

   a. Head          b. Glove          c. Hat          d. Arm

5. Short is to tall as fast is to: _____

   a. Quick          b. Slow          c. Big          d. First

6. Ruler is to measure as thermometer is to: _____

   a. Wind          b. Degrees          c. Weather          d. Temperature

7. Cup is to water as bag is to _____

   a. Paper          b. Plastic          c. Tear          d. Groceries

8. City is to states as tree is to _____

   a. Branches          b. Forest          c. Leaves          d. Bush

9. Teacher is to student as mother is to_____

   a. Child          b. Father          c. Love          d. Family

10. Chicken is to egg as cow is to: _____

   a. Farm          b. Hay          c. Milk          d. Meat

# Classifying

Classify the following words and write your best answer next to each word. It might be helpful to think of the word as a type of something. For example, if the word was *oak*, your answer would be *tree* (oak is a type of tree).

**Example**: Oak     Tree

| | | | |
|---|---|---|---|
| Cortland | _____ | Toyota | _____ |
| Coke | _____ | Timex | _____ |
| Parsley | _____ | Mars | _____ |
| Salmon | _____ | Merlot | _____ |
| Advil | _____ | Nike | _____ |
| Soccer | _____ | Plum | _____ |
| Spring | _____ | Hammer | _____ |
| Robin | _____ | Python | _____ |
| Tudor | _____ | Easter | _____ |
| Sleet | _____ | Gold | _____ |
| Turtle | _____ | Rose | _____ |
| Rye | _____ | Asia | _____ |
| Godiva | _____ | Bic | _____ |
| Corn | _____ | Dime | _____ |
| Surgeon | _____ | Derby | _____ |
| Saturn | _____ | Cheerios | _____ |
| Siamese | _____ | Poodle | _____ |
| Atlantic | _____ | Swiss | _____ |
| Penne | _____ | Buddhism | _____ |
| Alps | _____ | Michelin | _____ |

# Grouping

Circle the member that does not belong to the group.

| | | | | |
|---|---|---|---|---|
| 1. | Cement | Stone | Rock | Dirt |
| 2. | Look | Listen | Taste | Talk |
| 3. | Spinach | Corn | Grapefruit | Lemon |
| 4. | Soccer | Football | Basketball | Baseball |
| 5. | iPod | iPhone | iPad | Computer |
| 6. | Oil | Gas | Water | Antifreeze |
| 7. | Seek | Follow | Pursue | Recover |
| 8. | Tiger | Cheetah | Leopard | Giraffe |
| 9. | Europe | Asia | United States | Africa |
| 10. | Run | Hit | Goal | Home Run |
| 11. | Beagle | Collie | Poodle | Mongrel |
| 12. | Robin | Butterfly | Bat | Ostrich |
| 13. | Kennedy | Reagan | Lincoln | Clinton |
| 14. | Canine | Wisdom | Enamel | Incisors |
| 15. | Honda | Ford | Toyota | Volkswagen |
| 16. | End | Start | Begin | Commence |
| 17. | Cape | Tudor | Condo | Colonial |
| 18. | *Macbeth* | *Othello* | *The Raven* | *Romeo and Juliet* |
| 19. | Harvest | Oak | Birch | Maple |
| 20. | Chile | Nigeria | Brazil | Argentina |
| 21. | Aid | Help | Assist | Receive |
| 22. | Sneeze | Smell | Scratch | Sniffle |
| 23. | Laugh | Cry | Speak | Scream |
| 24. | Flexible | Bendable | Malleable | Rigid |
| 25. | Maine | Vermont | New York | Massachusetts |

# Categorizing

List two members of each group. An example is provided.

| | | |
|---|---|---|
| ***Example*: Cars** | **Ford** | **Honda** |
| 1. Planets | _____ | _____ |
| 2. Continents | _____ | _____ |
| 3. Cities | _____ | _____ |
| 4. Cereals | _____ | _____ |
| 5. Religions | _____ | _____ |
| 6. Sports | _____ | _____ |
| 7. Breads | _____ | _____ |
| 8. Cheeses | _____ | _____ |
| 9. Card Games | _____ | _____ |
| 10. Cats | _____ | _____ |
| 11. Oceans | _____ | _____ |
| 12. Spices | _____ | _____ |
| 13. Snakes | _____ | _____ |
| 14. Footwear | _____ | _____ |
| 15. House Styles | _____ | _____ |
| 16. Flowers | _____ | _____ |
| 17. Tools | _____ | _____ |
| 18. Italian Foods | _____ | _____ |
| 19. Occupations | _____ | _____ |
| 20. Authors | _____ | _____ |

# General Knowledge

Provide the answers to the following questions by writing your response on the line next to the question.

1.  How many sides does a pentagon have? _____

2.  Who is the current president? _____

3.  Name a famous author. _____

4.  How many Great Lakes are there? _____

5.  What is the capital of Italy? _____

6.  In what month is Memorial Day? _____

7.  Who was JFK? _____

8.  What is an arachnid? _____

9.  On which continent is the country Chile located? _____

10. Name a sports team from New York. _____

11. Name a famous military general. _____

12. Who invented the light bulb? _____

13. Name a famous football player. _____

14. Who wrote *Of Mice and Men*? _____

15. What is the capital of Texas? _____

16. What is a prosthetic used for? _____

17  Name a food high in fiber. _____

18. What is Taoism? _____

19. Who wrote *Romeo and Juliet*? _____

20. What does MPG stand for? _____

# Math

**Multiplication:**

| | | | | | |
|---|---|---|---|---|---|
| 2 | 7 | 3 | 6 | 5 | 4 |
| ×5 | ×7 | ×7 | ×9 | ×8 | ×9 |

| | | | | | |
|---|---|---|---|---|---|
| 11 | 17 | 10 | 23 | 14 | 8 |
| ×13 | ×4 | ×7 | ×5 | ×6 | ×8 |

**Addition:**

| | | | | | |
|---|---|---|---|---|---|
| 5 | 4 | 11 | 35 | 24 | 147 |
| +4 | +8 | +16 | +35 | +57 | +249 |

| | | | | | |
|---|---|---|---|---|---|
| 437 | 426 | 130 | 4347 | 246 | 8245 |
| +546 | +823 | +150 | +5428 | +617 | +7122 |

**Subtraction:**

| | | | | | |
|---|---|---|---|---|---|
| 7 | 6 | 14 | 35 | 117 | 349 |
| −4 | −3 | −13 | −18 | −39 | −133 |

| | | | | | |
|---|---|---|---|---|---|
| 713 | 256 | 165 | 370 | 3212 | 5432 |
| −417 | −137 | −135 | −269 | −1362 | −2345 |

# Similarities

Next to each pair, indicate how the two words are alike. An example is provided.

**Example**: Pen–Pencil                     Writing instruments

1. Lobster–Oyster     _____

2. Bacon–Ham     _____

3. Winter–Fall     _____

4. Hat–Coat     _____

5. Python–Boa     _____

6. Map–Compass     _____

7. Austin–Houston     _____

8. Beans–Peppers     _____

9. Alps-–Andes     _____

10. Kennedy–Lincoln     _____

11. Salt–Pepper     _____

12. Gold–Silver     _____

13. Happy–Sad     _____

14. Brazil–Chile     _____

15. Lethargic–Fatigued     _____

16. Praise–Punishment     _____

17. Mother–Father     _____

18. Hurricane–Tornado     _____

19. Eggs–Cheese     _____

20. Honda–Toyota     _____

# Synonyms and Antonyms

Next to each word in the list, write a word that means the same (synonym) and a word that means the opposite (antonym). An example is provided.

|  | **Synonym** | **Antonym** |
|---|---|---|
| *Example:* Large | Big | Small |
| 1. Tired | _____ | _____ |
| 2. Plain | _____ | _____ |
| 3. Secretive | _____ | _____ |
| 4. Lend | _____ | _____ |
| 5. Noisy | _____ | _____ |
| 6. Vanished | _____ | _____ |
| 7. Fresh | _____ | _____ |
| 8. Join | _____ | _____ |
| 9. Expand | _____ | _____ |
| 10. Purchase | _____ | _____ |
| 11. Help | _____ | _____ |
| 12. Sluggish | _____ | _____ |
| 13. Gather | _____ | _____ |
| 14. Fixed | _____ | _____ |
| 15. Easygoing | _____ | _____ |
| 16. Damp | _____ | _____ |
| 17. Clean | _____ | _____ |
| 18. Angry | _____ | _____ |
| 19. Courageous | _____ | _____ |
| 20. Ponder | _____ | _____ |

# Visual Matching

Find two of the same figures and label the inside of the pair the same number. The first one has been done for you (some figures will not have a match).

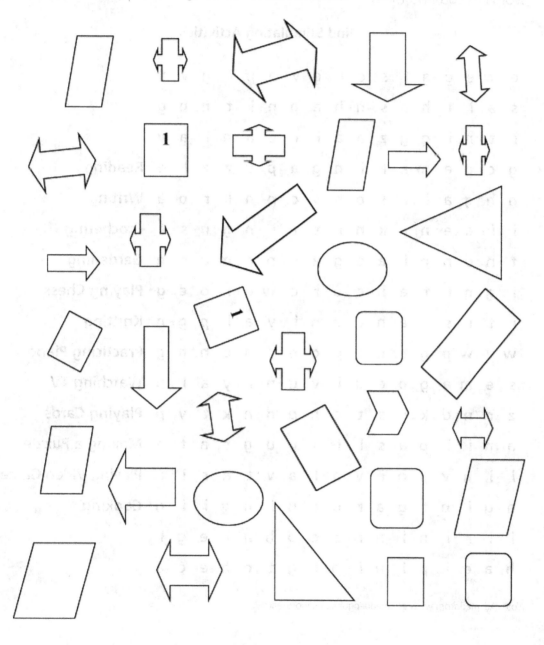

# Word Search

Find the words in the right-hand column hidden in the word box. Circle the words as you find them.

## Mind Stimulating Activities

| | | | | | | | | | | | | | | | | |
|---|---|---|---|---|---|---|---|---|---|---|---|---|---|---|---|---|
| e | w | e | g | g | l | s | c | l | g | v | g | p | i | g | y | t |
| s | a | i | t | h | a | s | n | h | a | p | n | l | t | n | p | g |
| i | t | n | i | g | g | z | a | a | i | r | c | a | n | i | a | v |
| g | c | g | e | m | a | k | i | n | g | a | p | u | z | z | l | e |
| n | h | g | a | i | i | s | o | n | s | c | p | n | k | r | o | a |
| i | i | a | e | n | r | k | n | i | t | t | i | n | g | n | s | t |
| t | n | o | r | p | i | a | e | g | a | i | p | r | m | d | r | n |
| i | g | n | i | t | e | h | c | o | r | c | w | e | r | o | e | g |
| r | t | l | s | s | e | h | c | g | n | i | y | a | l | p | g | n |
| w | v | w | p | g | r | o | t | p | o | n | c | d | c | n | n | g |
| s | e | m | a | g | o | e | d | i | v | g | n | i | y | a | l | p |
| z | r | n | d | k | i | s | t | c | n | p | d | n | k | t | y | p |
| a | n | i | i | p | a | s | l | i | s | i | u | g | t | a | t | a |
| i | i | n | v | p | o | i | y | a | t | a | v | t | a | s | i | i |
| a | g | i | p | t | g | a | r | d | e | n | i | n | g | i | i | g |
| i | i | r | i | n | l | n | r | r | c | o | h | n | i | e | g | i |
| h | a | e | i | p | i | n | i | h | i | g | t | o | h | e | c | a |

Reading
Writing
Crocheting
Gardening
Playing Chess
Knitting
Practicing Piano
Watching TV
Playing Cards
Making a Puzzle
Playing Video Games
Cooking

*Note*. Adapted from www.armoredpenguin.com/wordsearch/.

## Coping Statements

- These written exercises can help clients identify and practice coping statements and strategies to reduce stress and improve their functioning.
- Therapists can use the computer-facilitated therapy method to develop these statements in collaboration with the client.
- You can pick and choose to match your client's personality or goals or use the following examples to help your client generate their own coping statements.

## Behavioral Statements (*Action Statements*)

These exercises provide clients with specific behavioral directions and cues to assist them in practicing new coping behaviors and responses.

- "When I feel depressed, *I will go* for a short walk."
- "When I feel anxious, *I will practice* my breathing exercises."
- "*I will apply* for two jobs this week."
- "*I will call* my friend on Wednesday."
- "*I will make plans* to go out with my brother this weekend."
- "*I will start* to volunteer at the local food pantry on Saturday."

## I Statements (*Personality Statements*)

These exercises provide clients with personal self-referential coping statements that they can rehearse to promote their confidence in coping with their symptoms, stressors, and life challenges.

- "*I am a worthwhile person.*"
- "*I am strong* and can manage my depression."
- "*I am smart* and have always figured out how to cope with difficult situations."
- "*I have skills* and am well educated."
- "*I am the go-to person* in my family who everyone relies on."
- "*I have never given up* on anything."

327

# Appendix F

## Brief Assessment Tools

# Brief Assessment Tool

Using the following scale, rate how well you have been doing this past week in the following areas:

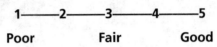

| 1 | 2 | 3 | 4 | 5 |
|---|---|---|---|---|
| Poor | | Fair | | Good |

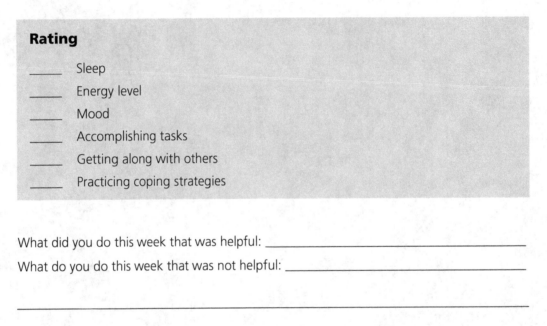

**Rating**

_____ Sleep

_____ Energy level

_____ Mood

_____ Accomplishing tasks

_____ Getting along with others

_____ Practicing coping strategies

What did you do this week that was helpful: _____

What do you do this week that was not helpful: _____

_____

Using the following scale, rate how well you have been doing overall in these areas:

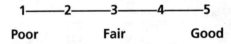

| 1 | 2 | 3 | 4 | 5 |
|---|---|---|---|---|
| Poor | | Fair | | Good |

**Rating**

_____ Progress toward therapy goals

_____ Accomplishing life tasks

_____ Mood

_____ Physical health

_____ Satisfaction with life and relationships

# Therapy Progress Tracker

This grid can be used to monitor your progress over 8 weeks in therapy. You can track your progress to determine how well you are doing in reaching your goals.

**Rating**

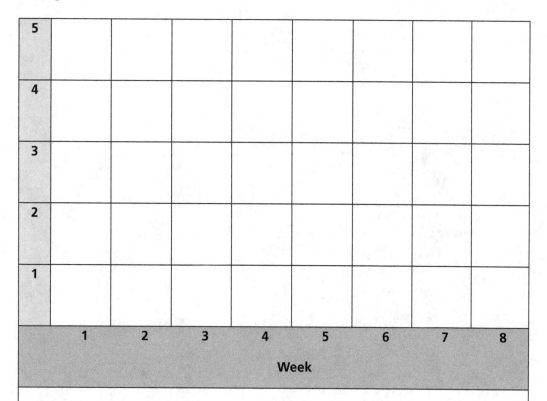

**Use this scale:**

1———2———3———4———5

Poor        Fair        Good

**Record your rating for each of the following.**

**Progress Toward Goals (P)**
**Overall Mood (M)**
**Use of Coping Strategies (CS)**

Use letters to distinguish these different areas on the grid: P, M, CS

# Appendix G

## Objectifying Therapy: Using Common Objects to Explain Therapy Concepts

| Object | Teaching Concept |
|---|---|
| Clay and stone | Flexibility versus rigidity |
| Small statue | Self and self-esteem |
| Ruler | Monitoring mood<br>Incremental change |
| Two plastic cups | "Worry cups"<br>Free-Floating versus problem-solving |
| One-pound dumbbell | Overusing certain mental muscles and learning to use different mental muscles |
| Two golf balls: white and black and grey | Black and white versus grey thinking |
| Two sets of glasses | Cognitive restructuring<br>(new glasses = new perspective) |
| Funnel | Focusing attention |
| On/off light switch | Categorical thinking |
| Dimmer light switch | Thinking in degrees |
| Coin in pocket | Tactile and visual reminder to practice a coping strategy |
| Plastic hamster wheel | Ruminating |
| Small spring | Stress: changing the tension |
| Radio with dials | Changing the thought channel<br>Adjusting the anger volume |

# Appendix H

## Coping Cards

| Coping Card | Coping Card |
|---|---|
| Coping Card | Coping Card |
| Coping Card | Coping Card |
| Coping Card | Coping Card |
| Coping Card | Coping Card |

# Appendix I

## Mini (Wallet) Diagrams

# Time Circles Diagrams

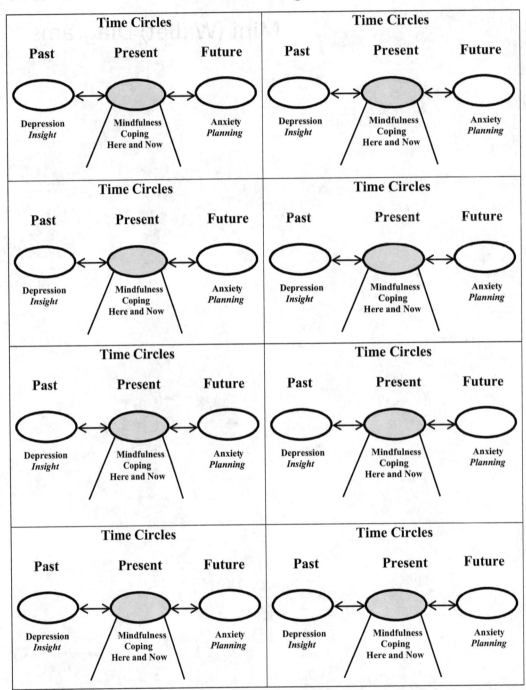

*Note.* Each diagram is approximately the size of a credit card and can be carried in your client's pocket, wallet, or purse. It can serve as a quick reminder of the coping strategies discussed when the diagram was used in the therapy session.

## Barometer Diagrams

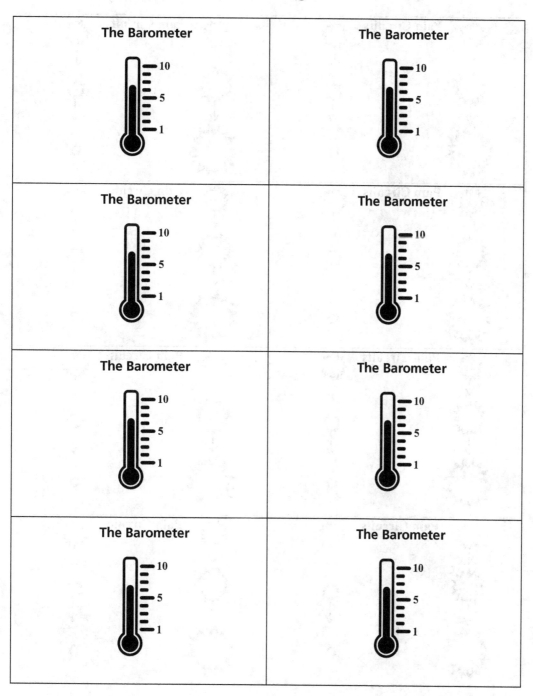

*Note.* Each diagram is approximately the size of a credit card and can be carried in your client's pocket, wallet, or purse. It can serve as a quick reminder of the coping strategies discussed when the diagram was used in the therapy session.

# Pain Circuits Diagrams

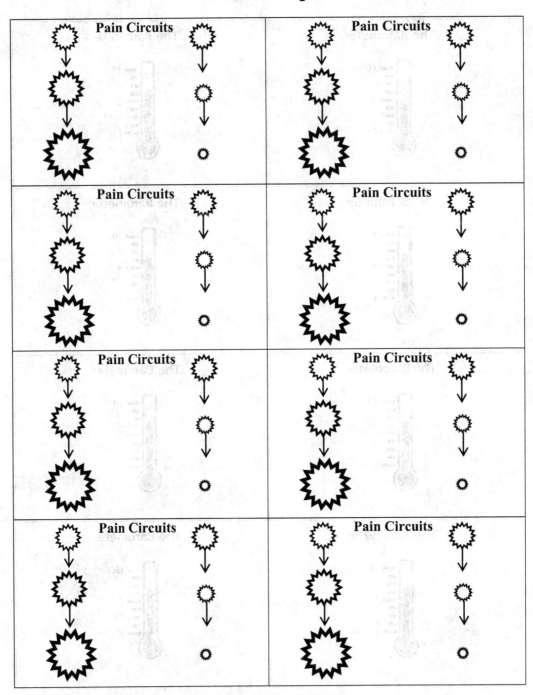

*Note.* Each diagram is approximately the size of a credit card and can be carried in your client's pocket, wallet, or purse. It can serve as a quick reminder of the coping strategies discussed when the diagram was used in the therapy session.

# Urges Diagrams

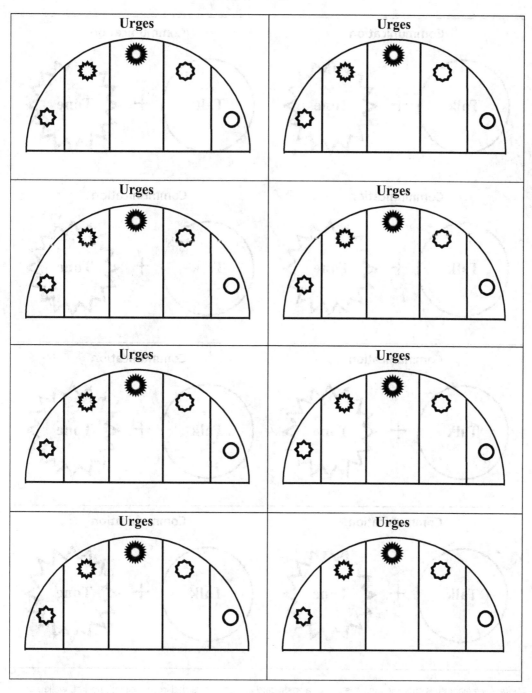

*Note.* Each diagram is approximately the size of a credit card and can be carried in your client's pocket, wallet, or purse. It can serve as a quick reminder of the coping strategies discussed when the diagram was used in the therapy session.

## Communication Diagrams

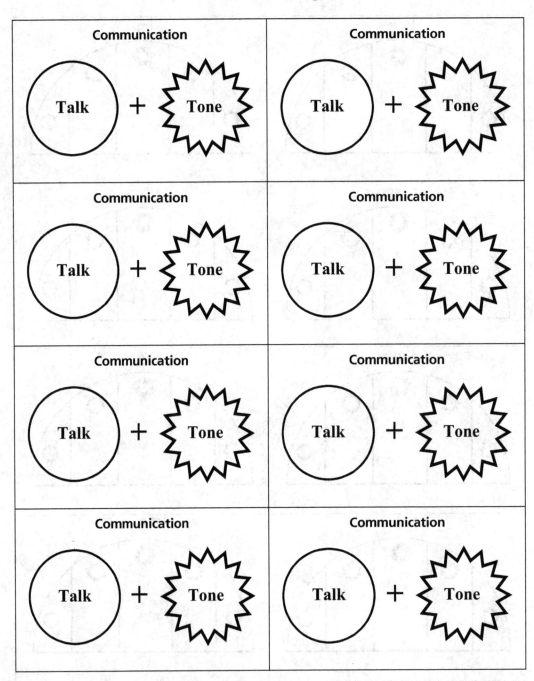

*Note.* Each diagram is approximately the size of a credit card and can be carried in your client's pocket, wallet, or purse. It can serve as a quick reminder of the coping strategies discussed when the diagram was used in the therapy session.

# Tree Diagrams

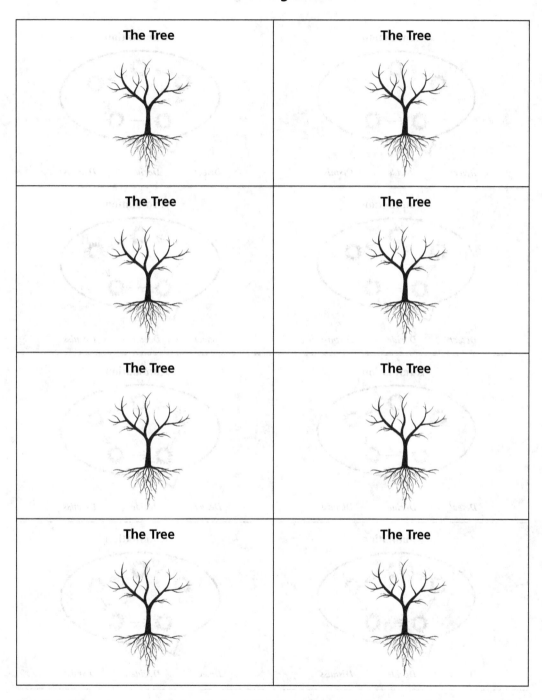

|  |  |
|---|---|
| **The Tree** | **The Tree** |
| **The Tree** | **The Tree** |
| **The Tree** | **The Tree** |
| **The Tree** | **The Tree** |

*Note*. Each diagram is approximately the size of a credit card and can be carried in your client's pocket, wallet, or purse. It can serve as a "quick reminder" of the coping strategies discussed when the diagram was used in the therapy session.

## Rumination Diagrams

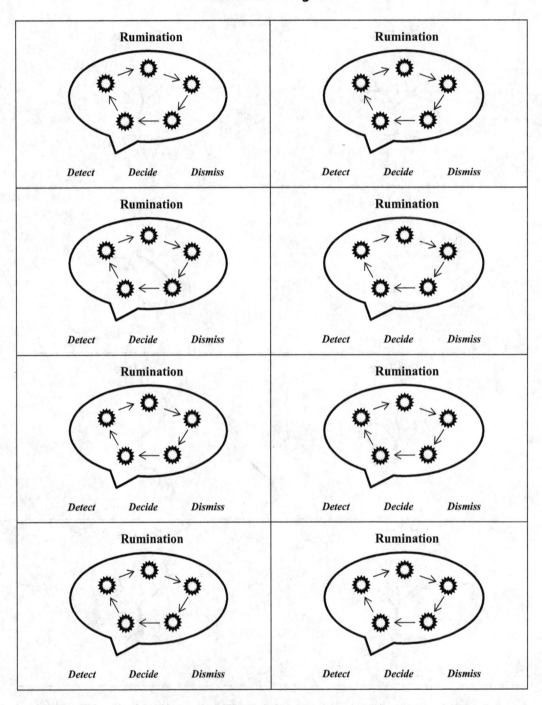

# Worry Diagrams

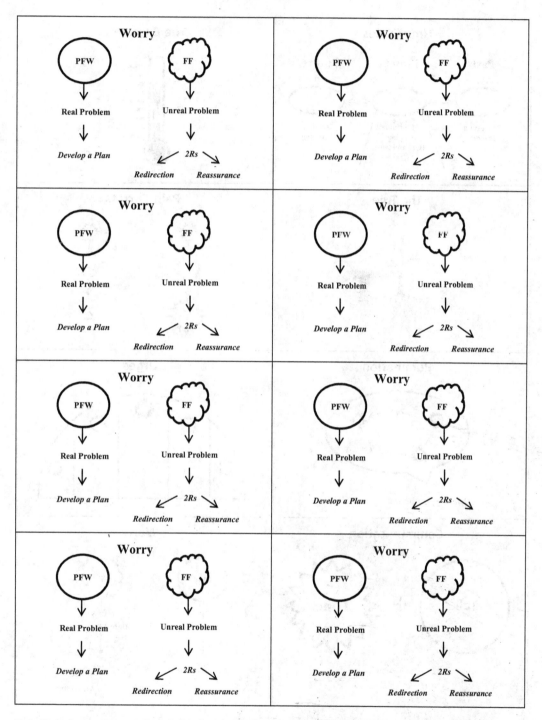

*Note.* Each diagram is approximately the size of a credit card and can be carried in your client's pocket, wallet, or purse. It can serve as a "quick reminder" of the coping strategies discussed when the diagram was used in the therapy session.

# Diagrams

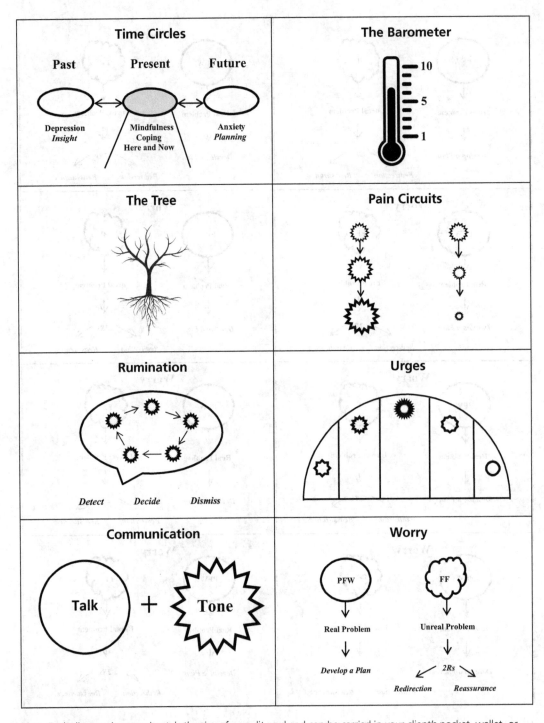

*Note.* Each diagram is approximately the size of a credit card and can be carried in your client's pocket, wallet, or purse. It can serve as a quick reminder of the coping strategies discussed when the diagram was used in the therapy session.

# Diagrams

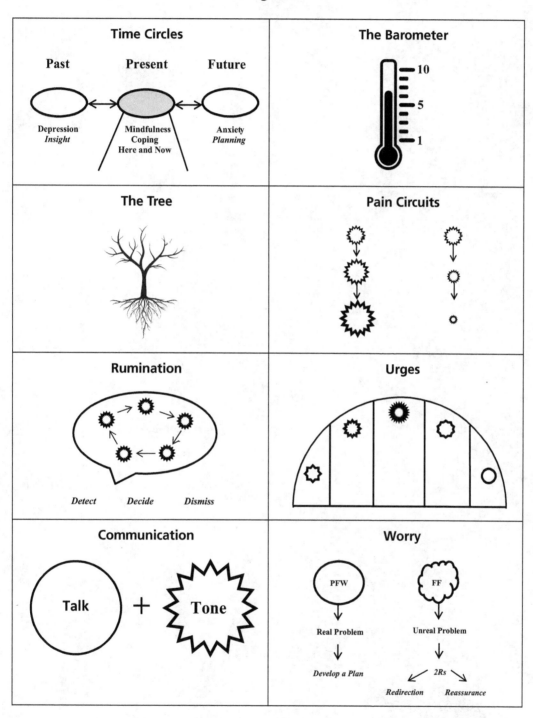

*Note.* Each diagram is approximately the size of a credit card and can be carried in your client's pocket, wallet, or purse. It can serve as a "quick reminder" of the coping strategies discussed when the diagram was used in the therapy session.

# Index

Note: Page numbers in **bold** refers to handouts, questionnaires and worksheets